WE SHALL OVERCOME

WE SHALL OVERCOME

PRESS PHOTOGRAPHS OF NASHVILLE DURING THE CIVIL RIGHTS ERA

Edited by Kathryn E. Delmez
Foreword by John Lewis

With Essays by Linda T. Wynn and Susan H. Edwards

FRIST ART MUSEUM *in association with*
VANDERBILT UNIVERSITY PRESS *Nashville, Tennessee*

Published in conjunction with the exhibition *We Shall Overcome: Civil Rights and the Nashville Press 1957–1968*, which was organized by the Frist Art Museum, Nashville, Tennessee.

EXHIBITION ITINERARY:

Frist Art Museum
March 30–October 14, 2018

Robert Churchwell Museum
Magnet School
November 30, 2018–May 24, 2019

Hiram Van Gordon Gallery,
Tennessee State University
March 15–April 30, 2021

Vanderbilt University Divinity School
August 1, 2022–May 31, 2023

EXHIBITION PRESENTING SPONSOR

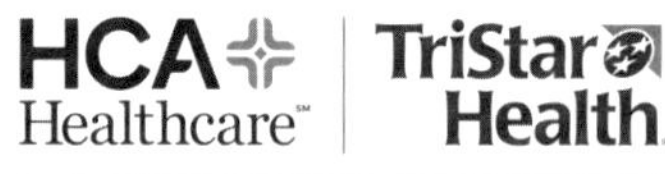

ADDITIONAL SPONSORS

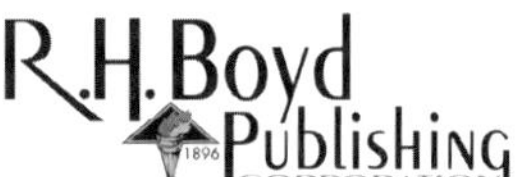

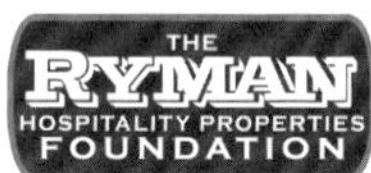

All images generously provided by *The Tennessean* and the Nashville Public Library, Special Collections, which houses the *Nashville Banner* archives.

Published by the Frist Art Museum
and Vanderbilt University Press
First paperback printing 2023

Front cover image:
Photo by Eldred Reaney, *The Tennessean*, April 16, 1960 (plate 34)
Courtesy of *The Tennessean*

Back cover images:
Photo by Gerald Holly, *The Tennessean*, June 19, 1963 (plate 58)
Courtesy of *The Tennessean*

Photo by Jack Gunter, *Nashville Banner*,
May 10, 1963 (plate 55)
Courtesy of the Nashville Public Library, Special Collections

Frist Art Museum

The Frist Art Museum is supported in part by

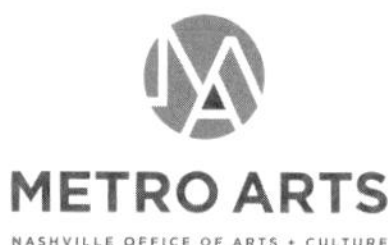

THE FRIST FOUNDATION

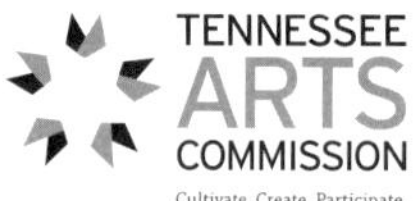

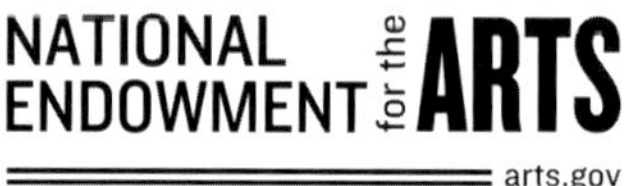

ISBN 978-0-8265-2221-4 (hardcover)
ISBN 978-0-8265-0576-7 (paperback)

This book was set in Arno Pro with Bebas Neue and Poynter Text used as display fonts.

Printed and bound in Canada by Friesens.

Library of Congress Cataloging-in-Publication Data on file
LC control number 2018014285
LC classification number LCC F444.N29 W44 2018
Dewey classification number 323.1196/0730768550904—dc23
LC record available at *lccn.loc.gov/2018014285*

The Frist Art Museum sits on land that Cherokee and Shawnee Native peoples, elders, and their ancestors call their homeland. We acknowledge and pay respect to them. We also acknowledge and offer deep gratitude to the land and water that support us.

Published with support from

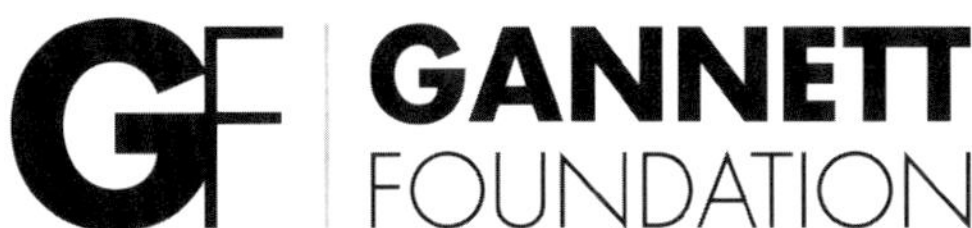

and made possible by the generosity of the following individuals:

Anonymous, in honor of Robert Churchwell Sr.
Samar Ali and Amr El Husseini
Kerry Brock and John Seigenthaler
Michael and Pamela Carter
Doreatha and André Churchwell
Ann and Tom Curtis
Vincent Durnan
Amy and Frank Garrison
Howard Gentry
Bernice and Joel Gordon
Janie Greenwood Harris, Esq.
The Healing Trust
Drs. Melvin N. and Marcelite D. Johnson
Robin and Bill King
Brooks and Bert Mathews
Freida and Lucius Outlaw Jr.
Alice Randall, David Ewing, and Caroline Randall Williams
Lisa and Mike Shmerling
Deborah Story
Vanderbilt University in honor of Rev. James Lawson
Matthew Walker
Gail, David, Samantha, and Nicholas Williams

CONTENTS

FOREWORD

The truth is sometimes hard to face. But we must face it. We must examine it. We must remember it. The truth will set us free. And the truth of the Nashville Civil Rights Movement is right here, between the pages of *We Shall Overcome: Press Photographs of Nashville in the Civil Rights Era.*

These photos are real portraits of what happened in the 1960s in Nashville, Tennessee. They were taken by photographers from the city's two major daily newspapers at that time, *The Tennessean* and the *Nashville Banner*. They reflect the struggle, the suffering, and the courage of people determined to end hatred, violence, and racism. They are a record of those who made our country more just and fair, and those who tried to crush justice and fairness.

I was there. I will never forget. But you did not have to be there, sitting at a lunch counter, riding a bus, or marching in the street to learn the lessons of history and apply them to today. Open this book. You will see photographs that document the bombings, the arrests, the beatings, and the pain and fear we felt as we were arrested, thrown into paddy wagons, and taken to jail.

These images also reflect hope and progress. We were just ordinary people with an extraordinary vision: that the nonviolent resistance taught by Martin Luther King Jr. and Mahatma Gandhi could help create a Beloved Community that values the dignity and the worth of every human being. We had faith that sacrificing our bodies to this ideal would ultimately change hearts and minds. Our protests were love in action. We wanted to redeem not only our attackers, but the very soul of America.

I believe we did so. But I also believe we must keep doing so. If our current political climate shows us anything, it is that old hatreds will reassert themselves if good people do not keep pressing the case for the Beloved Community.

Perhaps the greatest gift of Nashville's civil rights history is that it reminds us we can make a difference. No matter how fierce the adversary, no matter how organized the opposition, no matter how powerful the resistance, nothing can stop the movement of a disciplined, determined people motivated by justice. So, let's keep moving.

We have come a great distance in just a few decades. We still have a distance to go. We still need to change the social, political, economic, and religious structures around us. We still need a revolution of values and ideas in this nation and throughout the world. We still need to build a Beloved Community—a nation and a world at peace with itself.

This book reminds us that it was possible once. And it is possible still.

—Congressman John Lewis
US Representative for Georgia's 5th district

PREFACE

While fellow Southern cities such as Birmingham, Greensboro, and Little Rock may have been the focus of more headlines, Nashville played an important role in the Civil Rights Movement during the late 1950s and 1960s. In addition to being the first metropolis in the southeast to integrate places of business, Nashville was a hub for training students in nonviolent protest, many of whom became influential figures on the national stage. During an April 1960 speech at Fisk University, Dr. Martin Luther King Jr. himself said, "I came to Nashville not to bring inspiration, but to gain inspiration from the great movement that has taken place in this community." This legacy is worthy of reexamination fifty years after King's death, especially when race relations and social justice are again at the forefront of our country's consciousness. It also warrants an introduction to younger generations and the many newcomers to Nashville who may not be aware of its history. Finally, as so thoroughly described in David Halberstam's notable book *The Children*, this period reminds us that it is indeed our country's brave youth, often under the thoughtful guidance of elders, that can and will demand change, then and now.

The one hundred photographs featured here were taken between 1957, the year that desegregation in public schools began, and 1968, when the National Guard was called in to surround the state capitol in the wake of King's assassination in Memphis. Of central significance are images of lunch counter sit-ins led by students from local historically black colleges and universities that took place in early 1960. The photographs are sourced from the archives of Nashville's two daily newspapers at the time: *The Tennessean*, which was the more progressive publication, and the now-defunct *Nashville Banner*, a conservative paper whose leadership was less interested in covering events related to racial issues. Some of the photos in this book were selected to be published in the papers, but most were not, the disclosure of which reveals insight into the editorial process. Many of the images are published here for the first time. In several, photojournalists (and television crews) are visible, serving as a reminder of the presence of the camera and the rising influence of the media during these historic times. *We Shall Overcome* also offers an opportunity to consider the role of images and the media in shaping public opinion, something leaders in the movement were acutely aware of and a relevant subject in today's news-saturated climate.

This publication and the accompanying exhibition presented at the Frist Art Museum from March 30 through October 14, 2018, build upon a recent swelling of interest in the period throughout the city, evidenced by a major public artwork by Walter Hood commissioned by the Metro Arts Commission to a painted mural in North Nashville by the Norf Art Collective, both of which pay homage to local heroes of the movement. The photographs in this book, the first major publication devoted to images of Nashville during this turbulent era, depict a narrative that has moments of triumph and joy as well as pain and hate. And, while much change has come, some remind us that America is still struggling to achieve true racial equity, here in Nashville and around the country.

—Kathryn E. Delmez, curator

ACKNOWLEDGMENTS

In the 1960s, a generation of social activists emerged from the smoldering injustices they had inherited. They mobilized to confront authority, slowly at first and then with all just vigor, to challenge the status quo, reform legislation, expose special interests, and undermine the profit motive in political and military policy. The drive for equal rights and equal justice was a recurring effort throughout the twentieth century. At the core of our national disgrace are racial discrimination and injustice. Artists and photographers repeatedly found ways to engage in protest and question unconscious bias.

It is gratifying that a generation of young curators has taken up the mantle of ensuring that art promoting social justice remains visible and that conversations continue. Frist curator Kathryn Delmez has long wanted to organize an exhibition devoted to the Civil Rights Movement in Nashville. Her research and study culminated in the exhibition *We Shall Overcome: Civil Rights and the Nashville Press, 1957–1968*, which would be on view in the Conte Community Arts Gallery at the Frist, March 30 to October 14, 2018. No publication was planned.

After presenting a preview of the exhibition to the Board of Trustees, we received feedback suggesting that this project warranted a lasting document that would not only speak to a specific historical moment but also serve as a catalyst for future study at the Civil Rights Room of the Nashville Public Library and beyond. With the generous support of empathetic donors, we have been able to bring this book to fruition, offering gratis copies to branches of the Nashville Public Library, libraries in Metro Nashville Public Schools, Metro Council members, and members of the Tennessee State Assembly for distribution to libraries in their respective communities.

With characteristic enthusiasm, Ms. Delmez agreed to serve as editor for the publication and immediately began imagining the ideal content. We are grateful for her scholarship, work ethic, and poise in the face of compressed deadlines. While organizing the exhibition, Ms. Delmez contacted Caroline Vincent and Anne-Leslie Owens of the Metro Nashville Arts Commission, who offered suggestions and shared the wisdom of their experience planning *Witness Walls*, a public artwork marking Nashville's contributions to the Civil Rights Movement. We are very grateful for their early and generous support. They introduced Ms. Delmez to Professor Linda T. Wynn, who provided invaluable insight and direction for the exhibition.

Professor Wynn gave feedback on image selection, reviewed interpretative materials, and coordinated public programs presented in conjunction with the exhibition. Naturally, she was our first choice to write the essay for this book. Professor Wynn serves on the faculty of Fisk University in the Department of History and Political Science. She is also the assistant director for state programs at the Tennessee Historical Commission. Despite a heavy workload, she agreed. Her essay establishes the historical context for the Nashville protests, painting a vivid picture of Nashville in the years from 1957 to 1968.

The foreword herein was provided by Congressman John Lewis. We are humbled by his words and reminded that we are all called to action in the face of injustice. We thank John Seigenthaler Jr. and Katie Seigenthaler for facilitating his contribution. They have been generous and supportive colleagues throughout. During the organization of this publication and the exhibition it accompanies, we have been constantly mindful that our community and the world were changed by the courage of very young people, initially by six-year-old children bravely integrating public schools in the south and then teenagers, including Representative Lewis, who started a movement. We are forever in their debt and inspired by their courage.

The Civil Rights Room at the Nashville Public Library is an incomparable resource. Beth Odle, who oversees the photography archive in special collections, including the images from the *Nashville Banner*, has a deep knowledge of the material. In addition to guiding both Ms. Delmez and myself though the archive, she also provided detailed background information and leads on additional resources. Andrea Blackman, Special Collections division manager, gave important feedback on the project and generously allowed the Frist to modify for this publication the timeline featured in the Civil Rights Room.

At *The Tennessean*, Executive Editor Maria De Varenne was an indispensable advocate for this project. We thank her and everyone at Gannett Publications and the Gannett Foundation for all they did to help bring the exhibition and this publication to fruition. Photojournalist Larry McCormack, who worked for the *Nashville Banner* for many years before moving to *The Tennessean*, and archivist Richard Rogers provided valuable access to their well-organized and informative archive. Rogers responded quickly and thoroughly to myriad questions thrown his way during the research stage. McCormack and Rogers are passionately committed to preserving the integrity of historic images. We also thank former *Tennessean* reporter Dwight Lewis.

Ms. Delmez and I thank numerous members of the community for sharing experiences, including Beverly Boggs, Dr. André Churchwell, Ridley Wills II, and Carlton Wilkinson. Ms. Delmez humbly acknowledges the work of scholars and professionals who have devoted their careers to the subject of the Civil Rights Movement in Nashville. On her behalf, I thank DeLisa A. Minor Harris, Special Collections librarian at Fisk University, and Sharon Hull Smith, director of Special Collections at Tennessee State University (TSU), who facilitated study of their archives, specifically the student newspapers *The Fisk Forum* and *The Meter* (TSU). Sincere appreciation is due Karen Brown Dunlap, expert on the African American press in Tennessee, and Sandra Long Weaver, journalist and advisor to *The Meter.*

At Vanderbilt University, special thanks to Daniel Cornfield, professor of Sociology, and Larry W. Isaac, Gertrude Conaway Vanderbilt Professor of Sociology. Joseph Mella and Dean Martin Rapisarda presented an exhibition at the Vanderbilt University Art Gallery in 2016 on Perry Wallace, the first African American basketball player in the Southeastern Conference. They were generous colleagues from the start.

Reagan Petty, University of North Carolina, was an invaluable intern at an important moment in exhibition planning. Her research skills uncovered important information on the photojournalists from special collections and unearthed original clippings from *The Tennessean* and the *Nashville Banner.* Interns Mary Kathryn Alexander, Belmont University, and Ambar Gonzales, Fisk University, contributed valuable research, as did Vanderbilt University graduate student Katherine Schaffer, who assisted with compiling the timeline and bibliography in this book as well as content for the interactive computer program and app that accompany the exhibition.

This publication would not have been possible without the early support and commitment of trustees Gail Carr-Williams and Frank Garrison. We are indebted to them for recognizing the importance of publishing a lasting document of the project and for lead gifts from their families. We thank individual donors: Samar Ali and Amr El Husseini, Kerry Brock and John Seigenthaler, Pamela and Michael Carter, Doreatha and André Churchwell, Ann and Tom Curtis, Vincent Durnan, Amy and Frank Garrison, Howard Gentry, Bernice and Joel Gordon,

Janie Greenwood Harris, Esq., Drs. Marcelite and Melvin Johnson, Robin and Bill King, Brooks and Bert Mathews, Lucius and Freida Outlaw, Alice Randall, David Ewing, and Caroline Randall Williams, Lisa and Mike Shmerling, Deborah Story, Matthew Walker, and Gail, Dave, Samantha, and Nicholas Williams. We also gratefully acknowledge support from Vanderbilt University in honor of Rev. James Lawson and an anonymous gift in honor of Robert Churchwell Sr.

For reading early drafts of my essay I thank Angela Butler, Ellen Pryor, E. Thomas Wood, and, of course, Kathryn Delmez. Wallace Joiner secured image rights for all illustrations other than those provided by the Nashville Public Library and *The Tennessean.* We thank her for her cooperation and professionalism. At Vanderbilt University Press, we thank Michael Ames, director, for his warm and generous response to our proposal and his unflagging commitment to this project and civil rights in general. Also at Vanderbilt University Press, we thank designer Dariel Mayer for a visually compelling and thoughtful layout. Managing editor Joell Smith-Borne assured a seamless and precise manuscript.

Exhibition support was provided by HCA TriStar Health, presenting sponsor. Additional exhibition sponsors include R.H. Boyd Publishing Corporation and the Ryman Hospitality Properties Foundation. We gratefully acknowledge annual funding from the Metro Nashville Arts Commission, Tennessee Arts Commission, and the National Endowment for the Arts. For their steadfast support, we thank the Frist Foundation and the Frist Board of Trustees, especially Billy Frist, president and chair.

Finally, we are indebted to the photojournalists who documented the Civil Rights Movement in Nashville. They showed us then and in perpetuity the merits of a free press in a democracy. We thank them for the enduring legacy of their photographs.

—Susan H. Edwards, PhD
Executive Director & CEO

NASHVILLE

An Inspirational City

Linda T. Wynn

"There is a source of power in each of us
that we don't realize until we take responsibility."
—Diane J. Nash[1]

Most discussions about the African American struggle for equality, freedom, and justice in Nashville begin with the mid-twentieth century, when activists (most of them people of African descent) were in the process of overthrowing the Jim Crow laws that prevented them from being full-fledged citizens of the United States with all the rights and privileges accorded them by the Constitution. People seeking to learn about and understand the Modern Civil Rights Movement in Tennessee's capital city look not only to activists who were in the vanguard of desegregating schools or the veterans of sit-ins and freedom rides and those who battled to gain access to the ballot, but also to the reporting in local and national presses.[2] But African Americans in Nashville began the long trek to obtaining those rights granted by a civil society much earlier, in the nineteenth and early twentieth centuries. For example, one of the five cases in the Supreme Court's consolidated Civil Rights Cases of 1883, *Robinson and wife v. Memphis & Charleston Railroad*, was an antidiscrimination suit that began in Memphis; and in 1919 there was a silent march to Governor Thomas C. Rye's office to protest lynching. Despite these efforts, it was not until the United States Supreme Court's 1954 unanimous ruling in *Brown v. Board of Education of Topeka*, the 1955 case *Robert W. Kelley et al. v. Board of Education of City of Nashville* desegregating Nashville's public schools, and the 1958 formation of the Nashville Christian Leadership Council (NCLC), that Nashville's African American community laid the foundation for dismantling Jim Crow's racial segregation. Throughout this process, the local and national presses documented the journey toward attainment of civil and constitutional rights.

Newspapers in the early post–World War II era encountered a challenging, ongoing news story in the African American struggle for civil rights. African Americans' crusade for full civil rights exposed the profound difficulty the mainstream (white) press, both local and national, had in covering a movement that was wrestling with a fundamental aspect of America's social structure. Both those reporting the news and those responsible for disseminating it slowly came to terms with one of the greatest social and political campaigns of the twentieth century. While the mainstream Nashville press covered the school desegregation movement, it was somewhat dilatory in its coverage of the sit-ins conducted by students primarily from American Baptist Theological Seminary (now American Baptist College), Fisk University, Meharry Medical College, and Tennessee A&I State University (now Tennessee State University), the city's four historically black colleges and universities (HBCUs). African American newspapers and magazines, though, kept their communities informed about developments in the civil rights movement. In Nashville the African American press included the *Nashville Globe* (1906–1960), the *Nashville Commentator* (1948–1971), and the *Nashville World*. Civil rights leaders themselves published the *Nashville City Examiner* and the *Nashville News Star*. Occasionally the Nashville Christian Leadership Conference (NCLC) and the Student Nonviolent Coordinating Committee (SNCC) published newsletters.[3] Other papers, like the *Southern School News* published by the Southern Education Reporting Service (SERS), launched in Nashville in response to *Brown v. Board of Education*, reported on what happened in public education after school segregation became unconstitutional. Nashville's two largest white papers represented opposing views when it came to race relations. The *Nashville Banner*, the older of the two papers, adhered to the states' rights philosophy, while *The Tennessean* articulated a more progressive stance regarding race. In 1950, the *Banner*'s publisher, James Geddes Stahlman, an ultra-conservative tied to the segregationist policies of the Old South, hired Robert Churchwell Sr., the first African American reporter to work for a major southern newspaper (fig. 1). Churchwell covered "Negro News" and, after the *Brown* decision, education, but for the first five years of his employment he was barred from the newsroom and from attending meetings and was forced to work from home.[4]

When the Supreme Court announced its decision in *Brown v. Board of Education* on Monday, May 17, 1954, the Nashville white press reported two different points of view. The *Nashville Banner* , the only evening newspaper in Tennessee, shouted below its masthead "SEGREGATION OUT!" Notwithstanding the headline, the paper assured its readers that little would change locally.[5] Stahlman placed an editorial on the paper's front page. Although it denounced the "demagogic appeals" of protesters against the court's decision, it never deviated from its states' rights doctrine. The editorial called for a "reasoned and cautious treatment of the case presented to reconcile both national and States' Rights on the Constitution." The city's morning and Sunday paper, *The Tennessean*, under publisher Silliman Evans, while not completely endorsing the *Brown* decision, simply stated that school desegregation was the "law of the land." It further stated that those in the South would "be paying new honor to the principal of democracy they so readily profess, but on occasion, so reluctantly practice."[6]

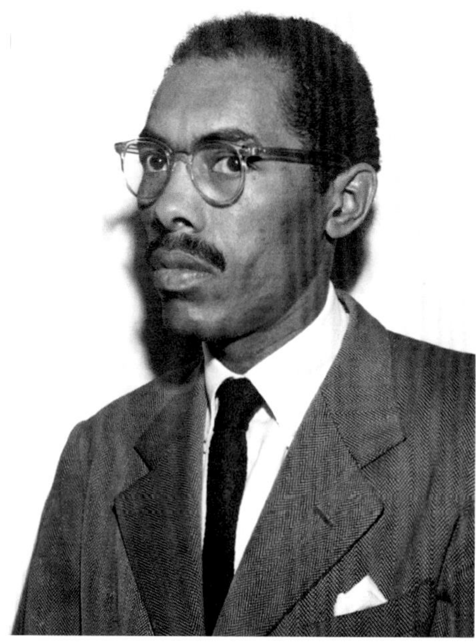

Figure 1. Robert Churchwell, the first full-time African American reporter in the South. Circa 1950. Courtesy of *Nashville Banner* Archives, Nashville Public Library, Special Collections

Soon after the *Brown* decision, attorney Z. Alexander Looby and the NAACP communicated with the Nashville Board of Education about initiating school desegregation. As foreseen by the *Banner*, change within the educational system did not come speedily. The following year, on May 31, 1955, the Supreme Court issued an ambiguous directive in the *Brown II* case that all public schools must desegregate "with all deliberate speed."[7] Most school boards placed their emphasis on "deliberate" rather than "speed." Consequently, Alfred Z. Kelley, an African American barber in Nashville, sought a legal reprieve for his son Robert, who faced having to go across town to Pearl, an African American high school, even though he lived within walking distance of the white East High School. With assistance from Looby and his law partner Avon N. Williams Sr., the Nashville NAACP, and the NAACP's Legal Defense Fund (LDF), in September 1955 a class action lawsuit, *Robert W. Kelley et al. v. Board of Education of City of Nashville*, was filed on behalf of Robert and twenty other African American students.[8] In December, attorneys amended the suit to include two white children who had also been refused admission to neighborhood schools. Their parents taught at Fisk University and lived in a predominantly African American neighborhood.[9] *Kelley* sought open admission to Nashville's schools without regard to race. A little more than a year later, in his ruling federal district judge William E. Miller ordered Nashville's Board of Education to formulate a desegregation plan no later than January 1957.[10] The Board of Education produced a document that became known as the Nashville Plan; it desegregated one grade per year, beginning with the first grade, but included a liberal transfer policy allowing students whose race was in the minority in their newly assigned schools to opt for a majority-status alternative, essentially allowing them to remain in segregated schools. When school board members voted on the proposed plan, the board's only black member, attorney Coyness Ennix, cast the sole dissenting vote. Judge Miller ordered the plan to be implemented in September 1957. Both of Nashville's major newspapers approved of the approach taken by the school board. For the *Banner* it was a "considerate" ruling; to *The Tennessean*, a "Victory for Gradualism."[11] According to the *Southern School News*, the Parents School Preference Committee, an ad hoc segregationist group, called upon the school board to abandon its desegregation plan.[12] The *Banner* endorsed the group's recommendation. The Nashville Plan became the law of the city, and other places across the South duplicated it.[13]

When the academic year began on September 9, eight elementary schools were to be desegregated: Buena Vista, Jones, and Fehr on the north side; Bailey, Caldwell, and Glenn on the east; Clemons, south of downtown; and Hattie Cotton, to the northeast. Thanks to extensive coverage by the city's newspapers, six of the eight schools captured the public's attention. However, Clemons and Hattie Cotton did not receive the same scrutiny from the media and did not attract the same rage.[14] Hattie Cotton experienced no significant disturbances during school hours when first-grader Patricia Watson, the lone African American student, entered the building. However, that night, at approximately 12:33 a.m., a blast disturbed the stillness of the night when the school's west wing was bombed (fig. 2). Earlier in the day John Kasper, a staunch segregationist originally from New Jersey, had been seen among the people protesting desegregation at several of the schools.[15] Kasper was arrested, and during the month of September editors at *The Tennessean* printed eight editorials about the Nashville Plan, Kasper and his co-conspirators, the dynamiting of Hattie Cotton, and the city police department's effective handling of the events. Likewise, the *Banner* praised law enforcement officials and their handling of Kasper, but it also wanted to "check and eradicate. . . the strife-breeding NAACP."[16] Beyond the local press, network television, newspapers across the country, and national magazines such as *Time* and *Newsweek* exposed Nashville as a hot spot along with Little Rock, Arkansas, and its Central High School. As the decade of the 1950s closed, Nashville and the rest of the nation witnessed a continuation of the movement to gain civil rights as students and others moved toward equality in America.

In January 1958, a year after the founding of the Southern Christian Leadership Conference (SCLC) by the Reverend Dr. Martin Luther King Jr. and other Southern ministers, Reverend Kelly Miller Smith Sr. (fig. 3), who had served on SCLC's board and was the pastor of the only downtown African American church, First Baptist Church Capitol Hill, established the Nashville Christian Leadership Conference (NCLC).[17] The nascent civil rights organization developed three objectives: increase voter registration; facilitate black employment, especially in the police department; and desegregate Nashville's lunch counters and restrooms in downtown stores.[18] The NCLC, after due

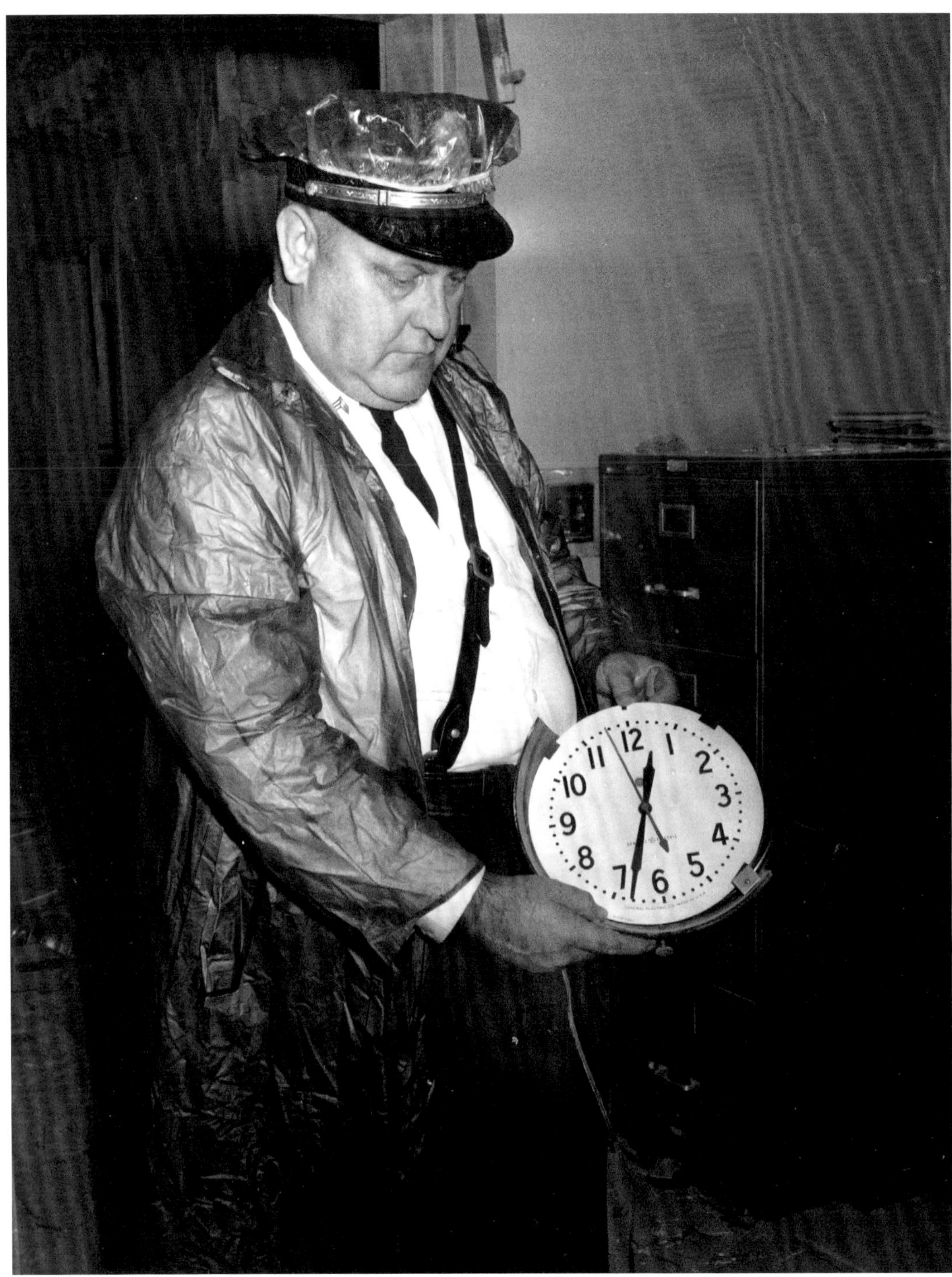

Figure 2. An officer displays a clock stopped at 12:33 a.m. when a dynamite blast damaged Hattie Cotton School. September 10, 1957. Photo by Dale Ernsberger, courtesy of *Nashville Banner* Archives, Nashville Public Library, Special Collections

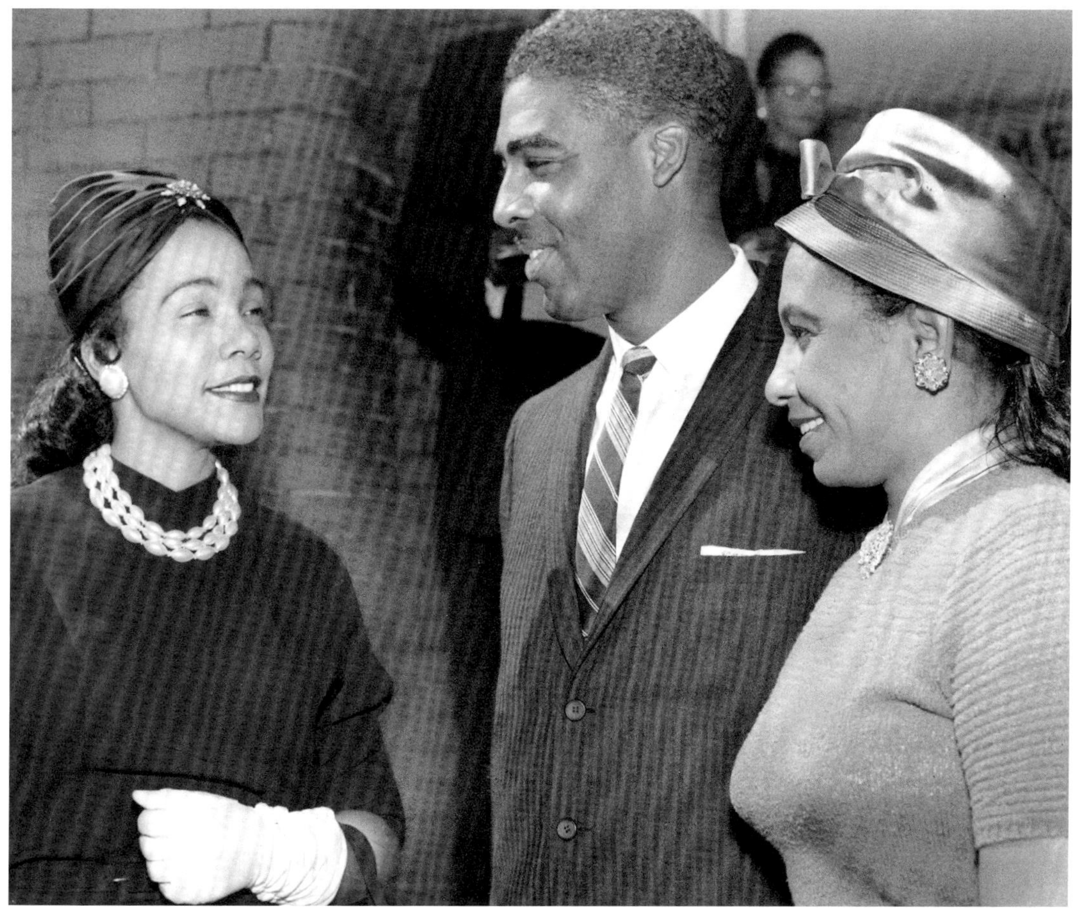

Figure 3. Rev. Kelly Miller Smith, pastor of First Baptist Church Capitol Hill, with Coretta Scott King and Mrs. D. Conrad Gandy. October 10, 1958. Photo by Bob Ray, courtesy of *Nashville Banner* Archives, Nashville Public Library, Special Collections

consideration, decided to move forward with desegregating the eateries in the city's central business district. Harvey's and Cain-Sloan department stores provided restaurants for those wishing to have a meal, and the district's five-and-dime stores, like Woolworth, McLellen's, and Kress, provided food in a more casual and less expensive setting. Before NCLC officials started their campaign to deconstruct the Jim Crow eateries, they initiated a dialogue with the stores' managers, but to no avail. In the fall of 1958, Reverend Smith and James Lawson, who had been called to the South by King and was a student in Vanderbilt University's Divinity School, conducted meetings and, to their surprise, attracted a small number of students from the city's HBCUs. Lawson held study sessions and workshops primarily at Clark Memorial Methodist and First Baptist Capitol Hill churches. As the student numbers grew, Lawson prepared them intellectually and mentally for the task of social desegregation and nonviolent protest. They read William Penn, Henry David Thoreau, Reinhold Niebuhr, and Gandhi, especially focusing on his concept of *satyagraha*, a philosophy of inner calm and resolution that enables one to embrace nonviolence as a way of life.[19]

Beginning in November of 1959, students and leaders of

NCLC conducted "test sit-ins" to confirm Nashville's exclusionary policy of racial segregation in downtown stores and, through the rest of November and December, planned their full-scale sit-ins for launching in January. However, they were delayed because adult leaders wanted more time to raise funds for bail, attorneys, and physicians. In the meantime, four male students from North Carolina Agricultural and Technical State College (now University) in Greensboro captured the nation's attention with their first sit-in at the Woolworth lunch counter on February 1, 1960.[20] Twelve days later, 124 Nashville students sought service at whites-only lunch counters in the city's central business district (plate 21). Led by Diane Nash, who later became the leader of the Nashville Student Central Committee, John Lewis, James Bevel, Bernard Lafayette, the Reverend C. T. Vivian, and others, their resolution shook Nashville's conservative foundation.[21] Throughout the sit-in campaign, students were arrested by the hundreds and beaten and abused by white antagonists (plates 28 and 23). In conjunction with the sit-ins, African Americans in Nashville initiated and sustained an "economic withdrawal" against downtown merchants, which proved especially impactful over the Easter holiday shopping season.

On April 17, 1960, Nashville students joined other students from across the region at Shaw University in Raleigh, North Carolina, and met with SCLC's acting director Ella Baker to form the Student Nonviolent Coordinating Committee (SNCC). Synonymous with the Nashville movement, Diane Nash was considered a favorite to become SNCC's first leader, but she lost to her Fisk colleague Marion Berry. "Diane was a devoted leader . . . but she was the wrong sex," said John Lewis. "There was a desire to emphasize and showcase black manhood."[22]

Just two days later, back in Nashville, attorney Z. Alexander Looby's home was bombed because of the prominent role he played in the civil rights movement not only in Nashville but statewide (plates 32 and 33). Fortunately Looby and his wife, Grafta (Mosby), were physically unharmed. In response, that afternoon thousands of African American and white protesters silently marched to the courthouse and confronted Mayor Ben West (plates 34, 35, and 36). After being interrogated by Nash and Reverend Vivian, the mayor affirmed the immorality of racial segregation, eventually agreeing that lunch counters should be desegregated. The next morning, *The Tennessean's* front-page headline read "INTEGRATE COUNTERS – MAYOR."[23] The evening of the twentieth, Dr. Martin Luther King Jr., speaking at Fisk University, said "I came to Nashville not to bring inspiration, but to gain inspiration from the great movement that has taken place in this community."[24] Within three months of the first sit-in, on May 10, 1960, Nashville became the first Southern city to begin desegregating its public facilities.[25]

Without doubt, the coterie of Nashville students produced one of the most, if not the most, dynamic of local movements. From the Nashville student movement came a group of conscientious leaders who traversed the southern region inspiring other activists and carrying the ethos of nonviolence they had learned from the Reverend James Lawson. The students played key roles in the Nashville sit-in movement and the formation of SNCC, and they would go on to be leaders in the Freedom Rides, the Birmingham campaign of 1963, and the struggle to gain voting rights in Selma, all events at the apex of the modern civil rights struggle. Consequently, the narrative of civil rights and its coverage in the Nashville press reflects the gamut of players, including young people and women, on the movement's battlefield; the stress and disruption it generated in the everyday life of the city; the role of the media, both print and radio/television; and the enormous obstacles and cruelty activists encountered.[26]

Although the first phase of the Nashville sit-in movement ended in May of 1960, systemic racism remained a problem. Over the next few years, more actions, including sit-ins and pickets, took place at restaurants, movie theaters, public swimming pools, and other segregated facilities.[27] Members of the Nashville student movement, under the leadership of Diane Nash, John Lewis, and others, played significant roles in the continuation of the Congress of Racial Equality's (CORE) Freedom Rides of 1961. In fact, fourteen students from Tennessee A&I State University were eventually expelled by order of Governor Bufford Ellington because of their participation in the Freedom Rides.

CORE and its director James Farmer initiated the bus rides though the southeast that tested the Supreme Court's 1960 *Boynton v. Virginia* decision that made it unconstitutional to racially segregate waiting rooms, restrooms, and lunch counters in interstate terminals. Encountering only a few problems during their first week of travel, the interracial group ran into a segregationist storm in Anniston, Alabama, on Mother's Day, May 14, 1961, when a vicious mob of more than one hundred angry whites brutally beat the Riders and fire bombed the bus (fig. 1, pg. 18). Another group of Riders was assaulted in the Birmingham bus station that day (fig. 4). These violent encounters, along with prodding from President John F. Kennedy's administration, caused Farmer to abort CORE's plans to ride to New Orleans. Nash, though, wondered why CORE allowed "violence to vanquish nonviolence."[28] Even after warnings from Farmer, Birmingham minister Fred Shuttlesworth, and US Justice Department representative John Seigenthaler of the Kennedy administration, members of the Nashville Student Movement left Nashville on May 17 for Birmingham. Upon their arrival, Theophilus Eugene "Bull" Conner, city commissioner of public safety, ordered the new group of Freedom Riders taken to jail. The Riders were released the following day at the Alabama state line, and Nash sent sit-in leader Leo (now known as Kwame) Lillard to pick them up and transport them back to Birmingham.[29] Three days later, despite the governor's pledge of protection, approximately three hundred white segregationists attacked the new group of Freedom Riders, which included thirteen students from Tennessee A&I State University, four from American Baptist College, two each from Fisk University and George Peabody College (all in Nashville), and one student from Atlanta's Spelman College,

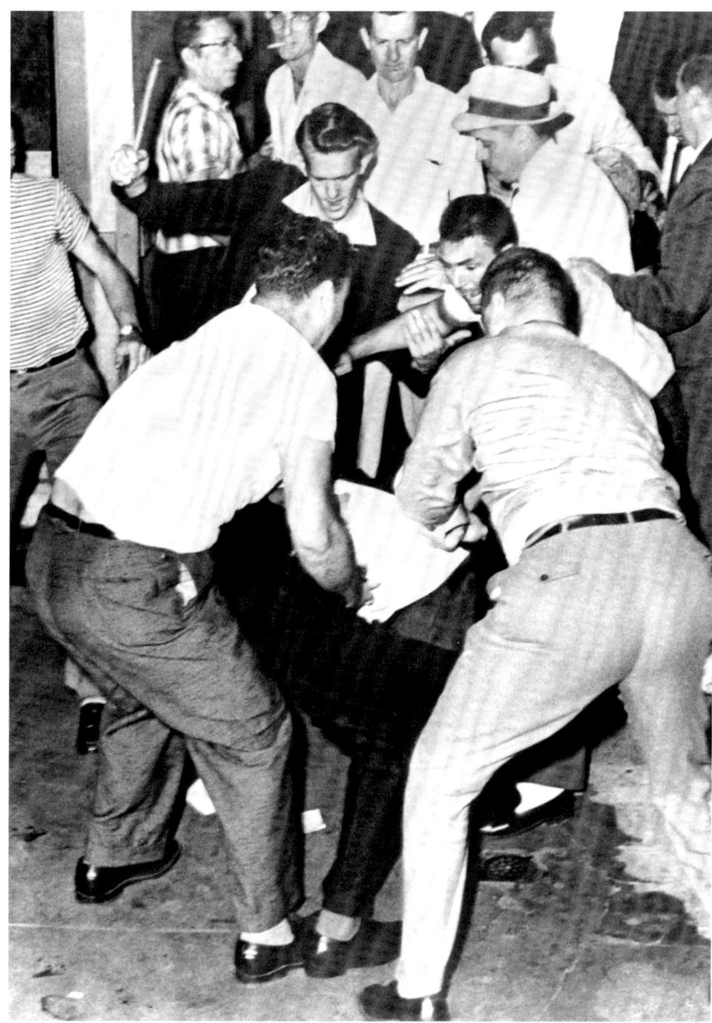

Figure 4. James Peck of New York, who was on one of the two Freedom Rider buses, is attacked at the bus station in Birmingham, Alabama. The other bus was burned in Anniston, Alabama. May 14, 1961. Photo by Tommy Langston, courtesy of Underwood Archives/Getty Images

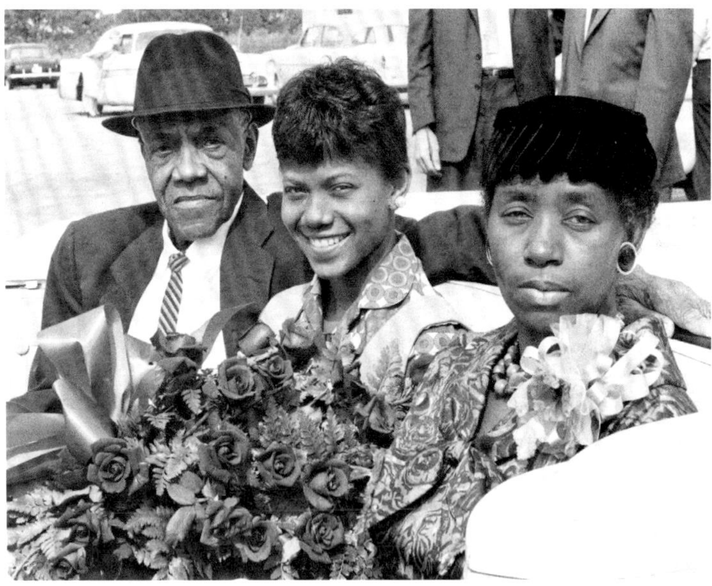

Figure 5. Three-time Olympic gold medal winner and Tennessee A&I State University track star Wilma Rudolph with her parents in a parade, which she insisted be desegregated, in her hometown of Clarksville, Tennessee. October 4, 1960. Photo by Bob Ray, courtesy of *Nashville Banner* Archives, Nashville Public Library, Special Collections

as well as Seigenthaler, as they pulled into at a bus depot in Montgomery.[30] The Riders remained undeterred and started out again four days after the Alabama assault. When the Riders arrived in Jackson, Mississippi, no fanatical white mobs awaited them. However, as they entered the whites-only waiting room, police immediately steered them into a paddy wagon and whisked them away to jail.[31] On September 22, 1961, in response to the Freedom Rides and under pressure from Attorney General Robert Kennedy and others in the Kennedy administration, the Interstate Commerce Commission (ICC) promulgated regulations prohibiting racial segregation in train and bus terminals, effective on November 1, 1961.

The day following the ICC's announcement, *The Tennessean* noted:

> As the Freedom Riders demonstrated, and as the [Civil Rights] commission pointed out, "many Negro interstate passengers are subjected to segregation in several forms in substantial parts of the United States," even today. . . . Those areas which seek to hold to the old order are again warned by the government that rights of all travelers in interstate commerce will not be denied. It is long past time for these areas to bow to the inevitable.[32]

During the modern civil rights era, sports also made contributions toward the easing of race relations. African Americans scored unprecedented points in the field of athletic competition and took positions against the region's code of racial segregation that at times placed them in harm's way. In 1960 Wilma Rudolph, a native of Clarksville, Tennessee, and a member of Tennessee A&I's famed "Tigerbelles," qualified for the 100 meters, the 200 meters, and the relay races in the Rome Olympiad. Not only did she qualify, Rudolph became the first American woman to win three gold medals. Her native city welcomed her home with a banquet and a parade. Like other student athletes, she protested by refusing to attend events held in her honor that were racially segregated. Clarksville officials capitulated, and Rudolph's celebration became the first desegregated event held in the city (fig. 5).

Later, during the 1964–65 academic year, Nashville experienced its first official desegregated athletic contest when the basketball teams from Pearl and Father Ryan high schools met at Municipal Auditorium on January 4. Although Father Ryan's team was predominately white, Willie Earl Brown, an outstanding African American athlete, played on the team's first string.[33] As game time approached, Pearl's coach Cornelius Ridley told *Tennessean* reporter Jimmy Davy, we "will surprise some people who believe all we do is run and shoot. We like to shoot, all right, but we do some other things too."[34] Although Pearl lost the game by one point, it proved that African American and white athletes could play on the same court without incident.

On July 2, 1964, President Lyndon Baines Johnson signed the Civil Rights Act of 1964 into law. This law amended the

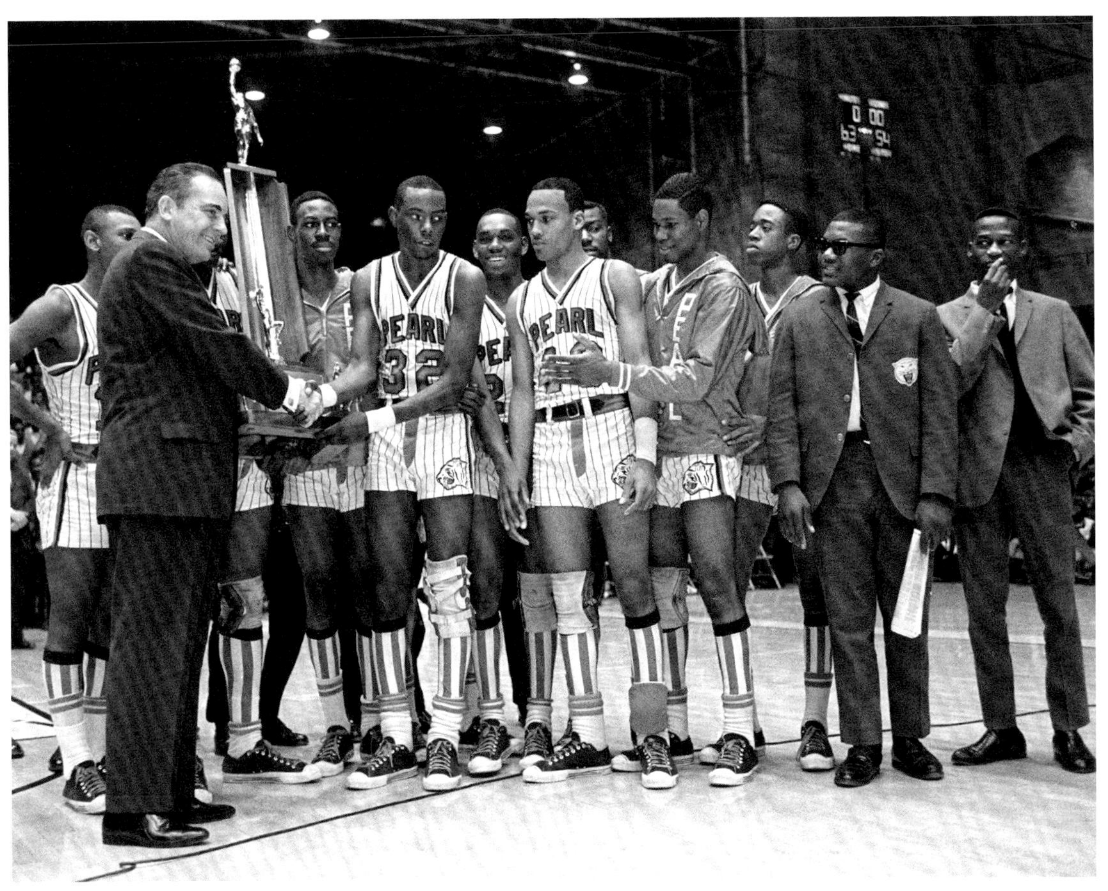

Figure 6. Governor Frank Clement presents the State Boys High School Basketball Championship trophy to Pearl High School's Tigers, who won the first integrated high school athletic competition in Tennessee. March 19, 1966. Photo by Bob Ray, courtesy of *Nashville Banner* Archives, Nashville Public Library, Special Collections

Civil Rights Acts of 1957 and 1960. The following year, on August 6, just as the academic year was beginning, President Johnson signed the 1965 Voting Rights Act. The first year that African Americans participated in the Tennessee Secondary School Athletic Association (TSSAA), Pearl's 1966 basketball team, with a perfect season, became the first all–African American team to win the state TSSAA Boys' Basketball Tournament (fig. 6).[35] After the season ended that spring, more than eighty colleges and universities attempted to recruit team member Perry E. Wallace Jr., a high school All-American and class Valedictorian. After much consideration, Wallace chose Vanderbilt University, becoming the first African American scholarship athlete to play basketball in the Southeastern Conference (SEC).[36] Segregationists' ire intensified. Wallace experienced racism at its worst, particularly at SEC schools in Alabama and Mississippi. Wallace's treatment at the University of Tennessee was not much better. There were threats of beatings, castration, and lynching. He endured physical abuse on the court that referees refused to acknowledge as fouls. Wallace was harangued, taunted, and threatened throughout his SEC career.

When racial malevolence confronted him, Wallace mentally retreated to the north Nashville school where he last experienced the comfort and solace of community support. "On that night in Starkville, Mississippi, Perry sang the Pearl High Alma

Mater," said his friend and high school and college classmate Walter R. Murray Jr. While coaches and teammates "chose not to see the racism," Wallace said, "I . . . wanted somebody to say, you're not crazy, I heard those people . . . calling you 'nigger' and threatening to hang you, I . . . want you to know I'm with you."[37] After Wallace's last season of play with the Vanderbilt Commodores, he was interviewed by Frank Sutherland of *The Tennessean*. The article appeared on March 9, 1970, entitled "Lonely 4 Years for VU Star: 'They Meant Well.'" Wallace's candor surprised many in both the African American and white communities.

On April 8, 1967, while Wallace was still at Vanderbilt, Stokely Carmichael (later known as Kwame Ture), the outspoken Black Power advocate and national head of SNCC, spoke at the university's Impact Symposium, as did Dr. Martin Luther King Jr., South Carolina senator Strom Thurmond, and poet Allen Ginsberg. Prior to Carmichael's speech, Stahlman's *Banner* started a campaign to prevent his appearance at Vanderbilt.[38] With Chancellor Alexander Heard's support, those who had invited Carmichael held steadfast in their commitment, and he addressed the Vanderbilt audience. Prior to speaking at the Impact Symposium, Carmichael addressed students at both Fisk and Tennessee A&I where he more boldly called for Black Power. Following Carmichael's speeches in Nashville, mayhem broke out, generally around the city's HBCUs. A *New York Times* report placed part of the blame on the *Banner* and those who had vociferously opposed Carmichael's Vanderbilt speech.[39]

A year later, Memphis sanitation workers staged a strike against unfair treatment and wages, after a malfunctioning garbage truck crushed Echol Cole and Robert Walker to death on February 1, 1968. City officials failed to respond to the workers' concerns, and, ultimately, this strike brought Martin Luther King to Memphis. A month after Cole and Walker's deaths, the National Advisory Commission on Civil Disorders issued its final report, which stated, "Our nation is moving toward two societies, one black, one white—separate and unequal."[40] The ongoing crisis in Memphis certainly supported the commission's report. King arrived in Memphis on March 18 and addressed a crowd of approximately twenty-five thousand. King praised their unity, saying, "You are demonstrating that we are all tied in a single garment of destiny, and that if one black person suffers, if one black person is down, we are all down."[41] The "drum major for justice" returned to Memphis on March 28 and led thousands of sanitation workers and sympathizers on a march through downtown. Unfortunately, the protests turned violent. The following day, over two hundred striking workers continued their daily march, carrying signs that read, "I Am a Man" (fig. 7).[42]

King returned to Memphis for the last time in early April. Addressing the audience at Mason Temple on April 3, King noted the "difficult days" that lay ahead. He asserted, "But it really doesn't matter with me now, because I've been to the mountaintop [and] I've seen the Promised Land." Continuing in the cadence of a Baptist preacher, he prophesied, "I may not get there with you. But I want you to know tonight, that we, as a people, will get to the Promised Land." The following evening while standing on the balcony of the Lorraine Motel, assassin James Earl Ray's bullet forever silenced King's voice. Rioting broke out in Memphis and across the nation, including Nashville, where National Guard troops were deployed and surrounded the state capitol (fig. 8). One week after the King assassination, President Johnson signed into law the Fair Housing Act, also known as the Civil Rights Act of 1968.

Although villainized by many during his life for the stances he took to push America toward adhering to its core principles, today the modern civil rights movement in Nashville and throughout global society amplifies King's message that "we are all caught in a network of mutuality."[43] Fifty years after his assassination, many do not recognize King's radicalism: his revolutionary vision, his identification with the poor, his unapologetic opposition to the Vietnam War, and his crusade against global imperialism. As Cornel West notes in *The Radical King*, "Although much of America did not know the radical King—and

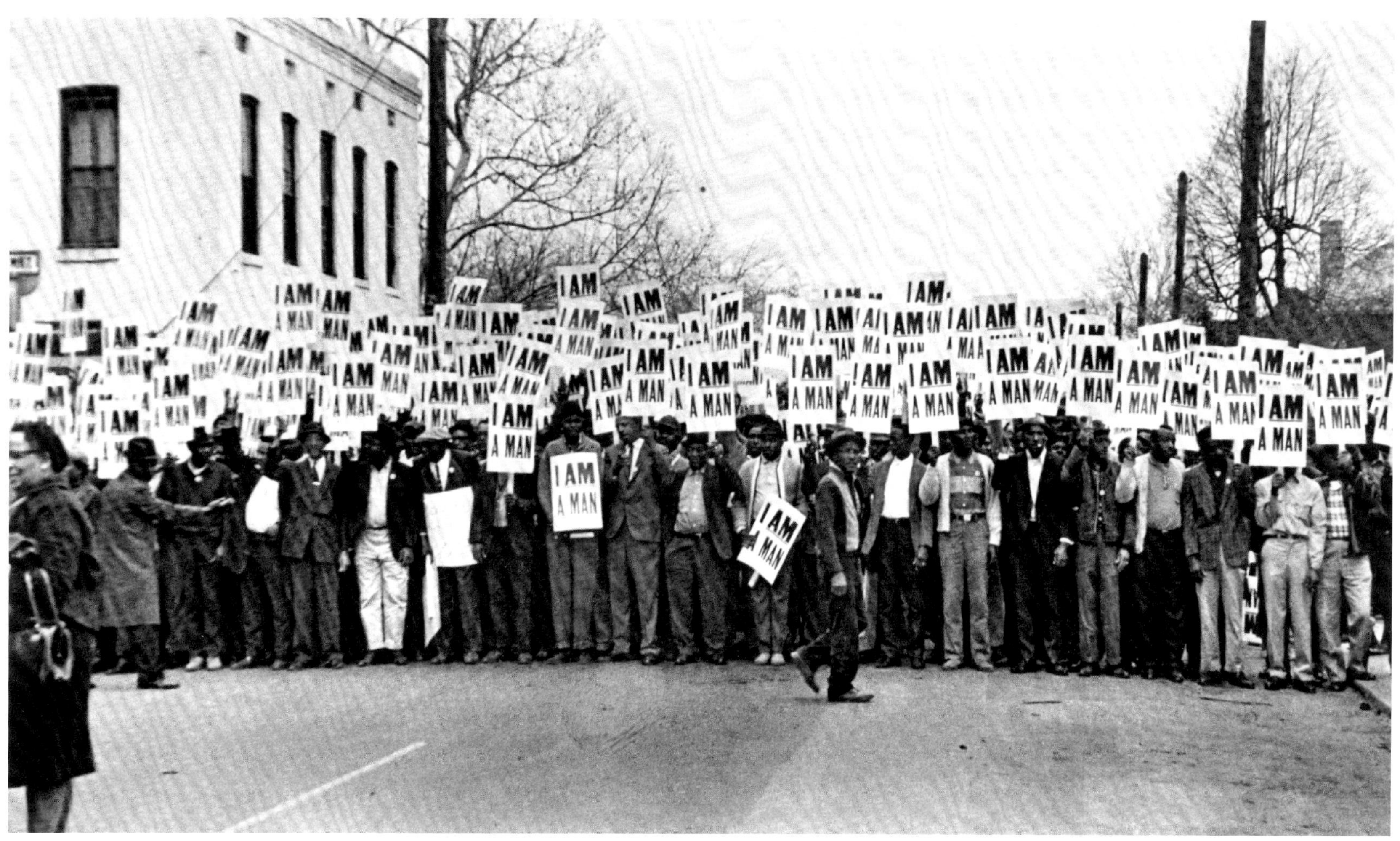

Figure 7. *I Am A Man, Sanitation Workers Strike, Memphis, Tennessee*. March 28, 1968 (printed 1994). Photo by Ernest C. Withers, courtesy of Bridgeman Images. Collection of Museum of Fine Arts, Houston, Texas, Museum purchase funded by the African American Art Advisory Association.

too few know today—the FBI and US government did. They called him 'the most dangerous man in America.'"[44] Yet, King's vision for an equitable American society, manifested by a yearning for racial, social, and economic justice, remains as germane now as it ever did.

Many who participated in the Modern Civil Rights Movement, both the young and the not so young, learned through their actions that the source of power was within each of them as they took responsibility to make Nashville, and indeed the world, a better place. "Struggle is a never ending process," said Coretta Scott King. "Freedom is never really won, you earn it and win it in every generation."[45]

NOTES

1. "Black Herstory: Recognizing and Remembering Some of the Most Powerful Women in Black History," The Black Institute, *www.theblackinstitute.org/black_herstory*.
2. The African American struggle of the 1950s and 1960s is referred to as the Modern Civil Rights Movement, which is designated by historians as beginning with the 1954 *Brown v. Board of Education* decision or in 1955 with Rosa Parks, the Reverend Dr. Martin Luther King Jr., and the Montgomery Bus Boycott. The movement did not end with King's death. It merely shifted to a new phase in which the changes the movement attained, and the ongoing impediments it confronted created a contemporary and more complex and rugged terrain of struggle. Today, movements like Black Lives Matter and others are a continuation of the Modern Civil Rights Movement.
3. Bobby L. Lovett, *The Civil Rights Movement in Tennessee: A Narrative History* (Knoxville: University of Tennessee Press, 2005), 25–26.

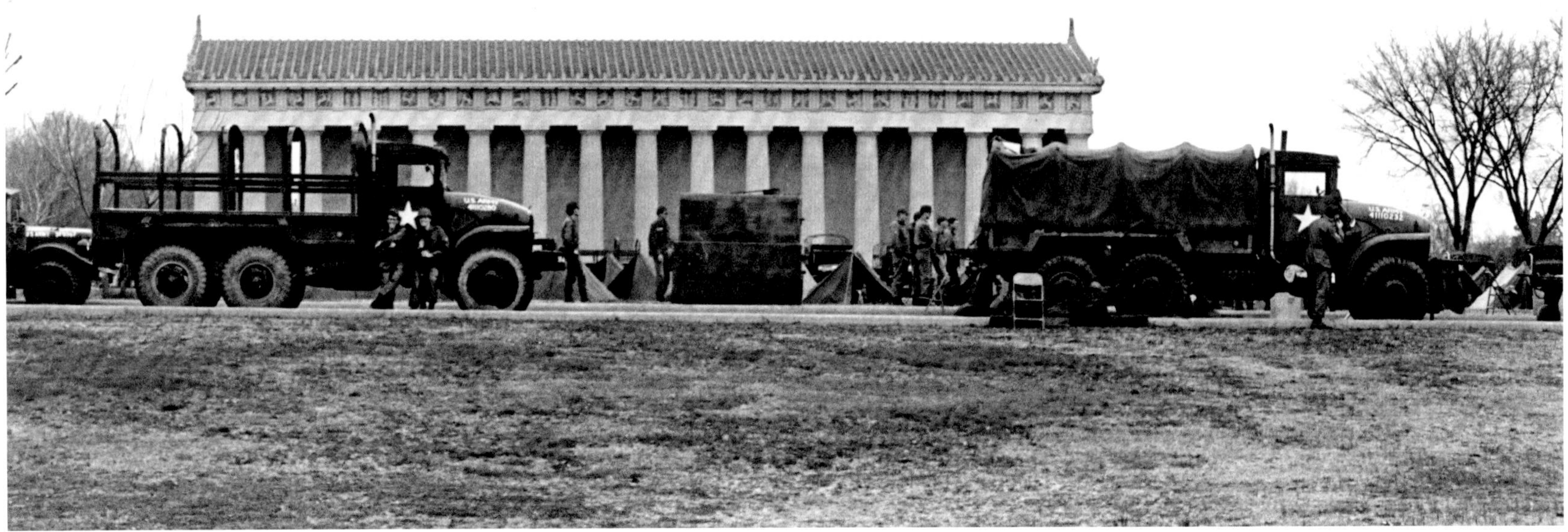

Figure 8. A convoy of Tennessee National Guardsmen in Centennial Park in the wake of Dr. Martin Luther King Jr.'s assassination. April 7, 1968. Photo by J. T. Phillips, courtesy of *The Tennessean*

4. According to Robert Churchwell Sr., he was hired by the *Banner* so the paper could start running pictures of "Negroes and Negro stories all over the paper, not just in one part." For five years, Churchwell wrote his stories at home and walked to the paper to deliver them to the city editor. "Robert Churchwell: VHFP Visionary," 2002, interview by Jerrard Davis, *www.visionaryproject.org/churchwellrobert*.
5. "Ruling Makes No Changes Immediately," *Nashville Banner*, May 17, 1954.
6. Hugh Davis Graham, *Crisis in Print: Desegregation and the Press in Tennessee* (Nashville: Vanderbilt University Press, 1967), 34–37, 43.
7. "Brown v. Board of Education (1955)," FindLaw, *caselaw.findlaw.com/us-supreme-court/349/294.html*.
8. Coincidently, this action came one hundred years after the opening of Nashville's first public school (for whites), Hume High and Grammar School.
9. Graham, *Crisis in Print*, 155–56.
10. Don Doyle, *Nashville since the 1920s* (Knoxville: University of Tennessee Press, 1985), 235. In the spring of 1956, nineteen of the twenty-two Southern members of the US Senate signed the Southern Manifesto in opposition to the *Brown* decision. The exceptions included Lyndon Johnson of Texas and Tennessee's Albert Gore Sr. and Estes Kefauver. US representative Percy Priest of Tennessee also did not sign the manifesto.
11. Graham, *Crisis in Print*, 157.
12. Graham, *Crisis in Print*, 156; *Southern School News*, August 1957, 6.
13. In 1971, US district judge L. Clure Morton ordered a massive cross-town busing plan to desegregate Nashville's public schools. *Kelley v. Board of Education*, the lawsuit filed in Nashville in 1955, was finally settled in 1998. See Doyle, *Nashville since the 1920s*; Lovett, *The Civil Rights Movement in Tennessee*; Ansley T. Erickson, *Making The Unequal Metropolis: School Desegregation and Its Limits* (Chicago: University of Chicago Press, 2016); and John Egerton, "Walking into History: The Beginning of School Desegregation in Nashville, Tennessee," *Southern Spaces*, May 4, 2009, *southernspaces.org/2009/walking-history-beginning-school-desegregation-nashville*.
14. Egerton, "Walking into History."
15. Egerton, "Walking into History"; Graham, *Crisis in Print*, 158.
16. Graham, *Crisis in Print*, 158.
17. Lovett, *The Civil Rights Movement in Tennessee*, 120.
18. Linda T. Wynn, "The Dawning of a New Day: The Nashville Sit-Ins, February 13–May 10, 1960," *Tennessee Historical Quarterly* 50, no. 1 (Spring 1991): 42–54.
19. Benjamin Houston, *The Nashville Way: Racial Etiquette and the Struggle for Social Justice in a Southern City* (Athens: University of Georgia Press, 2012), 87.
20. The four male students from North Carolina A&T were Joseph McNeil, Franklin McCain, Ezell Blair Jr. (Jibreel Khazan), and David Richmond. They became known as the "Greensboro Four." Greensboro, North Carolina, did not desegregate its lunch counters until July 25, 1960. According to Miles Wolff's *How It All Began: The Greensboro Sit-ins*, as a symbolic gesture to the protesters, the black employees at the Greensboro's Woolworth were the first to be served at the store's lunch counter. On July 26, 1960, every Woolworth in the country was desegregated, allowing for both whites and blacks to be served at the counters. The Greensboro sit-in was not the first. In August 1939, black attorney Samuel Wilbert Tucker organized a sit-in at the then-segregated Alexandria, Virginia, library. In 1942, the Congress of Racial Equality sponsored sit-ins in Chicago, as they did in St. Louis in 1949 and Baltimore in 1952. Also, a 1958 sit-in with high school students in Wichita, Kansas, was successful in ending segregation at every Dockum Drug Store in Kansas. Miles Wolff, *How It All Began: The Greensboro Sit-ins* (New York: Stein and Day, 1971).
21. Linda T. Wynn, "Diane Judith Nash: Agent of Social Change, Civil Rights Leader and Social Activist," *AME Church Review*, 123, no. 408: 68–94. Initially students elected Luther Harris and Earl Mays, who each served only a week as chair of the Student Central Committee. Subsequently, they elected Diane Nash as the third chair of the committee, an unusual feat for a woman during the 1960s. Also see Wynn, "The Dawning of a New Day."
22. Wynn, "Diane Judith Nash," 82.
23. David Halberstam, *The Tennessean*, April 20, 1960.
24. Garry Fullerton, "King Delayed by Bomb Scare," *The Tennessean*, April 21, 1960.
25. In March 1960, Mayor West formed a biracial committee composed of President Stephen J. Wright and students Audrey McDonald and Diane Nash of Fisk University, Tennessee A&I State University's President W. S. Davis and students Cupid Poe and Kenneth Frazier; and American Baptist College students James Bevel and Bernard Lafayette. Businesspersons included Lipscomb Davis, E. Donald Hart,

attorney and Nashville Community Relations Conference president George Barrett, B. B. Gullett of the Nashville Bar Association, and Madison Sarratt, vice-chancellor emeritus of Vanderbilt. Students continued their drive to desegregate lunch counters. On March 16, 1960, Peggy Alexander, Diane Nash, Stanley Hemphill, and Matthew Walker sat in at Greyhound's Post Restaurant and were served. The Greyhound Company quietly acknowledged that the Interstate Commerce Commission's ruling in 1955 required railways, bus stations, and airports to provide service to all. After the activists had been served, a white waitress attempted to cut a photographer trying to capture the scene. A group of "well-dressed" whites accosted the students and Walker suffered a "bad cut on the lip." See Wynn, "The Dawning of a New Day"; Houston, *The Nashville Way*, 83–122.

26. While it did not support the students' sit-in movement on its editorial pages, *The Tennessean* covered the protests with approximately seventy stories. James Stahlman, publisher of the city's evening paper the *Banner*, used his editorials, influence, and position on Vanderbilt University's Board of Trustees to have James Lawson, a divinity student at Vanderbilt, expelled for his involvement in student protests. See Gene Roberts and Hank Klibanoff, *The Race Beat: The Press, the Civil Rights Struggle, and the Awakening of a Nation* (New York: Knopf, 2006), 226; Wynn, "The Dawning of a New Day."
27. In November 1960 sit-ins resumed and did not end until 1964. Under pressure from the community, in May 1963 Mayor Beverly Briley appointed African Americans and whites to the Metropolitan Human Relations Committee. Two years later, the Nashville City Council replaced the advisory committee with the Human Relations Commission. See Doyle, *Nashville since the 1920s*, 252–54; Houston, *The Nashville Way*, 147–50.
28. Lynn Olson, *Freedom's Daughters: The Unsung Heroines of the Civil Rights Movement from 1830 to 1970* (New York: Scribner's, 2001), 184.
29. Wynn, "Diane Judith Nash," 85.
30. Students from Tennessee A&I State University included William Barbee, Catherine Burks, Carl Bush, Charles Butler, Allen Cason Jr., Lucretia Collins, Rudolph Graham, William Harbour, Patricia Jenkins, Frederick Leonard, William B. Mitchell Jr., Etta Simpson, and Clarence M. Wright; students from American Baptist College included Paul Brooks, Joseph Carter, Bernard Lafayette Jr., and John Robert Lewis; students from Fisk University included Susan Hermann, an exchange student from Whittier College, and James Zwerg, an exchange student from Beloit College; students from George Peabody College included Salynn McCollum and Susan Wilbur; Ruby Doris Smith was a student at Spelman College in Atlanta, Georgia. See Raymond Arsenault, *Freedom Riders: 1961 and the Struggle for Racial Justice* (New York: Oxford University Press, 2006), 537–38. For information on Ruby Doris Smith, who later became SNCC's executive secretary and the first and only woman to serve on the organization's executive committee, see Cynthia Griggs Fleming, *Soon We Will Not Cry: The Liberation of Ruby Doris Smith Robinson* (Lanham, MD: Rowman and Littlefield, 1998). Several riders and US Justice Department representative John Seigenthaler were beaten.
31. The Freedom Riders were tried and convicted for violating state law. At the trial, the prosecution accused the riders of trespassing. As their defense attorney Jack Young represented the riders, the judge turned his back. After Young finished, the judge immediately sentenced the activists to sixty days in the state penitentiary at Parchman Farm. See Arsenault, *Freedom Riders*, 209–58; "May 24, 1961: Freedom Riders Leave Montgomery, Arrive in Jackson and Arrested," Martin Luther King Jr. and the Global Freedom Struggle, *kingencyclopedia.stanford.edu/encyclopedia/chronologyentry/1961_05_24/index.html*.
32. *The Tennessean*, September 23, 1961, quoted in Graham, *Crisis in Print*, 211.
33. While *The Tennessean* had reported on Nashville's movement for civil rights, ironically on game day it covered the Dixie Flyers, the city's minor league ice hockey team, instead of the basketball game, stating that the Flyers' eight came winning streak, was "one of the most unbelievable performances in Nashville sports history." See Andrew Maraniss, *Strong Inside: Perry Wallace and the Collison of Race and Sports in the South* (Nashville: Vanderbilt University Press, 2014), 35.
34. Maraniss, *Strong Inside*, 35.
35. Linda T. Wynn, "Pearl High School: National and State Championships," in *Profiles of African Americans in Tennessee*, eds. Bobby L. Lovett and Linda T. Wynn (Nashville: Nashville Conference on African American History and Culture, 2007), n.p. In the spring of 1965, the state track meet was the TSSAA's first championship

to include African American high schools. Melrose High School of Memphis won the association's state championship. See Maraniss, *Strong Inside*, 72.

36. Along with Wallace, Vanderbilt recruited Godfrey Dillard from Detroit, Michigan, where he had attended an integrated Catholic high school and was a high-scoring guard on the basketball team. See Maraniss, *Strong Inside*, 101. Dillard suffered a knee injury his sophomore year and decided to leave Vanderbilt after he recovered. He went on to earn a bachelor's degree at Eastern Michigan University, a law degree from the University of Michigan, and a master's in international affairs at George Washington University. "A Conversation with Godfrey Dillard," Office for Equity, Diversity and Inclusion, Vanderbilt University (Oct. 10, 2016), *wpo.vanderbilt.edu/equity-diversity-inclusion/2016/10/10/a-conversation-with-godfrey-dillard*.
37. Perry E. Wallace Jr., Esq., interview with Linda T. Wynn, January 3, 1997. Also see Linda T. Wynn, "Wallace, Perry E., Jr. (1948–)" in *Tennessee Encyclopedia of History and Culture*, edited by Carroll Van West (Nashville: Tennessee Historical Society, 1998), 1029–30. Wallace passed on December 1, 2017. At Vanderbilt, Wallace was joined by Walter Murray, his classmate and class Salutatorian from Pearl High School. Murray later became the first African American member of the Vanderbilt Board of Trustees.
38. Lovett, *The Civil Rights Movement in Tennessee*, 206.
39. Doyle, *Nashville since the 1920s*, 255.
40. V. M. Briggs Jr., "Report of the National Advisory Commission on Civil Disorders: A Review Article," *Journal of Economic Issues* 2 (1968): 200–210. Available at *digitalcommons.ilr.cornell.edu/hrpubs/51*
41. "Memphis Sanitation Workers Strike (1968)," Martin Luther King Jr. and the Global Freedom Struggle, *kingencyclopedia.stanford.edu/encyclopedia/encyclopedia/enc_memphis_sanitation_workers_strike_1968*.
42. Michael K. Honey, *Going Down Jericho Road: The Memphis Strike, Martin Luther King's Last Campaign* (New York: W. W. Norton, 2007), 389; Larry Payne, a sixteen-year-old African American teenager, was killed on March 28, following the march in support of the Memphis sanitation workers.
43. Martin Luther King Jr. *Letter from a Birmingham Jail*, April 16, 1963. Available at *okra.stanford.edu/transcription/document_images/undecided/630416-019.pdf*.
44. Cornel West, *Martin Luther King, Jr.: The Radical King* (Boston: Beacon Press, 2015), x.
45. Coretta Scott King, *My Life with Martin Luther King, Jr.*, (New York: Henry Holt, 1993 [1969]), xiii.

THE NASHVILLE BEAT

Photojournalism during the Civil Rights Movement

Susan H. Edwards

During the turbulent 1960s, people across the country stood up, sat down, spoke out, protested, resisted, marched, mourned, and made a difference. Throughout it all, the fourth estate was front and center. Those working in print and broadcast media were imbued with a fervent sense of responsibility for holding government and its citizens accountable. Despite considerable disagreement on issues, all sides acknowledged the virtues of an independent press in a democracy. Photography, especially in the form of photojournalism, was a powerful ally. This essay concerns images of the Civil Rights Movement in Nashville that were made between 1957 and 1968 for the two white-owned local newspapers, the *Nashville Tennessean* and the *Nashville Banner*.[1] These images are contextualized with others used to influence public opinion. Their presumed veracity was fundamental to their power fifty years ago, and their relevance has not diminished over time.

Photojournalism originated in the nineteenth century in the era of the daguerreotype. In 1880, the half tone process was first used to accompany features that appeared in the *New York Daily Graphic*. At the turn of the century, illustrated journalism exploded with the production of publications such as *Collier's*, *New York World*, *Leslie's Weekly*, and *Harper's Weekly*. In the 1920s and early '30s, advances in cameras, film, and printing techniques revolutionized the sophistication of photography as a social weapon. Governments around the world realized the power of propaganda and quickly conscripted photography for political ends.[2]

In 1935, the Associated Press wire photo network was launched, allowing the transmission of news photos over telephone lines.[3] Images that appeared in *Survey Graphic*, *Look*, and *Life* magazines reached a national audience. By the 1960s, most photojournalists were using 35 mm cameras because they were lightweight and well suited to stopping action and capturing sudden dramatic circumstances such as those sparked by demonstrations and police responses.[4] When speed is paramount, print quality can suffer. Photographs of the Civil Rights era are impactful because of the urgency conveyed, grainy or slightly out-of-focus images notwithstanding.

In the 1960s, roughly 80 percent of American homes had television, but the printed page was still the medium that most Americans relied upon for news.[5] For many, the defining photographs of the Civil Rights era are by Joseph Postiglione (fig. 1), Charles Moore, Danny Lyons, Bruce Davidson, Ernest Withers, Gordon Parks, and Moneta Sleet Jr., and appeared in the *New York Times*, *Washington Post*, *Newsweek*, *TIME*, *Look*, *Life*, *Ebony*, *Jet*, and other national media. Still, amateur photographers, artists, documentarians, and photojournalists across the nation produced trustworthy images of familiar people and

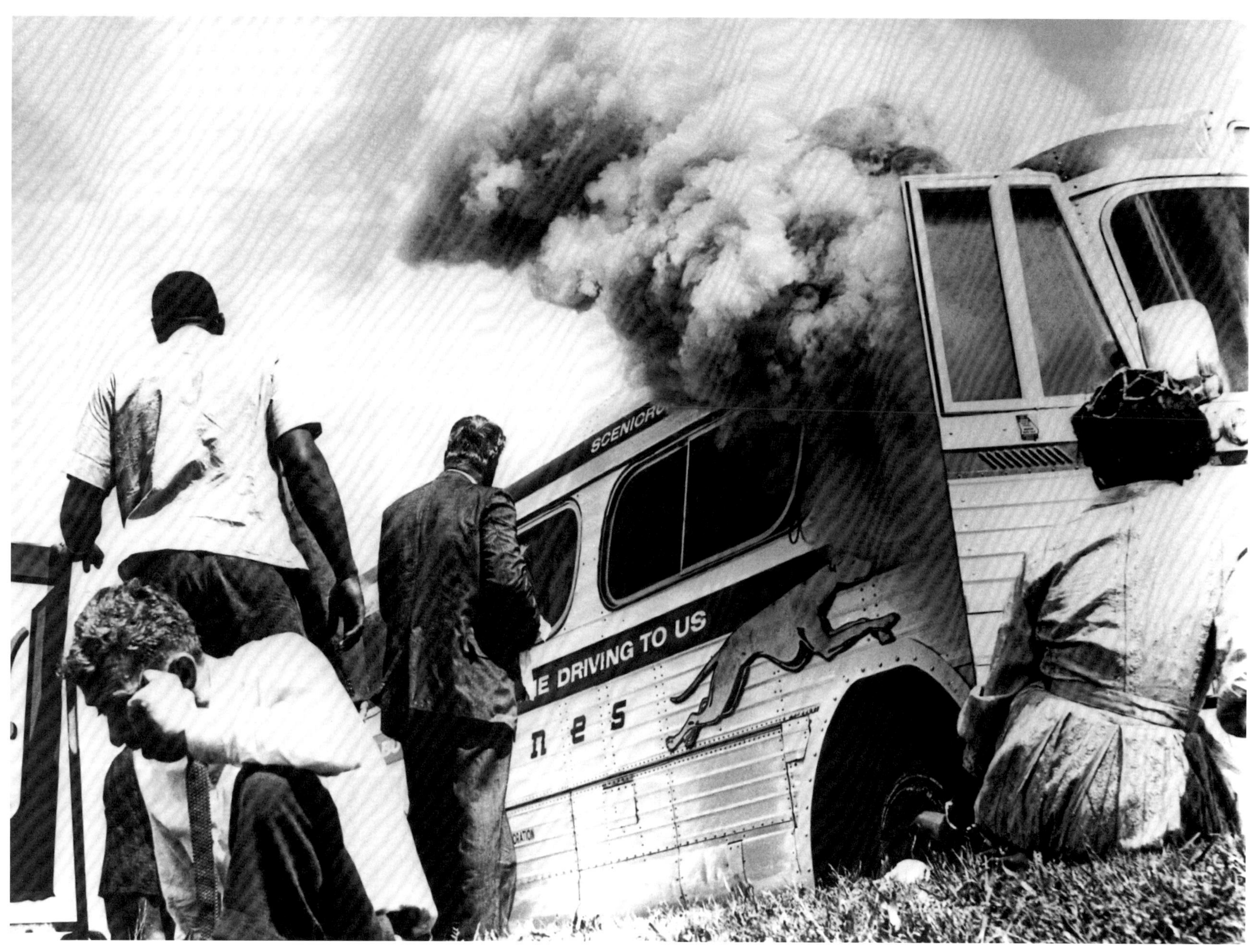

Figure 1. Freedom Riders on a trip through the southeast sponsored by the Congress of Racial Equality (CORE) sit on the ground outside their Greyhound bus after it was set afire by a group of whites who met the group on arrival in Anniston, Alabama. May 14, 1961. Photo by Joseph Postiglione, courtesy of Underwood Archives/Getty Images

places that changed hearts and minds locally to align over time with federal regulations.

In the 1960s, newspapers rarely used color photography except occasionally in advertising sections. Black and white images were trusted and associated with authenticity. With few exceptions, reformers from Jacob Riis (1849–1914) and Lewis Hine (1874–1940) to the Roosevelt administration's Farm Security Administration photographers relied upon black-and-white imagery for delivering social messages. Because photographs were deemed reliably true, they were also used as evidence in police work. Even though it was possible to manipulate images as early as the nineteenth century, long before digital cameras, those photographic techniques were more often reserved for photographs that were intentionally "art," rather than in the documentary mode.

During the years of segregation, Nashville's black-owned newspapers reported news of interest to the black community that rarely appeared in the white-owned newspapers.[6] To increase circulation in the African American community, *Nashville Banner* owner and publisher James Stahlman hired Robert Churchwell in 1950, the first African American journalist to work at a white-owned newspaper in the South. For the first five years of his employment, Churchwell was not seated in the press room but rather wrote copy at home and delivered it to the segregated newspaper office each morning.[7] Between 1957 and 1968, there was not a single African American photojournalist employed by either mainstream Nashville newspaper.[8]

From 1937 onward, *The Tennessean* and the *Nashville Banner* were housed in the same building and even shared printing presses, rolling out the more liberal *Tennessean* in the morning and the conservative positions of the *Banner* in the afternoon.[9] The editorial policies of *The Tennessean* and *Nashville Banner* date to the early twentieth century, but they intensified during the Great Depression, with the former being pro-labor and the latter supporting business interests. Silliman Evans Sr. purchased the *Nashville Tennessean* in 1937, in part to support Franklin Delano Roosevelt's agenda. Unionizing mines, tenant farms, and cotton mills was contentious and often labeled Communist, as were any efforts by the New Deal to redistribute wealth.[10]

The Civil Rights movement, also deemed Communist by some, unfolded in Nashville, Tennessee, under the watchful eyes of the press including the staff photographers (fig. 2).[11] The 1954 Supreme Court decision *Brown v. Board of Education of Topeka*, declaring segregated schools and education facilities unconstitutional, was a turning point for millions. Across the South, school districts began the process of unraveling systems of separate but "equal."

Nashville's grade-a-year plan for public school desegregation, which legally satisfied the court's standard of "all deliberate speed," started on September 9, 1957, when nineteen black first-graders attempted to integrate eight previously all-white schools.[12] Working for *The Tennessean*, Eldred Reaney photographed parents and students protesting in front of Buena Vista Elementary School in north Nashville (plate 7). White men, women, and children line both sides of the street, marching in protest. One man carries a placard reading, "Communists infiltrated our churches, now our schools." At the bottom a Bible verse, "2nd Peter 2–12," is referenced. More curiously the familiar citation John 3:16, *For God so loved the world, that He gave his only begotten son, that whoever believeth in Him should not perish, but have everlasting life*, appears beneath the hand-written words "Equal but Separate Rights."[13]

Although McCarthyism had been refuted by the late 1950s, any change in the status quo, whether fluoridated water or desegregation or rejection of religion, aroused exaggerated suspicions of Communist infiltration and influence. At least as offensive as a "Communist" to many Nashvillians was the presence of outside agitators, especially in 1957 with the arrival of Frederick John Kasper, a rabid segregationist, anti-Semite, member of the Ku Klux Klan, and northerner, whose bigotry had already disrupted school integration in Clinton, Tennessee.[14]

Six-year-old Patricia Watson successfully integrated Hattie

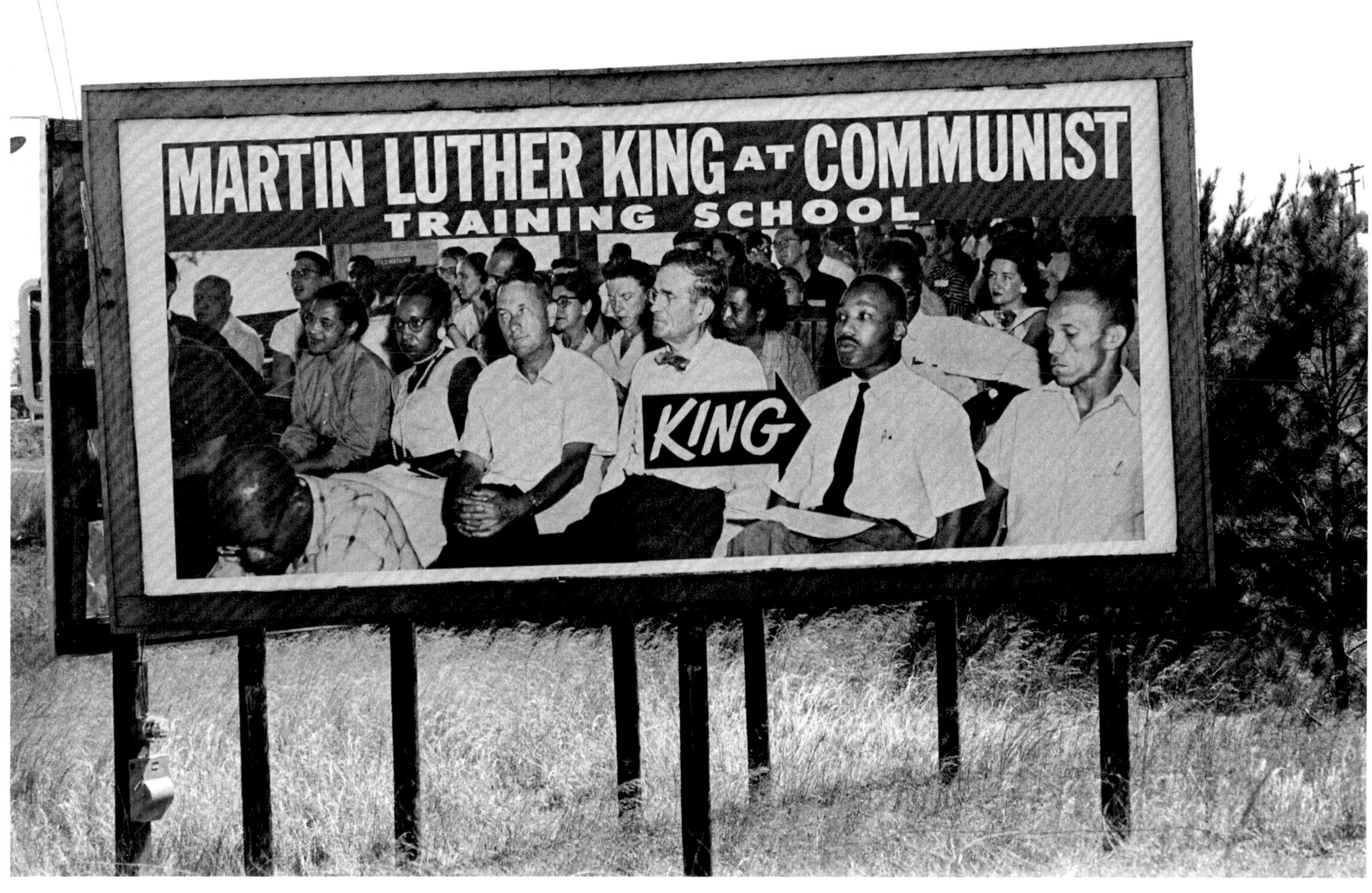

Figure 2. Billboard in Alabama with a photograph claiming to show Dr. Martin Luther King Jr. at a communist training school. The photo was actually taken in the 1940s at the Highlander Folk School in Monteagle, Tennessee. 1965. Courtesy of Getty Images/Bettmann/Contributor

Cotton Elementary School, where 139 white children remained through the end of the day. At 12:33 a.m. the following morning, a dynamite explosive blasted Hattie Cotton (plates 18 and 19). Later, Bill Goodman, working for the *Nashville Banner*, focused on Linda McKinley and Charles Elbert Ridley, the only two first graders to appear at Fehr Elementary School later that day (plate 17). The fear of another bombing frightened parents and children. Both the *Nashville Banner* and *The Tennessean* condemned the bombing.[15] Kasper was linked to the bombing but never indicted. In the end, only thirteen black children registered at white schools that September. Nashville public schools moved forward with the gradual integration plan, but private schools cropped up across Middle Tennessee to accommodate white flight.[16]

A NONVIOLENT SIT-IN OCCURRED in Greensboro, North Carolina, on February 1, 1960.[17] On February 13, sit-ins began in Nashville when students from American Baptist Theological Seminary (now American Baptist College), Fisk University, Meharry Medical College, and Tennessee Agriculture & Industry (A&I) State University (now Tennessee State University) took seats at the segregated lunch counters at Woolworth, S. H. Kress, and McLellan five-and-dime stores in downtown Nashville, asking to be served. The students had been in training for months with James Lawson, studying and practicing the methods of nonviolent protests. Lawson, a graduate student at the Vanderbilt University Divinity School, learned the methods of peaceful resistance when he was a Methodist missionary in India. Dr. Martin Luther King Jr., who met Lawson at Oberlin Theological School, had encouraged him to transfer to Vanderbilt because the South needed leaders like him.

Violence at the Nashville sit-ins was initiated only by the white hecklers, never the students. Vic Cooley from the *Nashville Banner* documented (plate 23) a black man at the Woolworth lunch counter being assaulted by white men who outnumber him more than ten to one. The peaceful demonstrator is in sharp focus, leaving the surrounding mayhem, including an advertisement for a 15¢ slice of German chocolate cake, slightly blurred. Another *Nashville Banner* photojournalist, Bill Goodman, recorded an empty lunch counter (plate 22). A sign states "Fountain Closed in Interest of Public Safety." The absence of customers and servers testifies to a loss of revenue, which ultimately would have an impact on the thinking of local merchants.

Editorials in the *Nashville Banner* couched James Lawson as an outsider and interloper as well as an agitator in favor of civil disobedience to an unlawful degree. James Stahlman, who, in addition to owning and publishing the *Nashville Banner*, was on the Board of Trust at Vanderbilt University, pressured Chancellor Harvie Branscomb and his fellow board members to expel Lawson from the Divinity School. Despite strong faculty support (plate 27), Lawson was forced to resign or be expelled. He refused to resign. His expulsion on March 3, 1960, prompted a national media scandal, multiple faculty resignations, the degradation of the Divinity School, harm to the reputation of Vanderbilt University, and the lasting regret of Branscomb.[18]

In the early months of the sit-ins, over 150 students were arrested. They were represented at trial by several attorneys including Adolpho A. Birch, Robert E. Lillard, Coyness L. Ennix Sr., Avon Williams Jr., and Z. Alexander Looby, whose home was bombed on April 19, 1960. The intensity of the blast was so powerful that 147 windows shattered in the Meharry Medical College alumni building across the street. Miraculously, no one was killed. *The Tennessean* photographer Joe Rudis captured John Thomas Martin sweeping debris (plate 33). He is dramatically silhouetted at work in the foreground. Through the window, citizens and the authorities inspect the Looby home.

Later that day, exasperated by violence and the resistance they were encountering, students began to march in silence from Fisk University down Jefferson Street. Along the way people from the community joined the procession in solidarity.[19] In an image by Jack Corn that ran in *The Tennessean* and that has been reproduced frequently in the intervening years, Diane Nash, C. T. Vivian, on her right, and Bernard Lafayette, on her left, lead with determination more than three thousand demonstrators to the steps of the Davidson County courthouse (plate 35). The historical moment is anchored in 1960 by vintage automobiles, the window style on the city bus, and the price of gasoline at 28¢ a gallon; but the resolve of the marchers is timeless.

On the courthouse steps, the demonstrators confronted Mayor Ben West. C. T. Vivian read a prepared text. Diane Nash called upon the mayor to take a stand against racial discrimination. Looking at the thousands of assembled protesters, the mayor realized that the students had the support of Nashville residents of all ages, many of whom were participating in the six-week boycott of downtown stores that had started on April 4. As recounted by author and historian Taylor Branch, Mayor West responded, "I appeal to all citizens to end discrimination, to have no bigotry, no bias, no hatred." Nash pressed, "Do you mean that to include lunch counters?" West admitted that he personally did not believe lunch-counter discrimination was right, leaving the final decision to the proprietors.[20]

The Tennessean and *Nashville Banner* seized upon different aspects of the mayor's answer. Neither newspaper mentioned the boycott, which was covered in the CBS documentary *Anatomy of a Demonstration* and in "Sit-In" on NBC's *White Paper*, narrated by Chet Huntley.[21] Merchants, who previously had feared a loss of business from whites, were significantly impacted by the loss of revenue from the black community exercising economic leverage to support the students. Merchants, however, claimed they were following the lead of Mayor West to desegregate. On May 10, six downtown stores began serving blacks.[22]

On November 10, John Lewis and two other African American students sat at the Fifth Avenue Krystal lunch counter, ordered, and ate ten-cent hamburgers. Their server poured water over their food and doused the students in cleansing powder, but the unperturbed students ate the food they had ordered and then left. Two hours later, Lewis and James Bevel returned and asked to speak with the manager who responded by locking the front door, turning on a fumigating machine, and leaving through the back door. Although the insect spray was nontoxic, Lewis and Bevel were locked inside and visibly choking when Assistant Fire Chief W. D. Gallaher was able to get the manager back to open the door.[23] *The Tennessean* photographer Jack Corn captured the students trapped behind a glass door (plate 43). Lewis stands on the right and Bevel on the left of a decal indicating membership in the National Restaurant Association dated 1960. Ambiguous reflections veil the physical space of those depicted, disrupting the expectation of figure placement—inside or outside, past or future, locked in a time/space warp, or somewhere in between. The *Nashville Banner* carried no coverage of the incident.

Ella Baker, executive secretary for the Southern Christian Leadership Conference (SCLC), was the driving force behind the creation of the Student Nonviolent Coordinating Committee (SNCC), a stand-alone organization that would engage youth to further the work of the SCLC and the National Association for the Advancement of Colored People (NAACP). Participants from the Greensboro, North Carolina, and Nashville sit-ins met at Shaw University in Greensboro in April 1960, electing Fisk University graduate school alumnus Marion Barry as its first chairman. Julian Bond was the first communications director. He and others understood the power of creating and disseminating images to further their message and at times to help raise funds for SNCC. John Lewis, who served as chairman from 1963 to 1966, said,

> It was the media that made it possible for the sit-in movement to travel around the South like wildfire. And it was the media that helped to translate the message and interpret to some degree not only the message, but the method. Because people saw these young black and white students sitting in peaceful, orderly, nonviolent fashion.[24]

In 1962, James Forman, SNCC executive secretary, hired Chicago photographer Danny Lyon as the official SNCC photographer.[25] Early protesters were deliberate in displaying

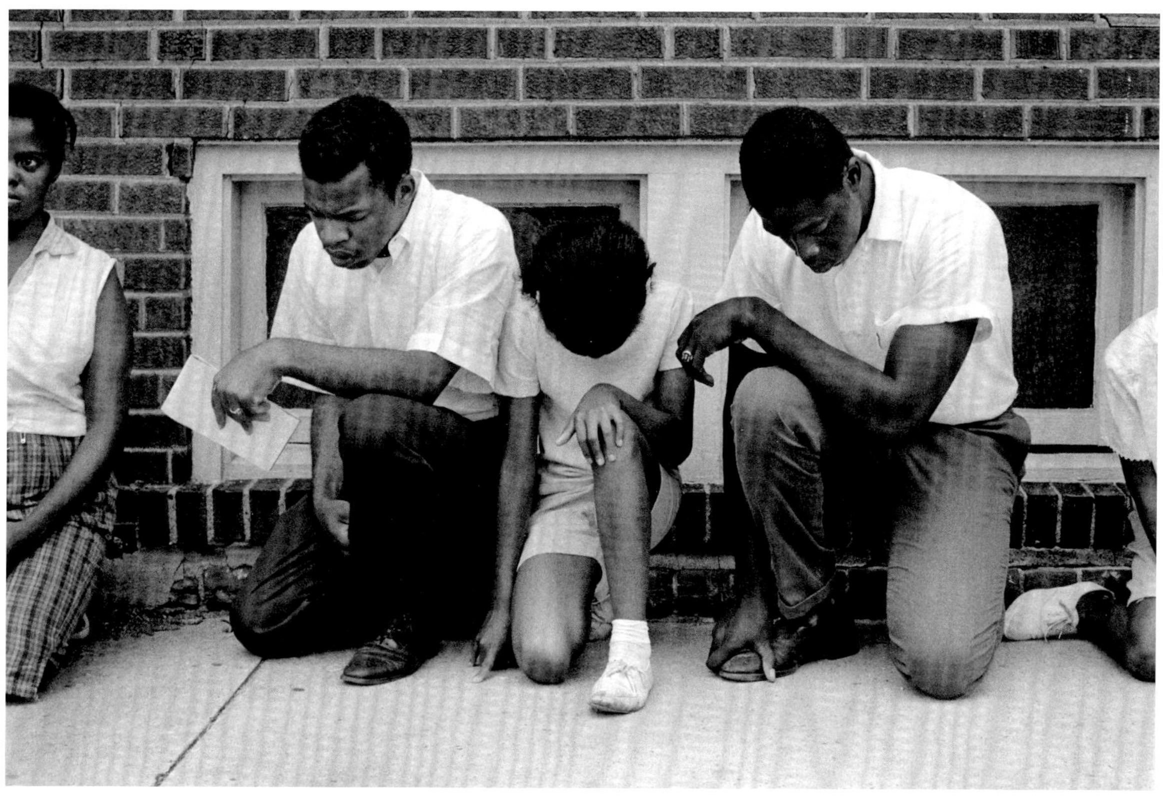

Figure 3. John Lewis (left) and others demonstrate at a segregated pool in Cairo, Illinois. 1962. Photo by Danny Lyon, courtesy of Danny Lyon/Magnum Photos

middle-class conformity by wearing their Sunday best, being polite, and remaining noncombative, intending to project themselves as honest people seeking constitutional rights.[26] Lyon's photograph of Lewis in prayer with a young girl and adult male outside a segregated swimming pool in Cairo, Illinois, was featured on ten thousand posters that sold for a dollar each to benefit SNCC (fig. 3).[27]

Posters had long been important in movements for organized labor, peace, and social justice. During the 1930s, posters and pamphlets illustrated with photographs were distributed by the Farm Security Administration (FSA) to influence public opinion and garner support for federal legislation designed to provide relief and recovery for those most affected by the Great Depression and to expose unfair labor practices.[28] In the Lyons photograph, the intent was not only to document the humility of the civil rights workers but also to enlist advocates to the movement. Leigh Raiford asks us to consider John Berger's position concerning how an image such as this one can challenge the world it represents while seducing viewers into it.[29]

As the 1960s progressed, national attention shifted to Alabama and Mississippi. Several of the Nashville activists participated in the Freedom Rides, but no Nashville photojournalists were assigned to cover their activities. Bombings, assaults, arrests, and murders changed the tenor of the movement. Disturbing images of the struggle were seen in *Time, Life, Newsweek,* and *US News and World Report,* awakening white Americans to the reality of Black America. Photojournalism was transitioning from illustrating text to a more powerful standalone documentation of the Civil Rights narrative.

On May 2, 1963, thousands of young people participated in the Children's Crusade in Birmingham. Hundreds were arrested and jailed. On the second day, Commissioner of Public Safety "Bull" Connor ordered the use of powerful water hoses, batons, and police dogs (fig. 4).[30] Children under brutal attack drew international criticism and sickened federal authorities, including President John F. Kennedy.[31] David Halberstam's thorough and poignant account of the civil rights movement in Nashville, *The Children*, points out that the nation was changed by young people who were barely out of their teens. Only a few years separated the crusaders in Birmingham from the young Nashville activists, still mobilized to desegregate libraries, restaurants, accommodations, swimming pools, and the YMCA. On May 10, 1963, *Tennessean* photojournalist Harold Lowe Jr. recorded a harrowing moment when Wharton Junior High School freshman Ewingella Bigham, only fifteen, lay unconscious in the street. The accompanying caption reports that she was injured during a near riot between white youths and black demonstrators. She had been struck with a patrolman's billy club. The *Banner* chose not to publish their similar photograph. Editorial policy often withheld inflammatory images for fear of inciting further unrest.[32] Both tell a truth that was uncomfortable in May 1963 and that is shocking to spectators today (plates 53 and 54).

American studies scholar Martin Berger writes that avoiding the most graphic images of brutality neutralizes the responsibility for abuse. Still, a fixation on the spectacle of violence can distract us from the hard, slow, relentless work required for reform. Berger warns that images of aggression, whether bombings, beatings, attack dogs, fire hoses, or nonviolent demonstrators being burned with cigarettes, reinforce blacks as victims and allow room for well-meaning whites to dissociate themselves from heinous crimes and fail to identify with the implicit narrative of systemic oppression.[33]

On August 27, 1963, blacks and whites boarded buses to travel to Washington, DC, for the March for Jobs and Freedom (plate 60). The following day, Dr. Martin Luther King Jr. delivered the famous "I Have a Dream" speech in front of the Lincoln Memorial to more than two hundred thousand people (fig. 5). John Lewis, then SNCC chairman, also spoke, issuing an impassioned plea for meaningful legislation. He expressed frustration with calls for patience. The time for freedom was "now." He urged continued marching, in the spirit of love and the spirit of dignity, to ensure brotherhood and true peace in the image of God and democracy.[34]

Peace remained elusive. Civil Rights worker and field secretary for the NAACP Medgar Evers was assassinated on June 12, 1963. On September 15, the Sixteenth Street Baptist Church in Birmingham, Alabama, was bombed, killing four young girls. Two more black children were killed in Birmingham the same day.[35] On November 22, President John F. Kennedy was assassinated. The nation was stunned (plate 61). The following day Lyndon Johnson was sworn in as president, and the crucible of civil rights passed to him.

In March 1964, heavyweight champion of the world, Cassius Clay Jr., announced his conversion to the Islamic faith, changing his name to Muhammad Ali. The following month, on April 27, more than three hundred demonstrators sat in front of Morrison's Cafeteria on West End Avenue in Nashville. Police moved in to disperse the crowd: violence ensued. *The Tennessean* and the *Nashville Banner* ran illustrated features. At least five photographers were sent by *The Tennessean* to cover the demonstrations and the police reactions. After three days, seventy-six demonstrators had been arrested. In one unpublished image, a white woman is dragged on the ground by three police officers, one with billy club raised (plate 64). The photojournalist captures how passions escalated as the crusade continued, intensifying actions and reactions.

On June 21, 1964, three Civil Rights workers volunteering for "Freedom Summer," James Chaney, Michael Schwerner, and Andrew Goodman, were abducted and murdered in Philadelphia, Mississippi. Their bodies were not found until August 4. In the meantime, on July 2, President Johnson signed the Civil

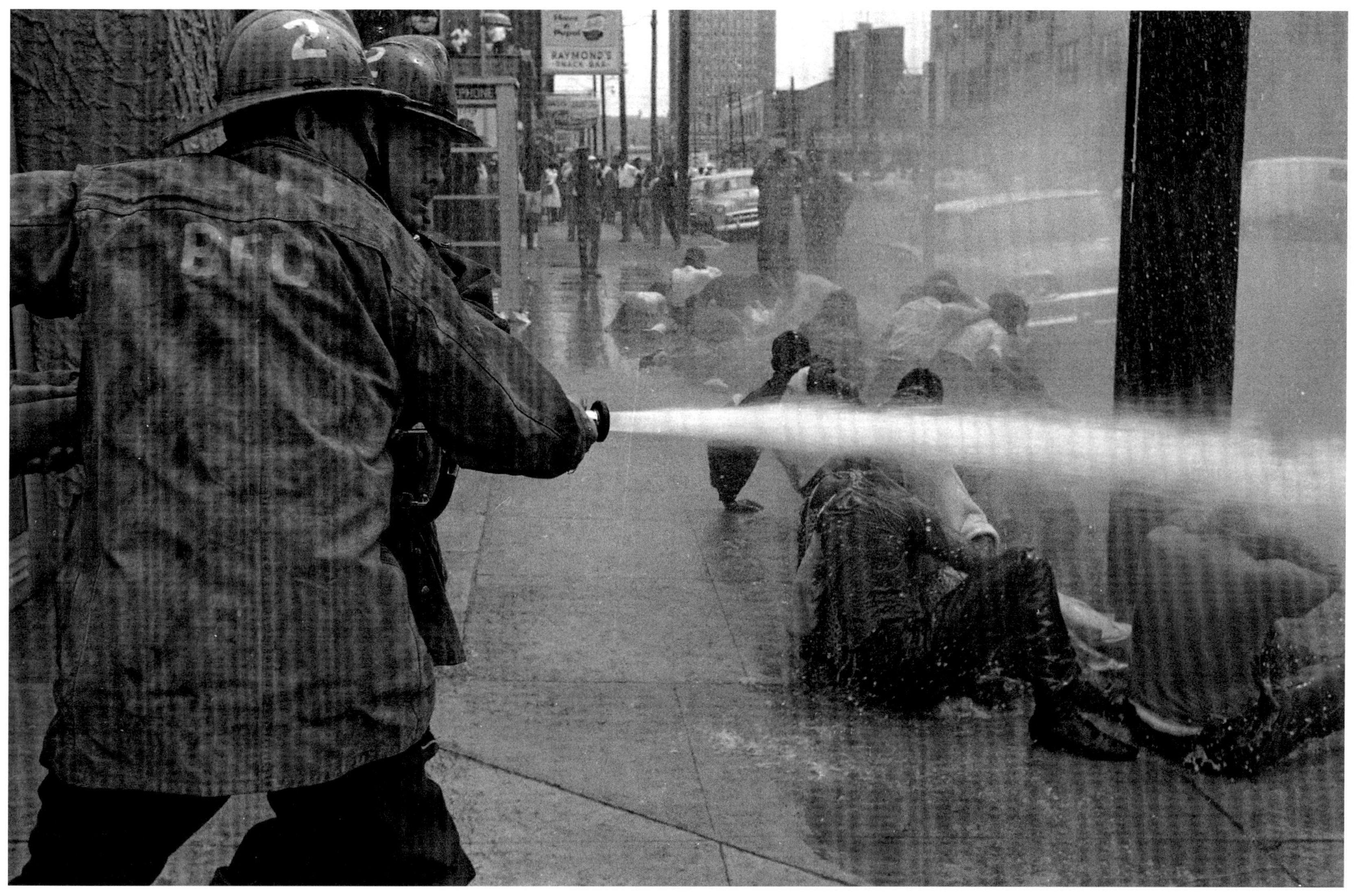

Figure 4. Firefighters aim firehoses at anti-segregation demonstrators on a sidewalk on 17th Street North, near Kelly Ingram Park, Birmingham, Alabama. Police officers used both firehoses and dogs to break up the demonstration. May 1963. Photo by Charles Moore, courtesy of Getty Images

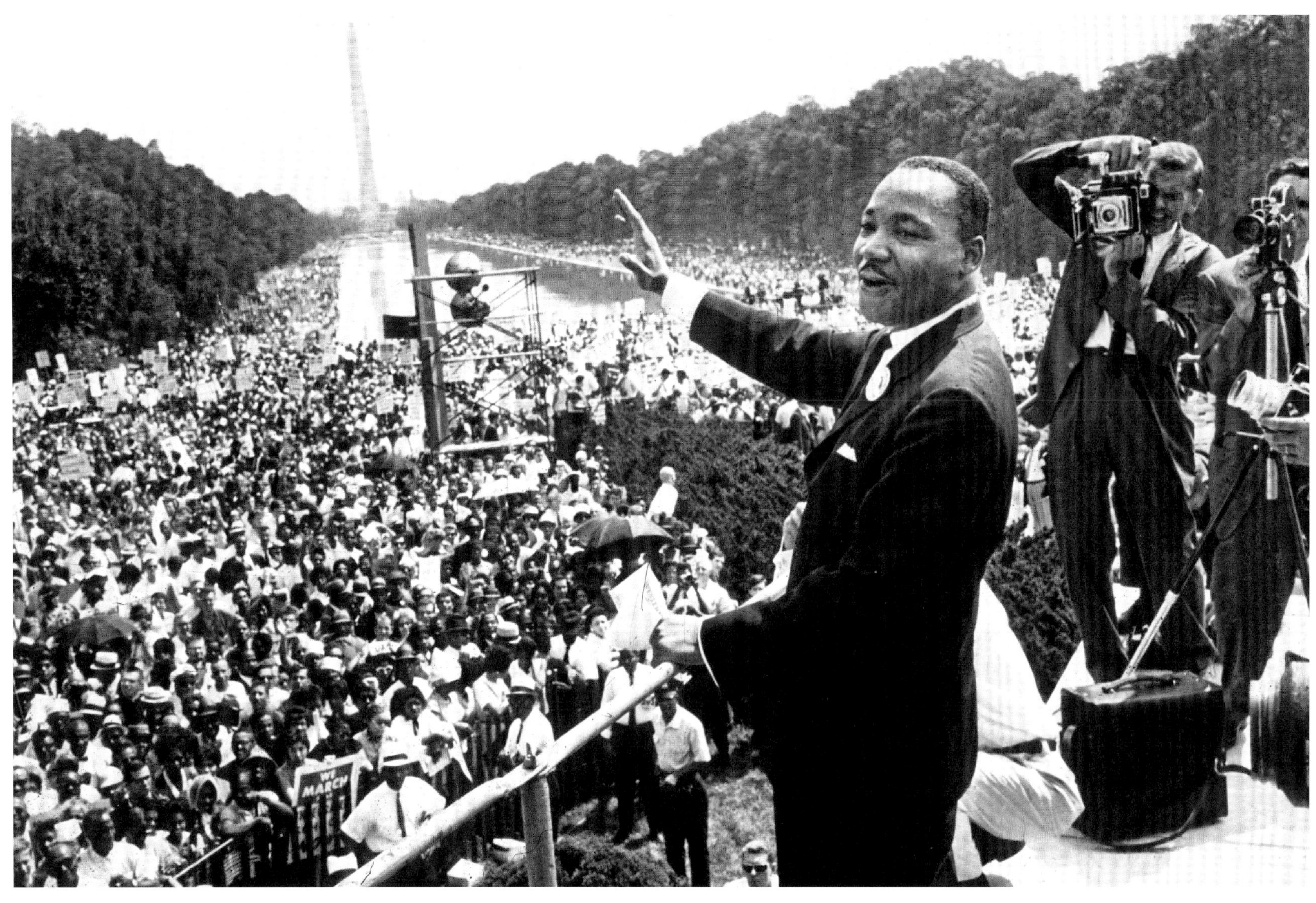

Figure 5. Dr. Martin Luther King Jr. waves to the crowd during the March in Washington for Jobs and Freedom. August 28, 1963. Courtesy Bridgeman Images

Rights Act of 1964, prohibiting discrimination in public places and in the workplace based on race, color, religion, sex, or national origin. In late August, Fannie Lou Hamer gave her "I Question America" speech at the Democratic National Convention where she claimed before the Credential Committee the legitimacy of the Mississippi Freedom Democratic Party (MFDP) as the only political party in Mississippi that was open to voters of all races (fig. 6). Hubert Humphrey was dispatched to offer a compromise that the MFDP did not accept. In October, Dr. Martin Luther King Jr. was awarded the Nobel Peace Prize.

Within a year, on February 21, 1965, Malcolm X was assassinated. On August 6, President Johnson signed the Voting Rights Act of 1965, designed to overrule state and local laws that prevented African Americans from exercising their right to vote guaranteed under the Fifteenth Amendment (1870) to the Constitution of the United States.

Martin Luther King Jr. expanded his commitment to nonviolence in a speech delivered to an audience of clergy and laymen on April 4, 1967, at Riverside Church in New York City, calling for peace in Vietnam.[36] Three days later, April 7, he was a featured speaker at the Vanderbilt University two-day IMPACT symposium, along with Stokely Carmichael, Allen Ginsberg, and Strom Thurmond. *The Tennessean* covered the conference, which attracted an estimated 4,500 to Vanderbilt's Memorial Gym (plate 70).

Carmichael, who had succeeded John Lewis as chairman of SNCC, pushed to end white supremacy rather than just overthrow segregation. He cited economic and educational disparity as formidable barriers to advancement for black people. Furthermore, he warned that entrenched power structures oppressed all poor people, thereby changing the rhetoric from one of racial equality to one of class struggle. While in Nashville, the eloquent and articulate Carmichael made several public appearances. The first was at Fisk University on April 6, where he spoke against the war in Vietnam and about the importance

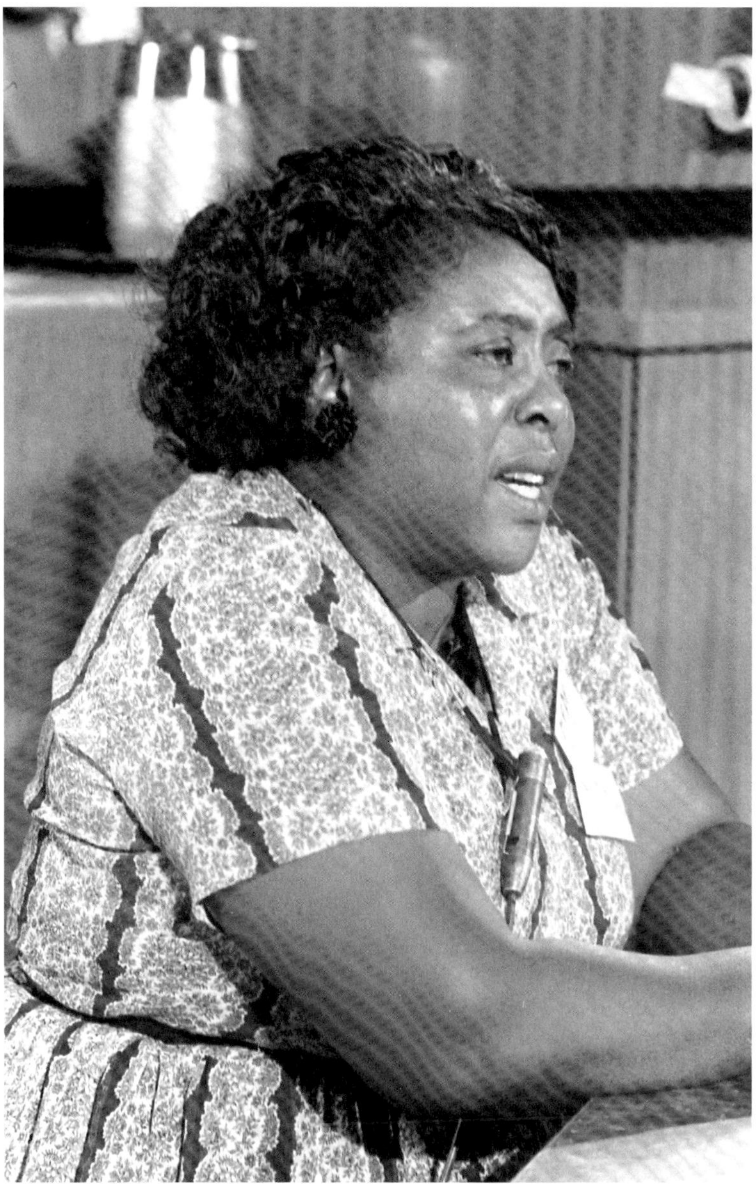

Figure 6. Fannie Lou Hamer, Mississippi Freedom Democratic Party delegate, at the Democratic National Convention, Atlantic City, New Jersey. August 1964. Photo by Warren K. Leffler, courtesy of the Library of Congress, Prints and Photographs Division

of education for black people. The following day at Tennessee A&I, Carmichael addressed the students in a more radical tone about the systemic repression of poor people (plate 71). Dressed in jeans and shirtsleeves, Carmichael called for students to "organize and take over this city." He agitated for black power, which was threatening to middle-class blacks as well as the white establishment.[37] On Saturday, April 8, he spoke at Vanderbilt University dressed in a three-piece suit and tie, recalling how the students schooled in nonviolent protest dressed in their Sunday best for the 1960s sit-ins.

On the evening of April 8, 1967, civil unrest erupted in Nashville with rock-throwing that escalated to gunfire, property damage, and looting. After three days of rioting, nearly ninety people were arrested. The local media referred to Carmichael as the militant leader of SNCC, a Communist, and an outside agitator. He was accused of inciting a riot.[38] Black and white leadership came together quickly. Within the week, students and concerned citizens gathered to demonstrate for peace and to protest what they saw as police brutality. The cause of the Nashville riot has never been determined despite a thorough investigation by the FBI and the Kerner Commission.[39]

The following year, on April 4, 1968, Dr. King, who was in Memphis to support striking sanitation workers, was assassinated at the Lorraine Motel (fig. 7). Anger, hurt, and frustration erupted. Riots broke out in cities across the country, including Nashville. Local law enforcement was inadequate for restoring order. This time, tanks rolled in. A photograph of the National Guard stationed around the Tennessee State Capitol building is a chilling depiction of authority, regimented and regulated. Disorderly conduct and the messy work sometimes required to ensure democracy are out of sight (plate 100).

The process of securing civil rights and overturning segregation that began in 1954 with *Brown v. Board of Education* slowed but was not abandoned. Calls for law and order gained momentum in the face of the rising influence of black militancy. By 1968, the black middle-class had a vested interest in building on the progress to date. Popular culture was making inroads with depictions of blacks transcending victimhood in films such as *Guess Who's Coming to Dinner* and *In the Heat of the Night*, the 1967 film that won the Academy Award for best picture on April 10, 1968, in a ceremony that was postponed two days because of King's assassination.

With the assassination of Bobby Kennedy just a few months later in June, Hubert Humphrey became the Democratic nominee for president. In November, Richard Nixon was elected. By the late 1960s, the priority of still photographs of the Civil Rights movement was being eclipsed by a growing presence of images related to the war in Vietnam in print and on television. Yet, as writer and journalist Edward P. Morgan acknowledges, it is through media photographs that many people remember or learn about the 1960s. He notes, "absent the graphic imagery, the sixties era may well have been significantly different."[40]

Early images of civil disobedience evoked sympathy at home and abroad, including that of young Bronx High School of Science student Stokely Carmichael.[41] "When we reproduce Civil Rights photographs today with the same framing that dominated media accounts in the 1960s, we inadvertently enforce the status quo. Before we can 'write the final page' of the Civil Rights era, we must reframe the iconic photographs and develop a more progressive canon of images."[42]

The contribution of the Nashville sit-ins to the history of the Civil Rights movement is well documented, not as the first but as the most well-organized. For months, students trained and practiced the methods of nonviolent protest. Many important leaders and intellectuals of the movement had a connection to Nashville: Martin Luther King Jr., James Lawson, Diane Nash, John Lewis, C. T. Vivian, Marion Barry, James Bevel, and Bernard Lafayette, among others. Fifty years after the assassination of Dr. King, photographs such as those made for *The Tennessean* and the *Nashville Banner* have acquired a patina burnished by the courage and sacrifices of the organizers as well as those of local, everyday citizens. Photojournalists working for Nashville

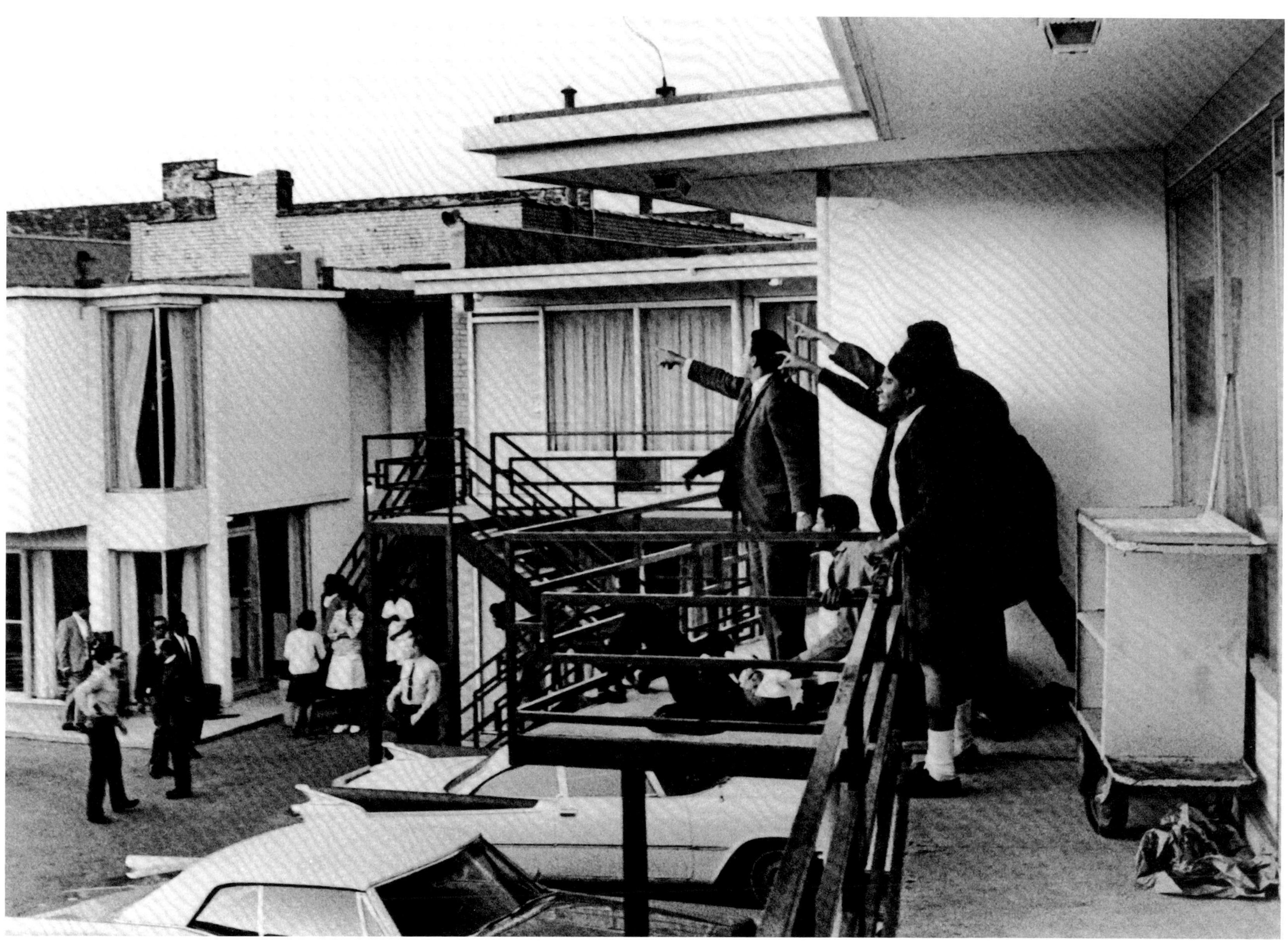

Figure 7. Civil rights leader Andrew Young (left) and others on the balcony of the Lorraine Motel point toward where the gun shots came from as Dr. King lies mortally wounded at their feet. April 4, 1968. Photo by Joseph Louw, courtesy of The *LIFE* Images Collection/Getty Images

media did not produce iconic images of the movement. Their work, however, demonstrates that the most accurate telling of the struggle is conveyed less by the spectacle of violence than by the long and emotional process of breaking away from the way things had always been.

NOTES

1. The *Nashville Tennessean*, first published in 1907, became *The Tennessean* in 1972, and was purchased by the Gannett Corporation in 1979. At the request of the paper's executive editor, Maria De Varenne, and to ensure clarity for contemporary readers, the newspaper is referred to as *The Tennessean* in this essay.
2. Michael L. Carlebach, *American Journalism Comes of Age* (Washington, DC: Smithsonian Institution Press, 1997), 1–2. See also Leah Ollman, *Camera as Weapon: Worker Photography between the Wars* (San Diego, CA: Museum of Photographic Arts, 199), 1.
3. Julian Cox, *Road to Freedom: Photographs of the Civil Rights Movement, 1956–1968* (Atlanta, GA: High Museum of Art, 2008), 22.
4. Cox, *Road to Freedom*, 23. Brian Coe, *Camera: From Daguerreotypes to Instant Pictures* (New York: Crown Publishers, 1978), 50, 232. Photographer, historian, and librarian Beth Odle at the Nashville Public Library confirmed that a limited number of photographs in the archive were made with a 4×5 in. Graflex Speed Graphic camera. Later and briefly, some photographers used a 2½ in. press camera, but photographs made after 1960 were made with 35 mm cameras (Interview with the author December 30, 2017). The Special Collections Division of the Nashville Public Library includes the Civil Rights Room and the *Nashville Banner* Archives. Andera Blackman, Elizabeth Coleman, and Beth Odle are not only generous colleagues, they are also the co-curators and collaborators for the publication *Visions and Voices: The Civil Rights Movement in Nashville and Tennessee* (Nashville: Nashville Public Library, 2007).
5. Gene Roberts and Hank Klibanoff, *The Race Beat: The Press, the Civil Rights Struggle, and the Awakening of a Nation* (New York: Alfred A. Knopf, 2006), 321. Also, Cox, *Road to Freedom*, 22.
6. See "Who Speaks for the Southern Negro," in Hugh Davis Graham, *Crisis in Print: Desegregation and the Press in Tennessee* (Nashville, TN: Vanderbilt University Press, 1967), 251–68, 331.
7. Interview with his son André Churchwell, MD, December 19, 2017. The Smithsonian National Museum of African American History and Culture commemorates Robert Churchwell's accomplishment in an exhibit that includes the reporter's portable typewriter, hat, and coat. In 2010, the name of Wharton Elementary School was changed to Robert Churchwell Museum Magnet Elementary School.
8. Billy Easley, an African American photojournalist, was hired by John Seigenthaler Sr. at *The Tennessean* sometime after 1962. Easley worked primarily in the darkroom until the late '60s.
9. During the 1950s, while the Tennessee State Legislature was grappling with whether to approve Daylight Saving Time (DST), the Nashville newspapers displayed two different time zones on a shared outdoor clock. *The Tennessean* side faced west with Central DST, and the *Banner* side showed Central Standard Time (CST). John Seigenthaler, "*The Tennessean*: 108 Years and Counting," *The Tennessean*, November 20, 2015. *www.tennessean.com/story/news/local/2015/11/20/tennessean-nashville-newspaper-history/76100780*.
10. In Tennessee the influential Highlander Folk School, founded by Myles Horton, an educator and proponent of integration, women's rights, and nonviolent resistance, taught or mentored many leaders of the Civil Rights Movement, including Rosa Parks, Martin Luther King Jr., and John Lewis. Horton was labeled a Communist for his progressive views, and in 1961 the state closed Highlander Folk School, but not before Horton's influence set in motion a movement to secure equal rights for disenfranchised people of color. Horton's wife, Zilphia, is credited with helping convert hymns to anthems for the Civil Rights Movement, including *We Shall Overcome*, *Keep Your Eyes on the Prize*, *We Shall Not Be Moved*, and *This Little Light of Mine*.
11. With gratitude to W. Ridley Wills II, who mentioned seeing this billboard in Nashville. Interview with the author, December 21, 2017.
12. John Egerton, "Walking into History: The Beginning of Desegregation in Nashville," *Southern Spaces*, May 4, 2009. *southernspaces.org/2009/walking-history-beginning-school-desegregation-nashville*. Wallace Westfeldt, "Full Attendance Asked for Start of Classes Here," *The Tennessean*, September 9, 1957, A1. "Crowds Threaten

but 19 Negroes Enter 7 Desegregated Schools," *Nashville Banner*, September 7, 1957, A1. Numbers later revised.

13. King James Version.
14. See "The Crucible at Clinton," in Graham, *Crisis in Print*, 91–113.
15. In an editorial, Silliman Evans Jr. wrote "a short rise to fame ended abruptly here when an agitator met face-to-face the spirit of a firm lady, long deceased: Hattie Cotton." *The Tennessean*, editorial, September 14, 1957, A1. James Stahlman offered a $1,000 reward for information regarding the bombing. "Lawless Elements Must Go," editorial, *Nashville Banner*, September 10, 1957, A1.
16. Father Ryan Roman Catholic High School integrated in 1954. The Roman Catholic Church acted promptly to integrate parochial schools across the country following the *Brown v. Board* decision. Notably, at that time Catholic schools were same-sex, and the integration of same-sex schools presented a less threatening possibility of miscegenation, which remained a felony in Tennessee until 1967. Roger D. Hardaway, "Race, Sex, and Law: Miscegenation in Tennessee," *Journal of East Tennessee History* 74 (2000): 24–37.
17. Sit-ins occurred in Chicago in 1943 and in St. Louis and Baltimore in 1949 and 1953, and in "some sixteen southern and border cities in the late 1950s. . . . The media and the nation had not paid much attention." Henry Hampton and Steve Fayer with Sarah Flynn, *Voices of Freedom: An Oral History of the Civil Rights Movement from the 1950s through the 1980s* (New York: Bantam Books, 1991), 51.
18. "No Place in Nashville for Inciters of Strife," *Nashville Banner* editorial, March 1, 1960, A4. Lawson is compared to John Kasper, the outside segregationist involved with Nashville school desegregation and the bombing of Hattie Cotton Elementary School: "his [Kasper's] capacity for mischief shows in the crisis he has brought on race relations not only the city but at other points in the South which he has visited on that mission of incitement." See also Ray Waddle, "Days of Thunder: The Lawson Affair," *Vanderbilt Magazine*, Fall 2002, 35–43.
19. Hampton, Fayer, and Flynn, *Voices of Freedom*, 65–66. In early March 1960, Mayor Ben West had convened a Special Committee on Sit-In Demonstrations that included George Barrett, F. Donald Hart, Dr. W. S. Davis, Madison Sarratt, Lipscomb Davis, Dr. Stephen Wright, B. B. Gullett, and students from Fisk, Tennessee A&I, and American Baptist College. Photograph, "Nashville Mayor Ben West's special committee on sit-in demonstrations confers . . ." by Jimmy Ellis, in "George Barrett Over the Years," gallery on *The Tennessean* website, *www.tennessean.com/picture-gallery/news/local/2014/08/27/george-barrett-over-the-years/14671367*.
20. Taylor Branch, *Parting the Waters: America in the King Years, 1954–63* (New York: Simon and Schuster, 1988), 295; and David E. Sumner, "The Local Press and the Nashville Student Movement, 1960" (PhD diss., University of Tennessee, 1989), 74–75.
21. Both documentaries are on view in a permanent installation at the Civil Rights Room at the Main Library of the Nashville Public Library.
22. Sumner, "The Local Press," 110–15. In July of that year, J. B. Lippincott Company published the Pulitzer Prize–winning novel *To Kill a Mockingbird*.
23. For a detailed account of the incident, see Branch, *Parting the Waters*, 379–80.
24. Sumner, "The Local Press," 189.
25. By the time Lyon left in 1964, there were photographers of various races and ethnicities working full-time for SNCC, including Joffre Clark, Fred deVan, Bob Fletcher, Doug Harris, Rufus Hinton, Julius Lester, Norris McNamara, Francis Mitchell, Clifford Vaughs, Mary Varela, Tamio Wakayama, and Dee Gorton. Harris and Fletcher took part in a weekend-long tutorial offered by Richard Avedon. Others received training from Matt Herron, a former student of Minor White. Dorothea Lange served as advisor for the Southern Documentary Project which Herron conceived and directed to produce a visual record of the Civil Rights Movement. Leigh Raiford, "'Come Let Us Build a New World Together': SNCC and Photography of the Civil Rights Movement," *American Quarterly* 59, no. 4 (December 2007): 1139, 1156.
26. Martin A. Berger, *Seeing through Race: A Reinterpretation of Civil Rights Photography* (Berkeley: University of California Press, 2011), 120.
27. Danny Lyon, *Memories of the Southern Civil Rights Movement* (Santa Fe, NM: Twin Palms Publishers, 2010), 26. See also Raiford, "'Come Let Us Build,'" 1129–57.

28. Raiford, "'Come Let Us Build,'" 1138. See also F. Jack Hurley, *Portrait of a Decade: Roy Stryker and the Development of Documentary Photography in the Thirties* (New York: Da Capo Press, 1977).
29. Raiford, "'Come Let Us Build,'" 1138. John Berger, "Uses of Photography," in *About Looking* (New York: Vintage, 1980); see also Geoffrey Batchen, "Vernacular Photography," in *Each Wild Idea: Writing, Photography, History* (Cambridge: MIT Press, 2001).
30. Beverly Boggs said that parents allowed their children to participate in the Children's Crusade assuming their innocence would protect them from retaliation because parents could lose their jobs. Interview with the author November 12, 2016.
31. Edward P. Morgan, *What Really Happened to the 1960s: How Mass Media Culture Failed American Democracy* (Lawrence: University Press of Kansas, 2010), 122. Also see Taylor Branch, *Pillar of Fire: America in the King Years, 1963–65* (New York: Touchstone, 1998), 87.
32. See "Lost Images of Civil Rights," in Berger, *About Looking*, 112–56.
33. Berger, *About Looking*, 159–60.
34. "Rep John Lewis' Speech at March on Washington," August 27, 1963. Published on YouTube on February 7, 2016, by Dallas Co. Schools. *www.youtube.com/watch?v=tFs1eTsokJg.*
35. The children killed in Birmingham on September 15, 1966 were Denise McNair (11), Carole Robertson (14), Addie Mae Collins (14), and Cynthia Wesley (14) at the Sixteenth Street Baptist Church; Virgil Ware (13), shot while riding on the handlebars of his brother's bike by a youth who was an Eagle Scout; and Johnnie Robinson (16), shot by police for throwing rocks at a car. Berger, *About Looking*, 140.
36. For an explanation of the early and late phases of the Civil Rights movement, as well as King's migration of priorities to the needs of poor people and against the war in Vietnam, the FBI harassment and threats he experienced, and his break with the establishment, see Cornel West, "The Paradox of the Afro-American Rebellion," in *The 60s Without Apology*, ed. Sohnya Sayre, Anders Stephanson, Stanley Aronowitz, and Frederic Jameson (Minneapolis: University of Minnesota Press/Social Text, 1984), 44–58.
37. Tom Ingram, "Carmichael Accuses Negroes of Yielding to 'White Lies,'" *The Tennessean*, April 7, 1967, 7. See also Bill Carey, "A Vanderbilt Guest Starts a Riot," April 2, 2008, 3-5. Nashvillepost.com/business/education/article/20400112/a-vanderbilt-guest-starts-a-riot, 3.
38. Scott Frizzell, "Not Just a Matter of Black and White: The Nashville Riot of 1967," *Tennessee Historical Quarterly* 70, no. 1 (Spring 2011): 26–51. See also Jennifer Hendricks, "Stokely Carmichael and the 1967 IMPACT Symposium: Black Power, White Fear, and the Conservative South," *Tennessee Historical Quarterly* 63, no. 4 (Winter 2004): 284–304.
39. "OEO, Riot Figure Linked," *St. Petersburg Times* (Times Wire Service), August 4, 1967, 10-A. Also see National Advisory Commission on Civil Disorders, *The Kerner Report: The 1968 Report of the National Advisory Commission on Civil Disobedience* (New York: Pantheon Books, 1988).
40. Morgan, *What Really Happened*, 117.
41. Morgan, *What Really Happened*, 117–19.
42. Berger, *About Looking*, 160.

PLATES

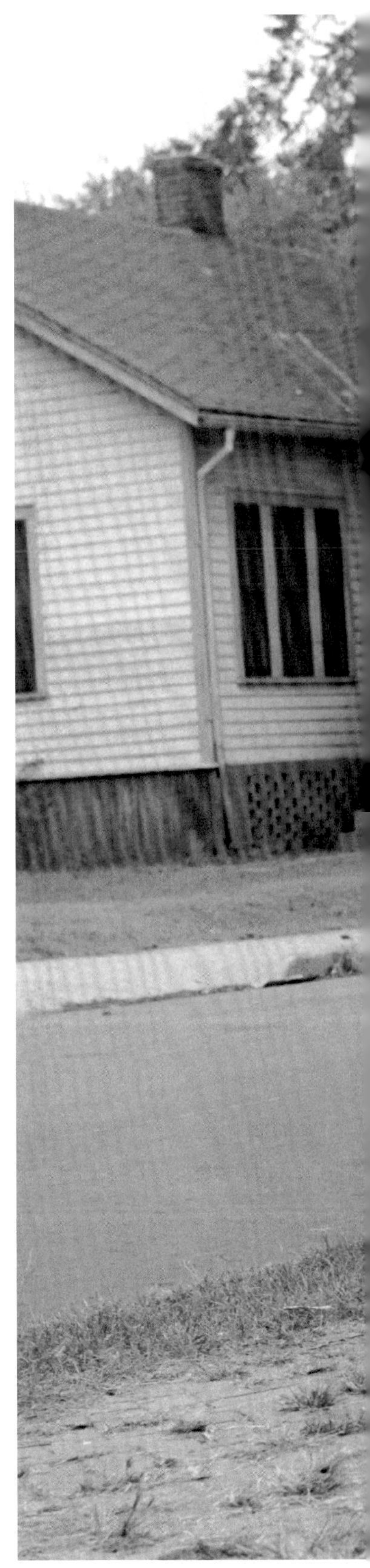

PLATE 1

John Malone, *Nashville Banner*

SEPTEMBER 9, 1957

On the first day of the new school year, Grace McKinley escorts her daughter Linda Gail McKinley and Rita Buchanan (far left) to Fehr Elementary School through a crowd of segregationists and protesters. Courtesy of the Nashville Public Library, Special Collections

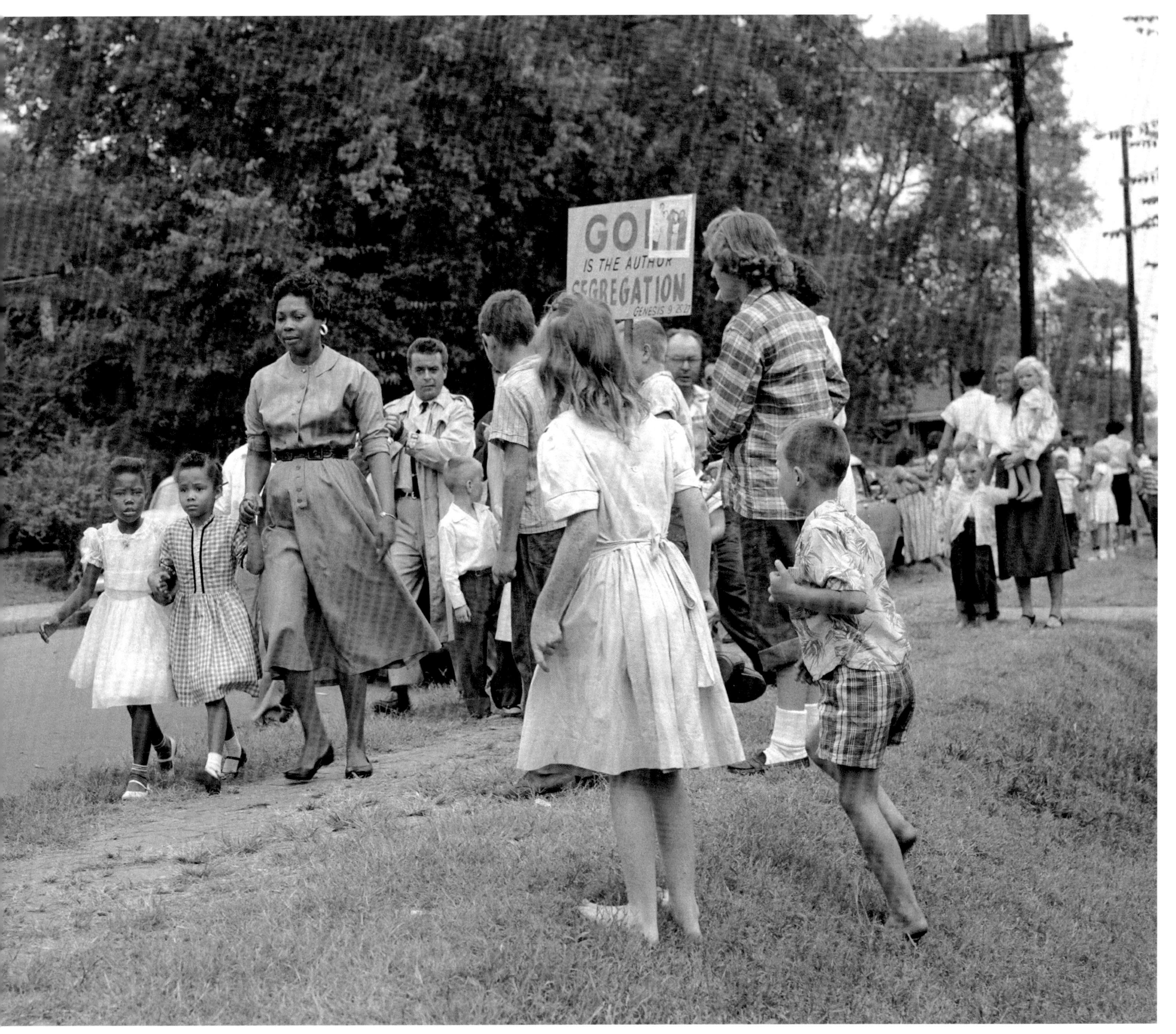
GO
IS THE AUTHOR
SEGREGATION
GENESIS 9

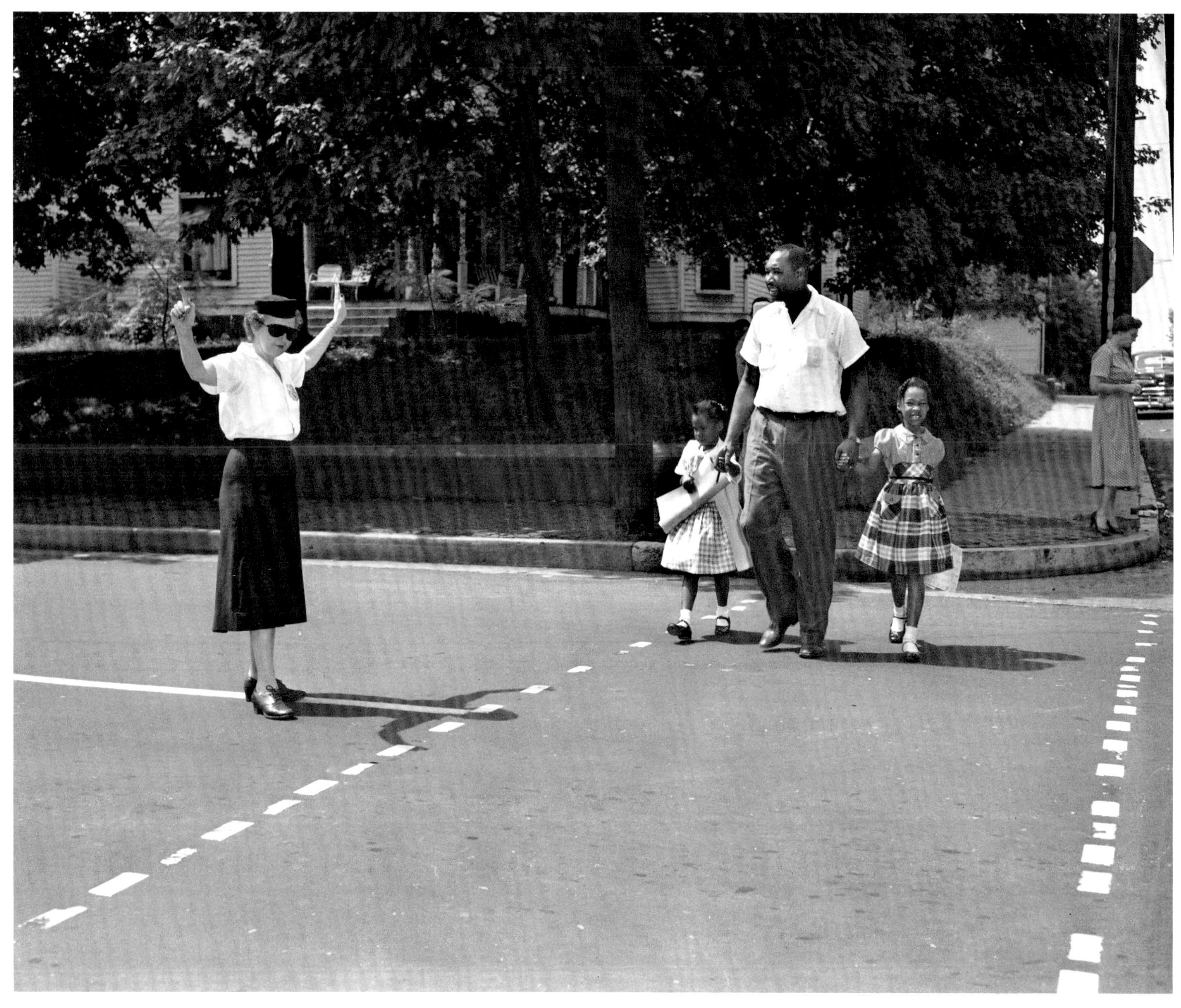

PLATE 2

Bob Ray, *Nashville Banner*

SEPTEMBER 9, 1957

Harold Street walks his daughter Lajuanda Street (right) and her friend Jacqueline Griffith (left) to Glenn Elementary School. Courtesy of the Nashville Public Library, Special Collections

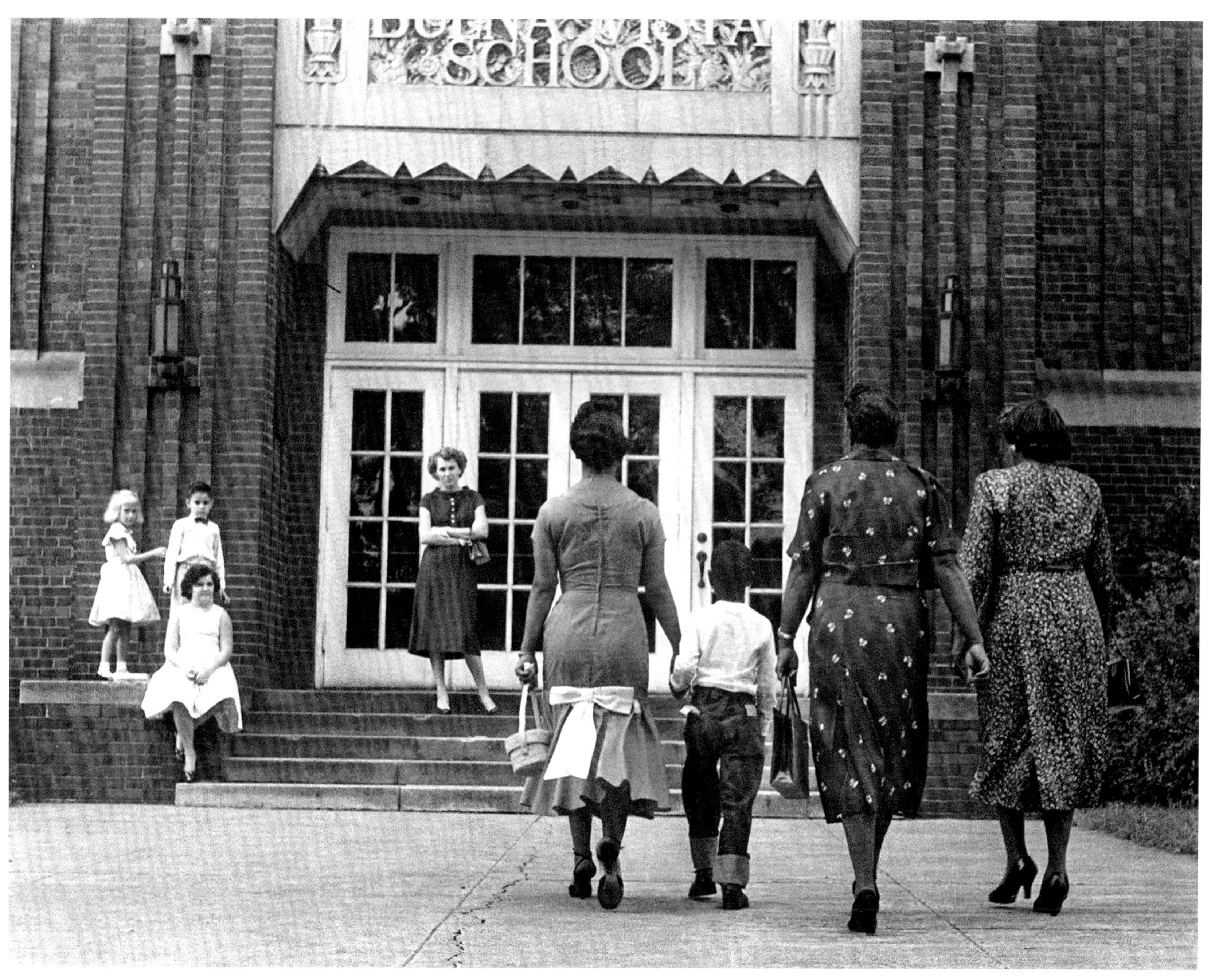

PLATE 3

Eldred Reaney, *The Tennessean*

SEPTEMBER 9, 1957

Erroll Groves (center) holds the hand of his mother, Iridell Groves, as they walk into Buena Vista School on the first day of desegregation in Nashville's public schools. Courtesy of *The Tennessean*

PLATE 4

Howard Cooper, *The Tennessean*

SEPTEMBER 9, 1957

Pencil and paper in hand, first-grader Marvin Moore walks with his mother, Maude Baxter, as his father talks with a reporter on the first day of school. They are heading to the all-white Jones School, where Marvin will be one of the four students to integrate it.
Courtesy of *The Tennessean*

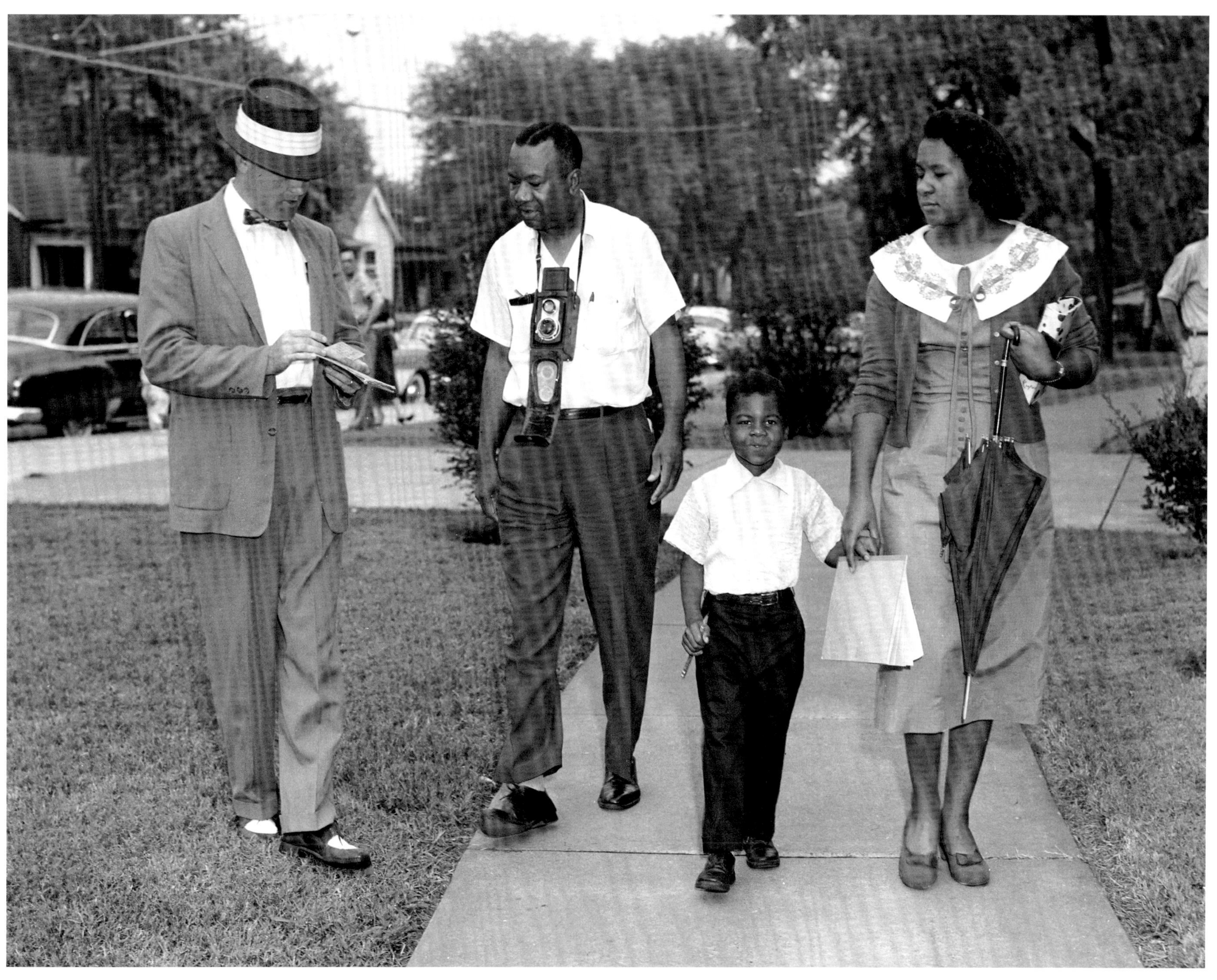

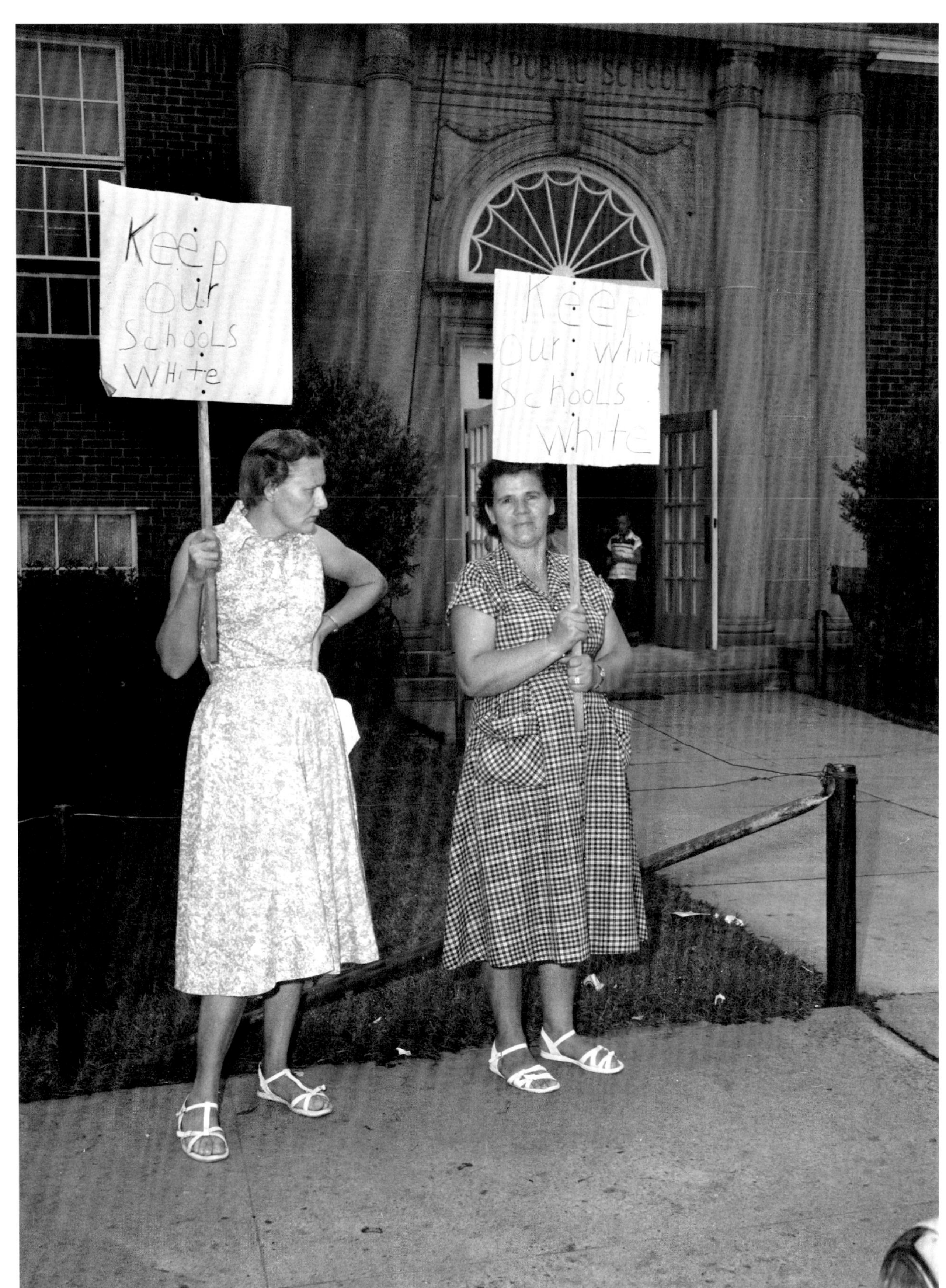

PLATE 5

Staff photographer, *Nashville Banner*

SEPTEMBER 9, 1957

Segregationists protest outside Fehr Elementary School in North Nashville. Courtesy of the Nashville Public Library, Special Collections

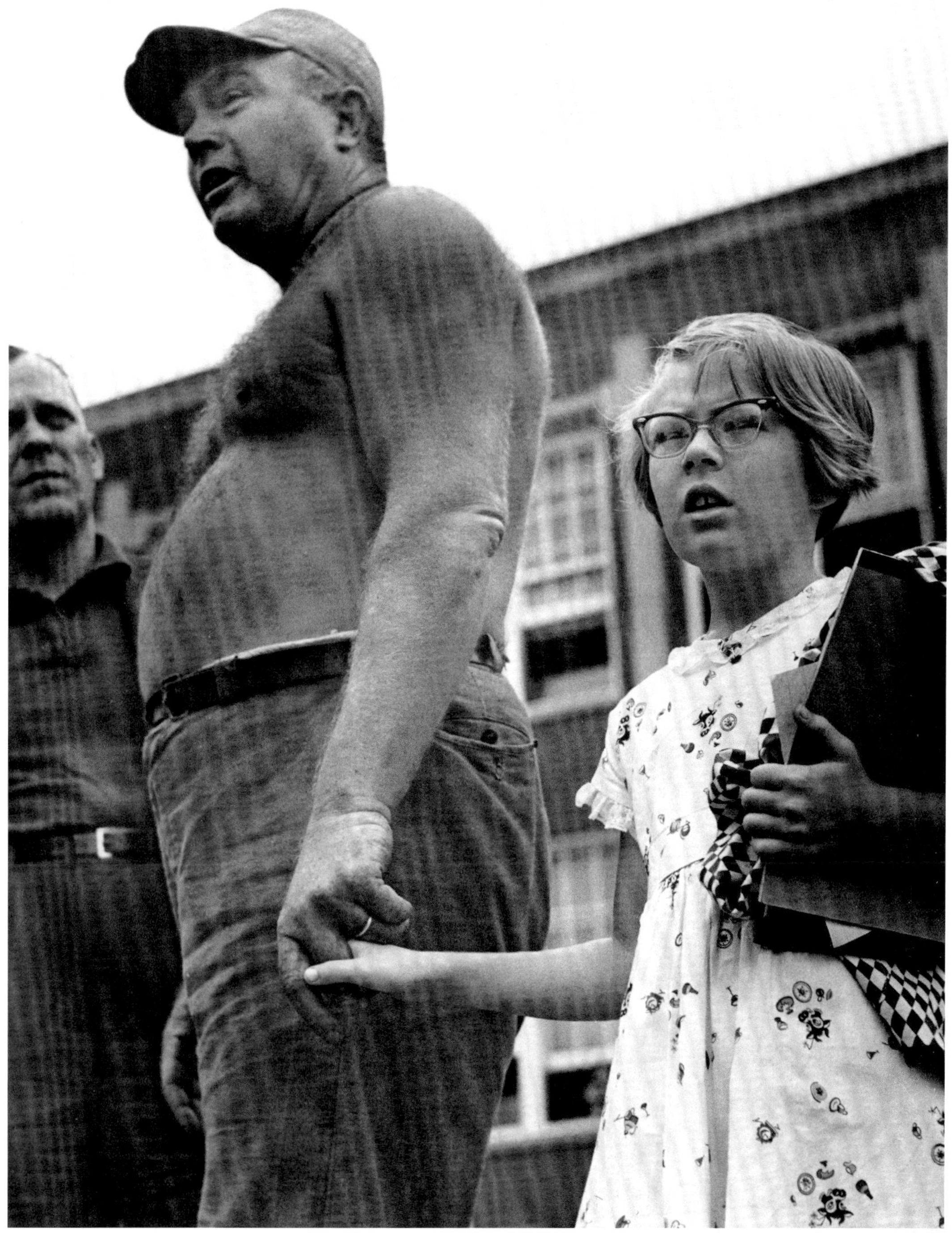

PLATE 6
Eldred Reaney,
The Tennessean
SEPTEMBER 9, 1957
J. B. Lokey leads his seven-year-old daughter out of Caldwell Elementary School. He decided to withdraw his child until things "get settled."
Courtesy of *The Tennessean*

PLATE 7

Eldred Reaney, *The Tennessean*

SEPTEMBER 9, 1957

Protesters, including defrocked minister Fred Stroud, are in front of Buena Vista School, where three African American children walked through the front door on the first day of desegregation. Courtesy of *The Tennessean*

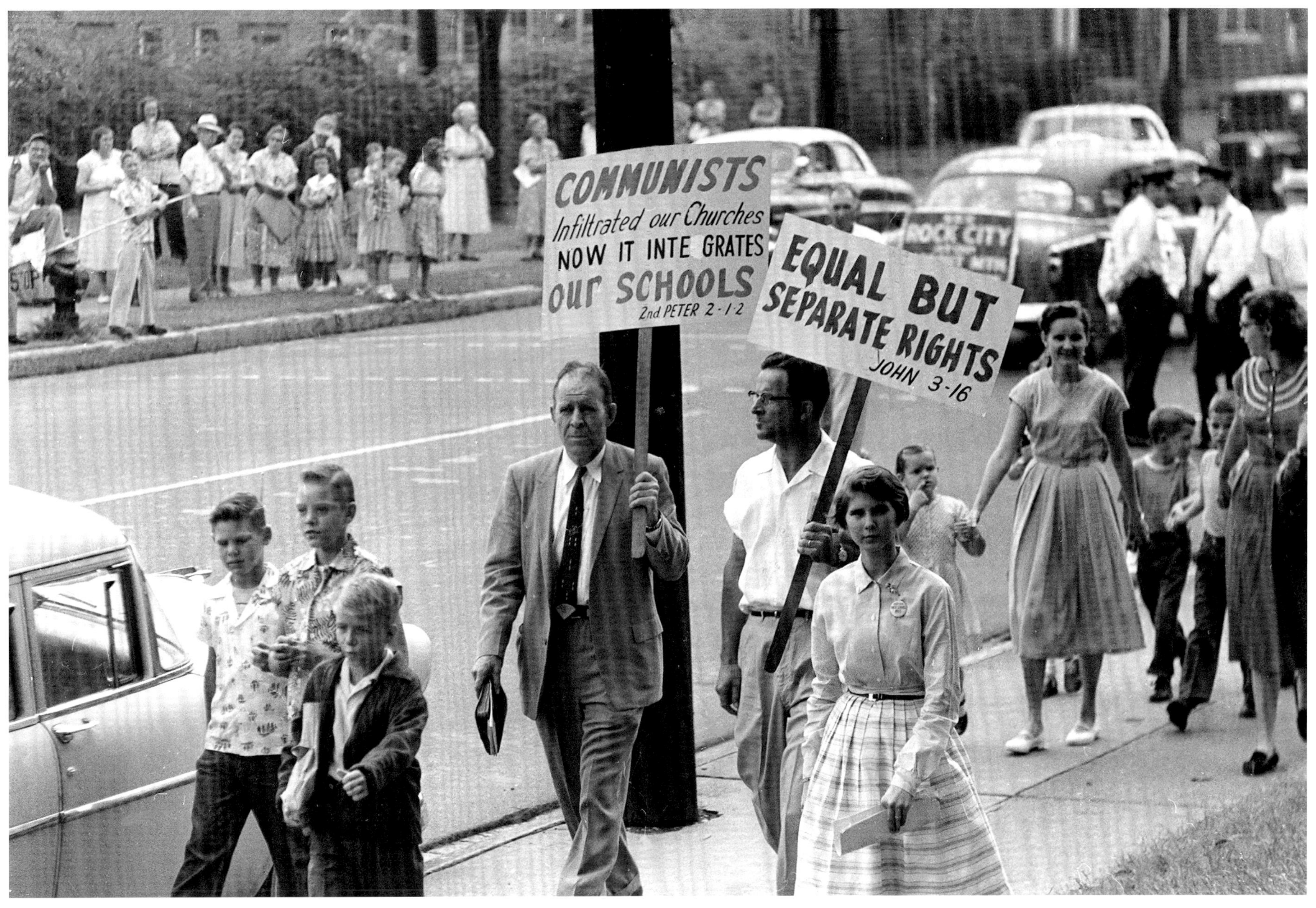
COMMUNISTS
Infiltrated our Churches
NOW IT INTE GRATES
our SCHOOLS
2nd PETER 2-1-2
EQUAL BUT
SEPARATE RIGHTS
JOHN 3-16
ROCK CITY

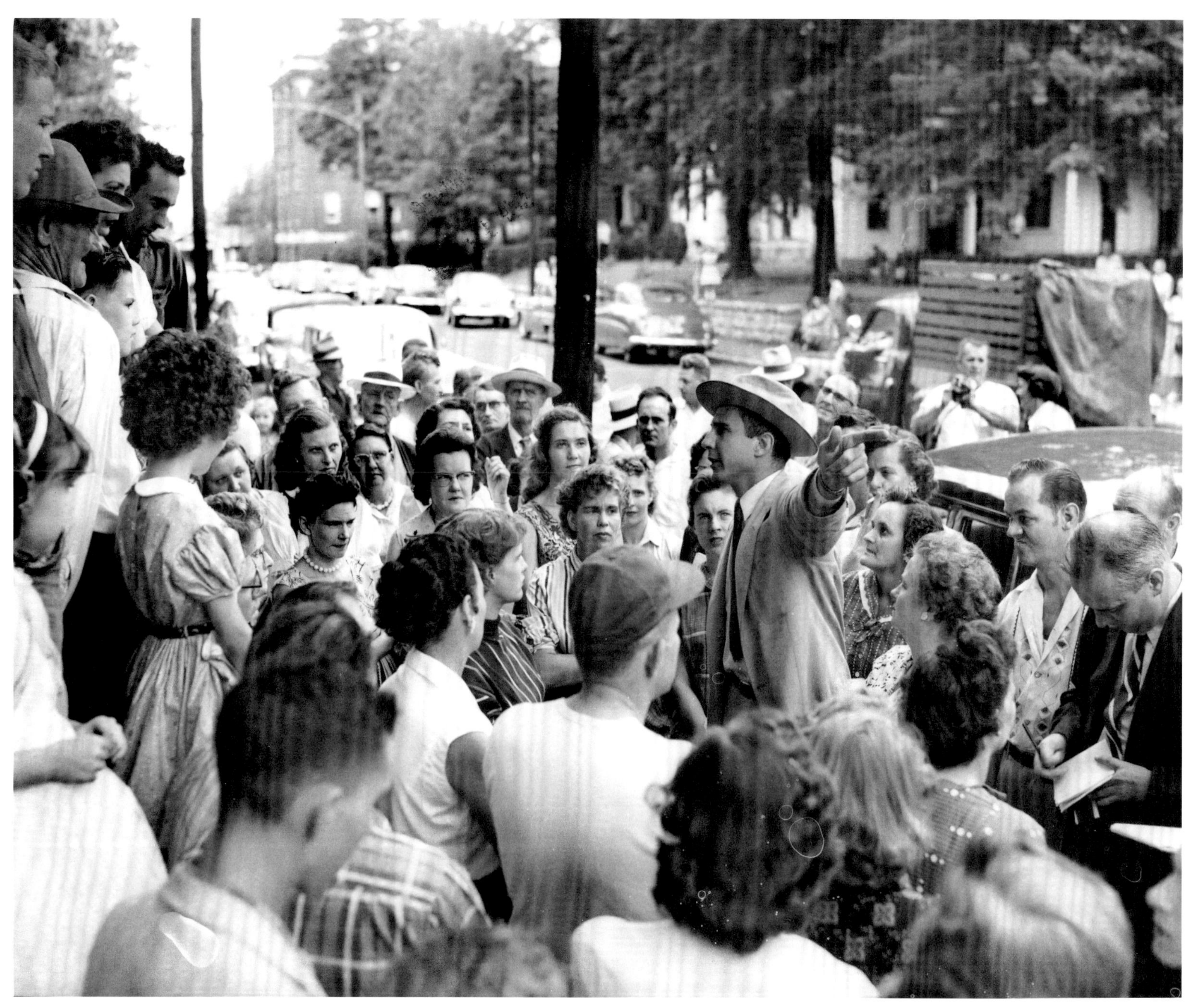

PLATE 8

Bob Ray, *Nashville Banner*

SEPTEMBER 1957

Northerner John Kasper, leader of a White Citizen's Council and a staunch segregationist, came to Nashville to protest school desegregation. Here he speaks to a crowd in front of Glenn Elementary School.

Courtesy of the Nashville Public Library, Special Collections

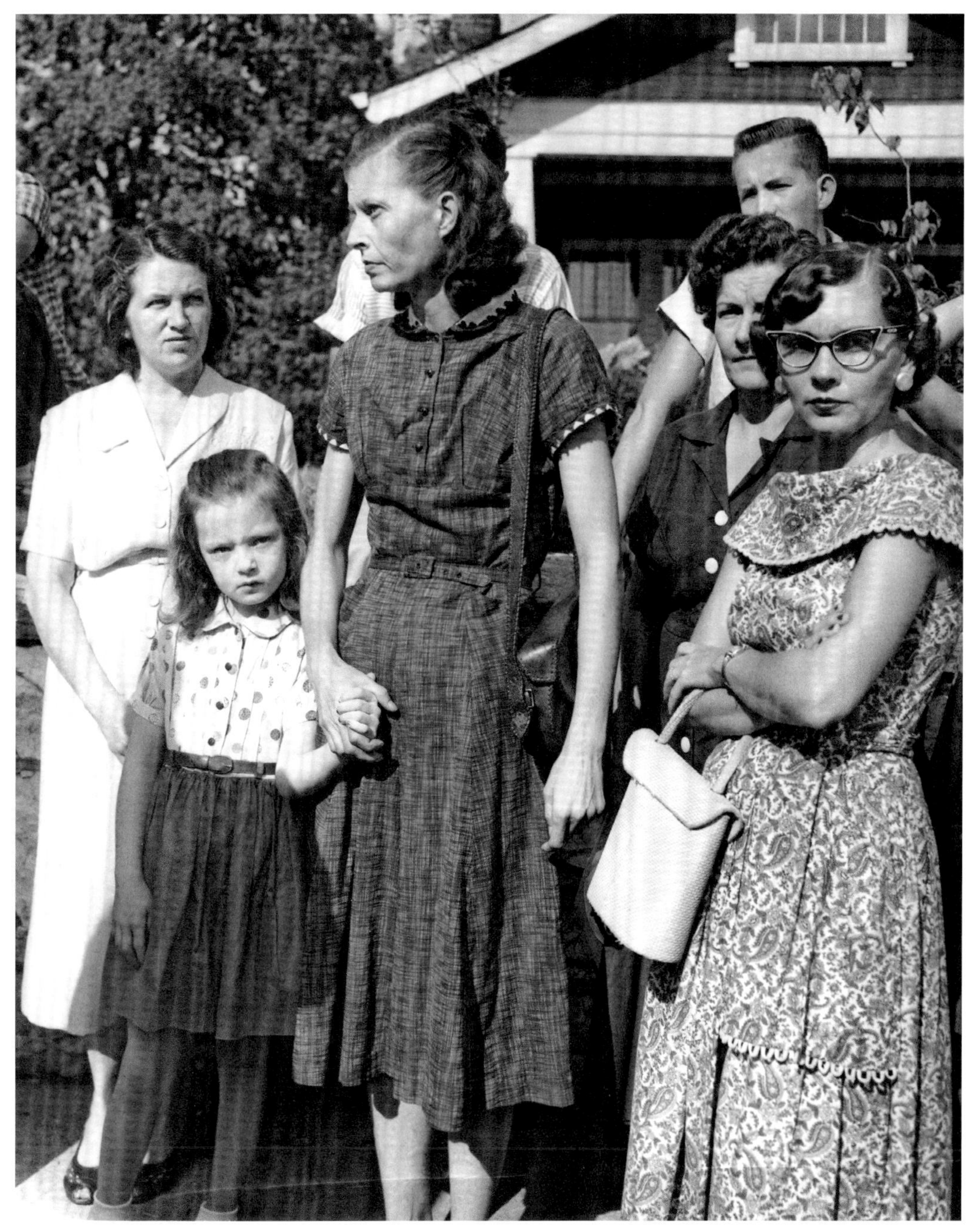

PLATE 9

Bob Ray, *Nashville Banner*

SEPTEMBER 9, 1957

Parents and a young girl on the first day of desegregation at Glenn Elementary School in East Nashville.

Courtesy of the Nashville Public Library, Special Collections

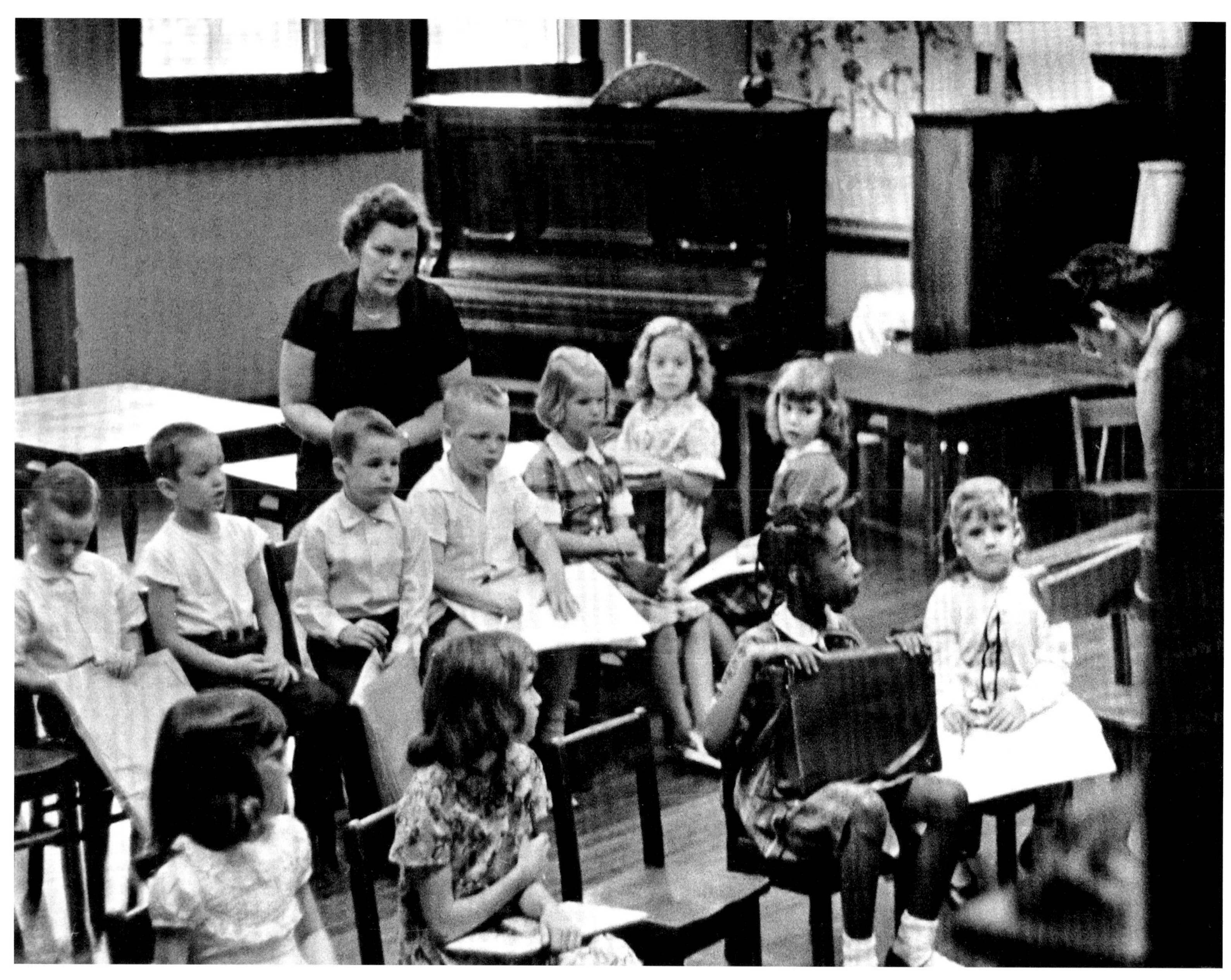

PLATE 10

Jack Corn, *The Tennessean*

SEPTEMBER 9, 1957

First graders sit quietly in a classroom at Glenn Elementary School as the fall term begins. Holding a school satchel is six-year-old Lajuanda Street, one of two African American children integrated into the school on the first day. Courtesy of *The Tennessean*

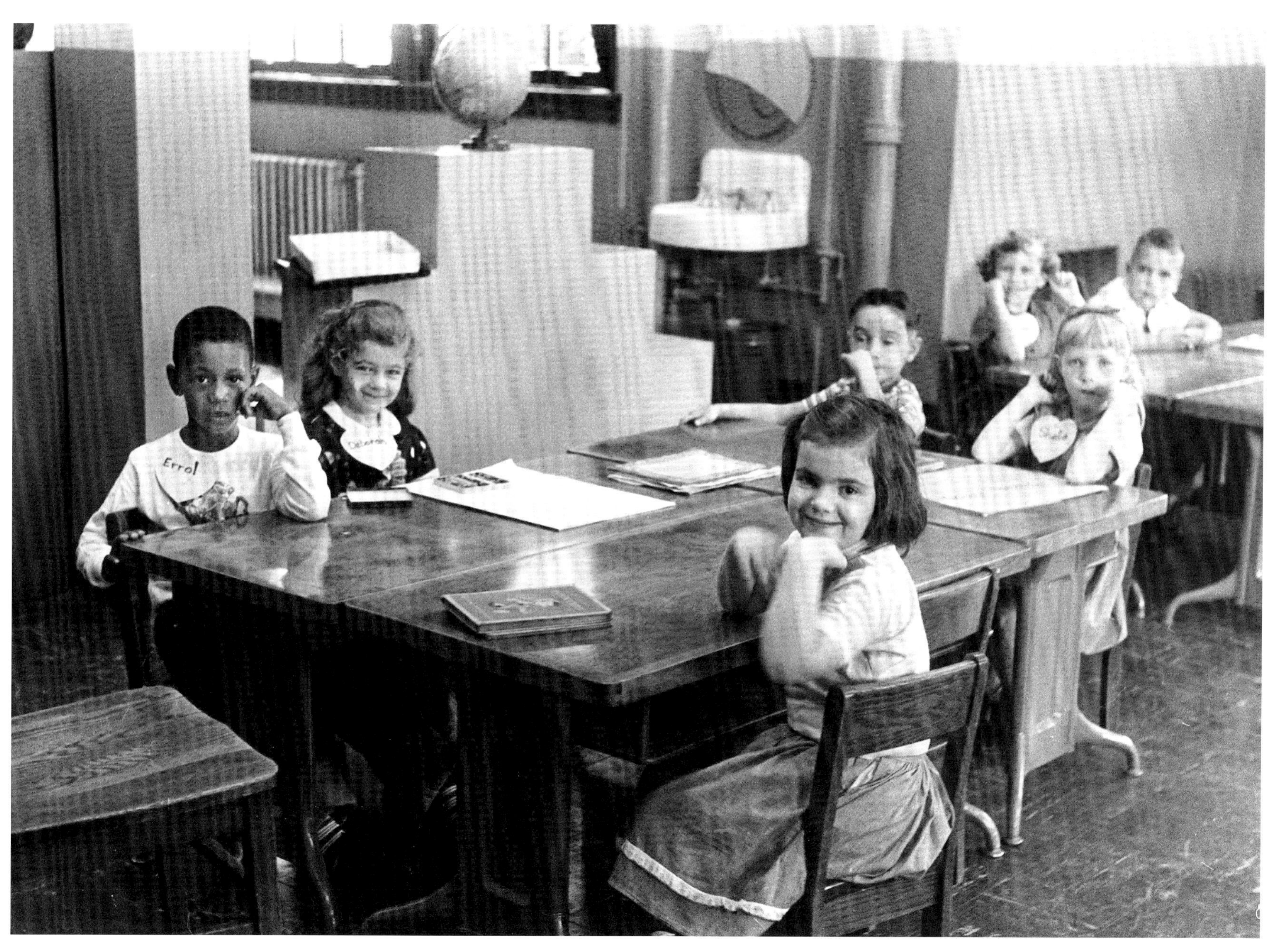

PLATE 11

Eldred Reaney, *The Tennessean*

SEPTEMBER 9, 1957

Erroll Groves (left) sits with his new classmates at Buena Vista School.

Courtesy of *The Tennessean*

PLATE 12

Staff photographer, *Nashville Banner*

SEPTEMBER 9, 1957

Closely watched by the police and the press, Grace McKinley and her daughter Linda Gail McKinley and her friend Rita Buchanan leave Fehr School.

Courtesy of the Nashville Public Library, Special Collections

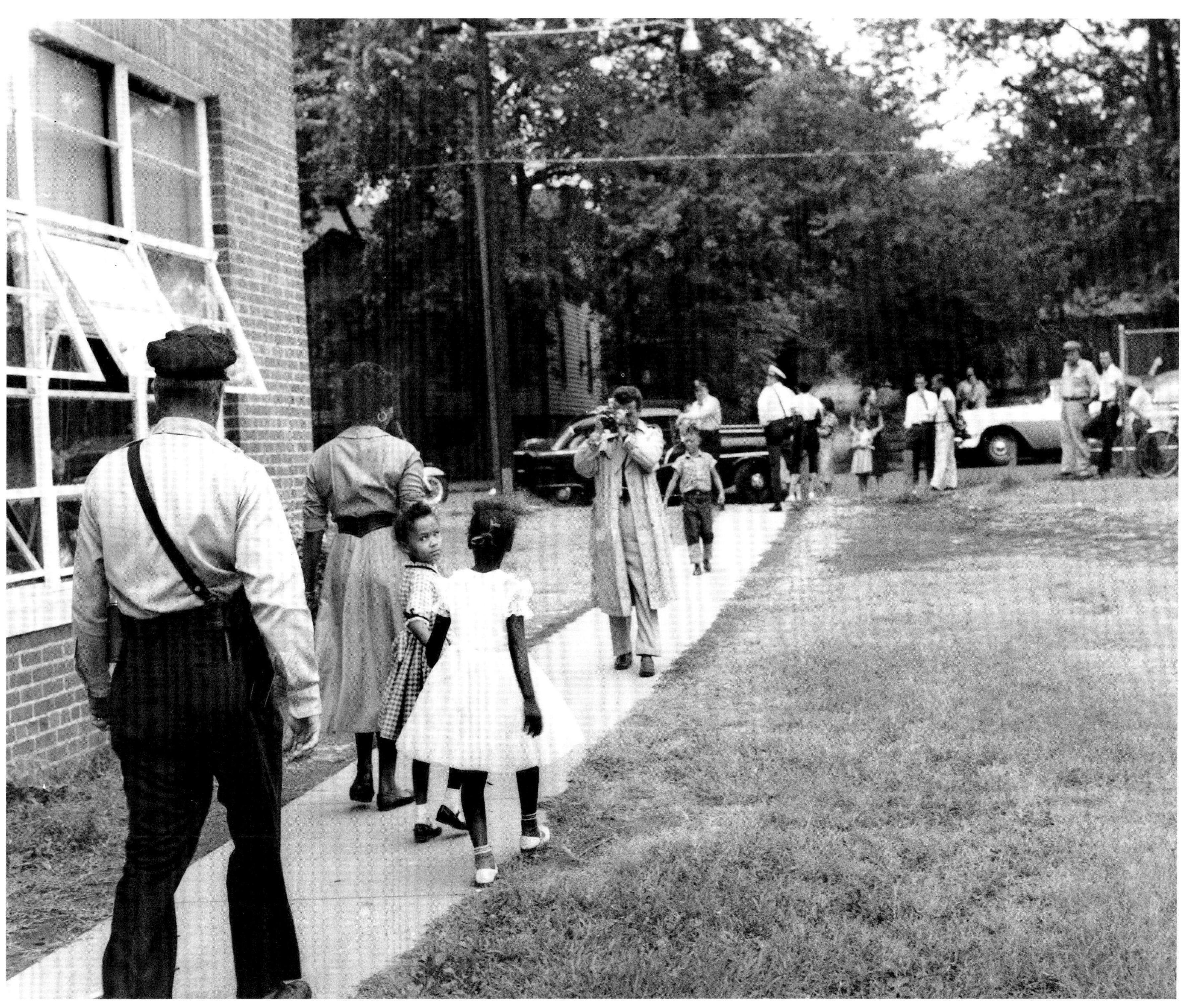

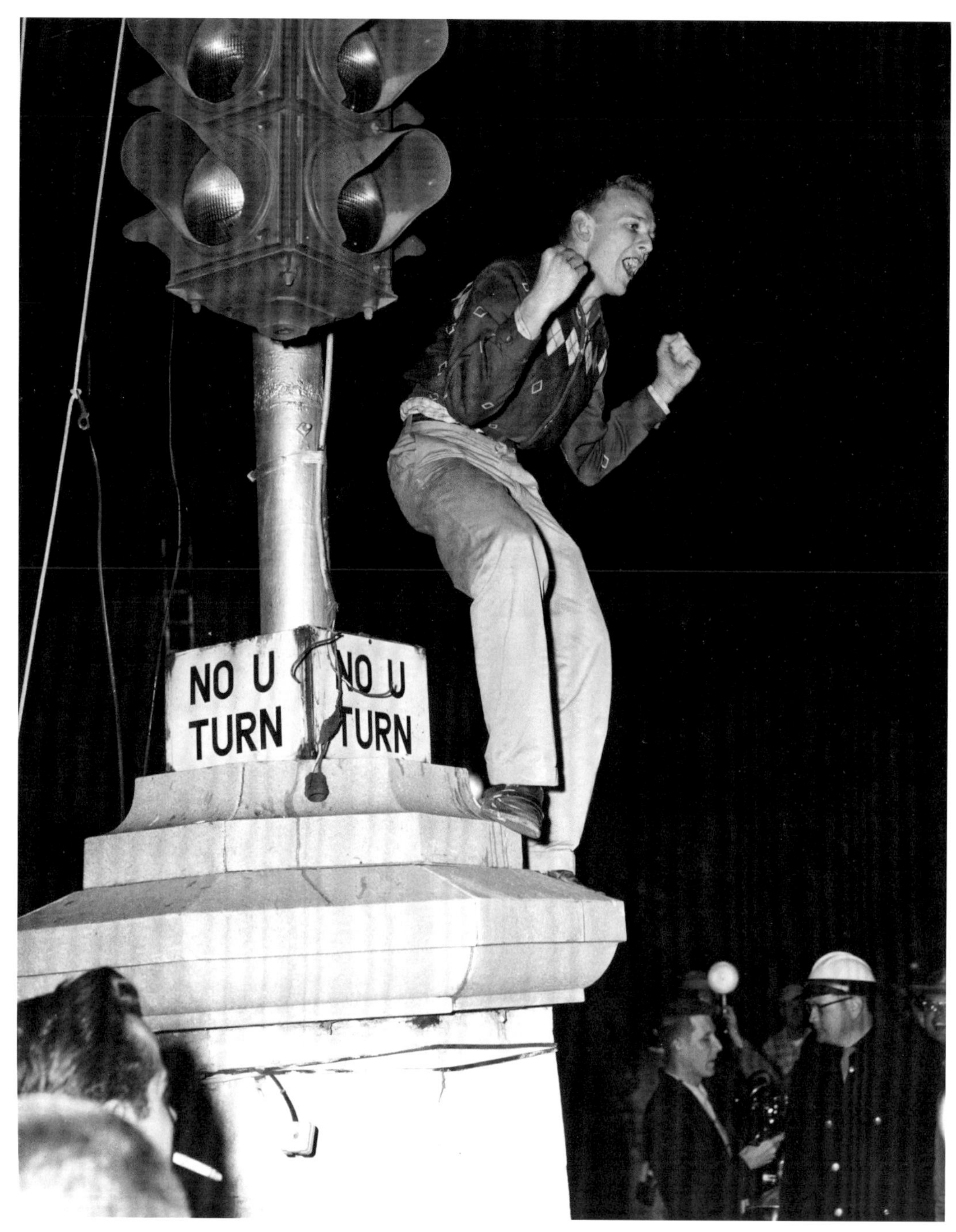

PLATE 13
Paul Schleicher, *Nashville Banner*
SEPTEMBER 8 OR 9, 1957
Although local officials, including Police Chief Douglas Hosse, vowed to uphold the law and protect the students, some people passionately protested the plan to desegregate the public schools. Courtesy of the Nashville Public Library, Special Collections

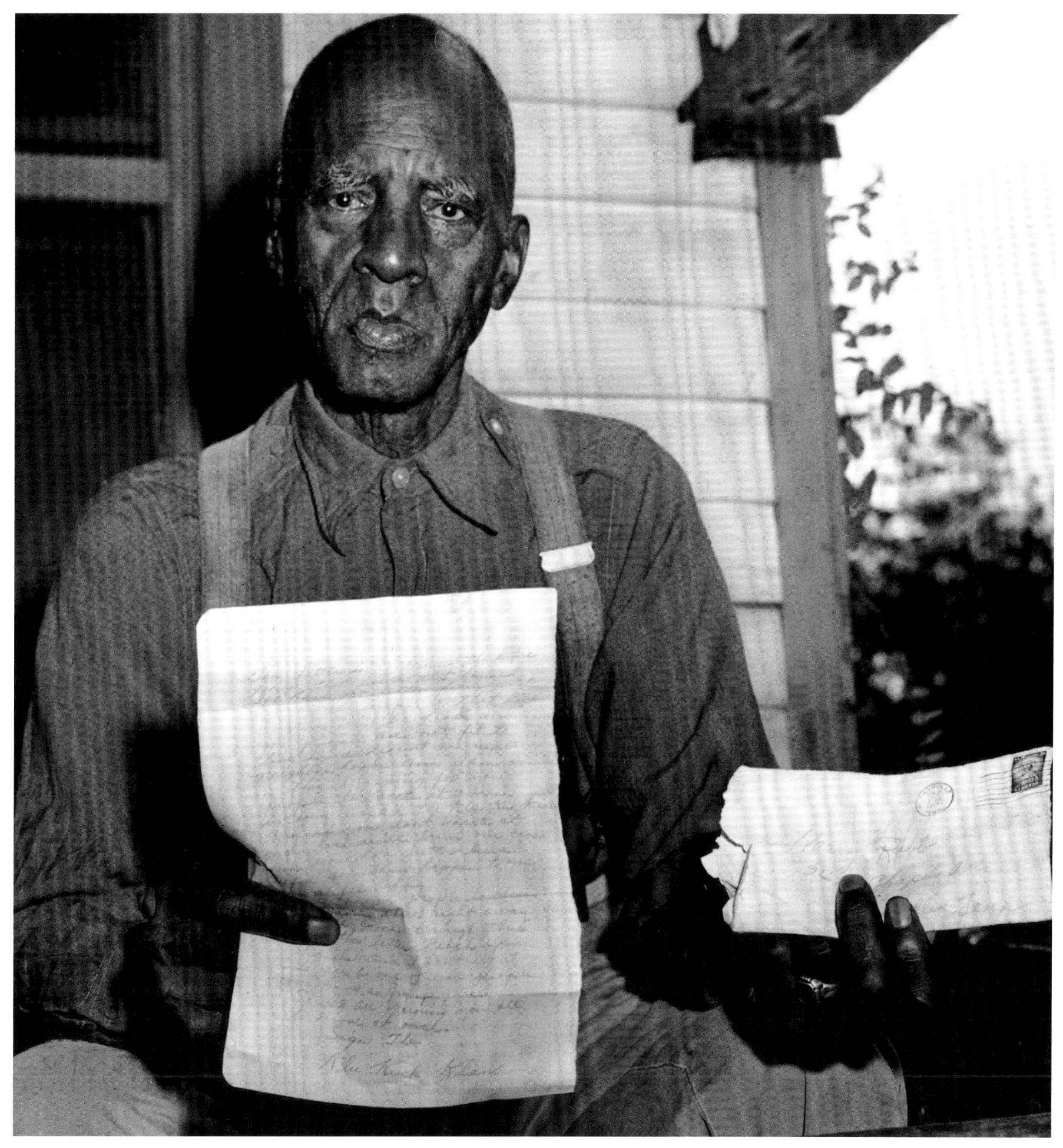

PLATE 14

Bill Preston, *The Tennessean*

SEPTEMBER 10, 1957

Harry Robb shows a letter his family received from a Ku Klux Klan member a week after his granddaughter, Era May Bailey, was to enroll in the all-white Bailey School. The letter threatened a cross-burning if the family did not move.

Courtesy of *The Tennessean*

Printed in the paper on September 10, 1957

PLATE 15

Paul Schleicher, *Nashville Banner*

SEPTEMBER 10, 1957

A crowd gathers near Hattie Cotton School in East Nashville following the bombing of its east wing shortly after midnight. One six-year-old African American girl had attended classes there the previous day. Courtesy of the Nashville Public Library, Special Collections

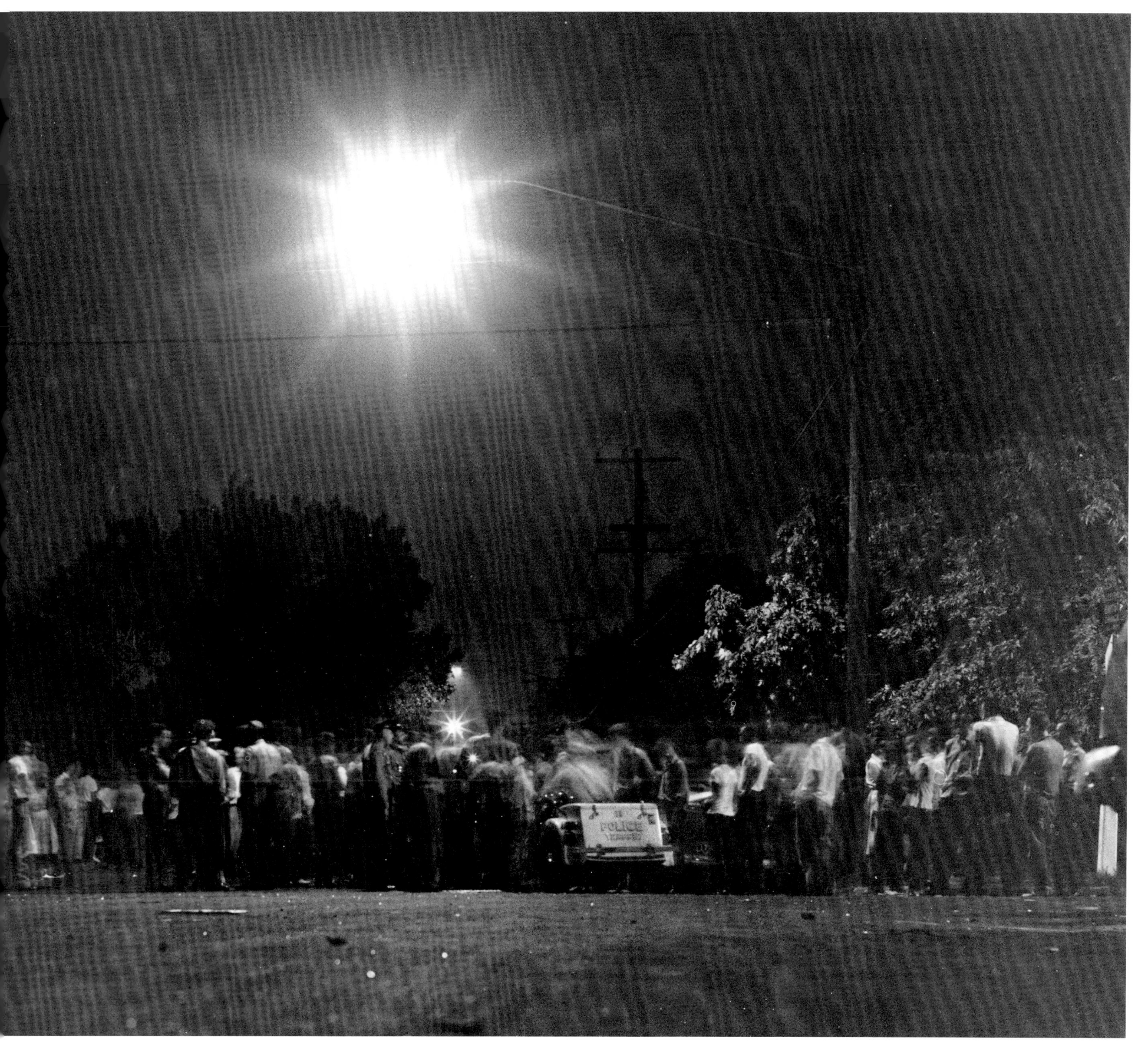
POLICE

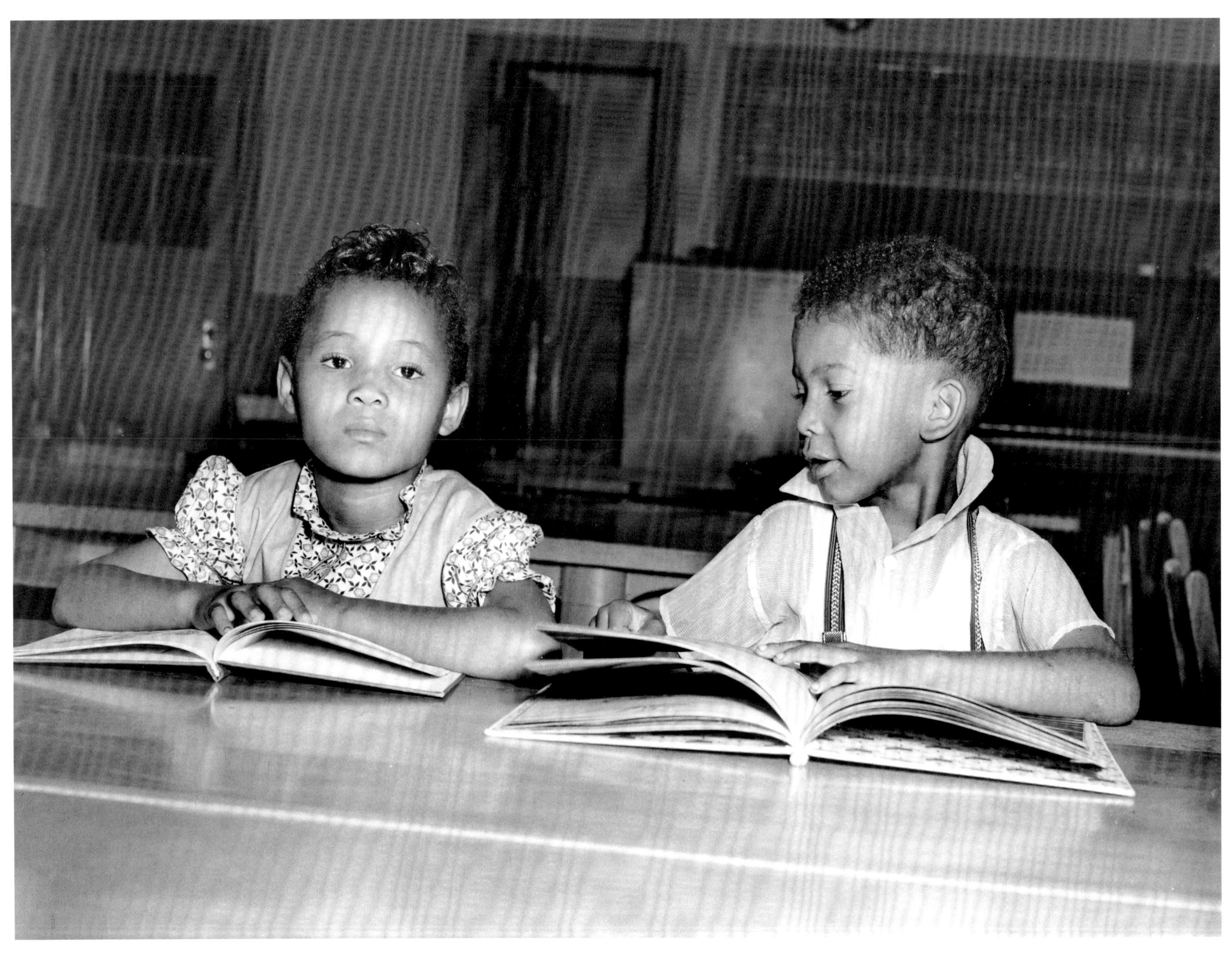

PLATE 16
Bill Goodman, *Nashville Banner*
SEPTEMBER 10, 1957
Linda McKinley and Charles Elbert Ridley at Fehr Elementary School.
Courtesy of the Nashville Public Library, Special Collections

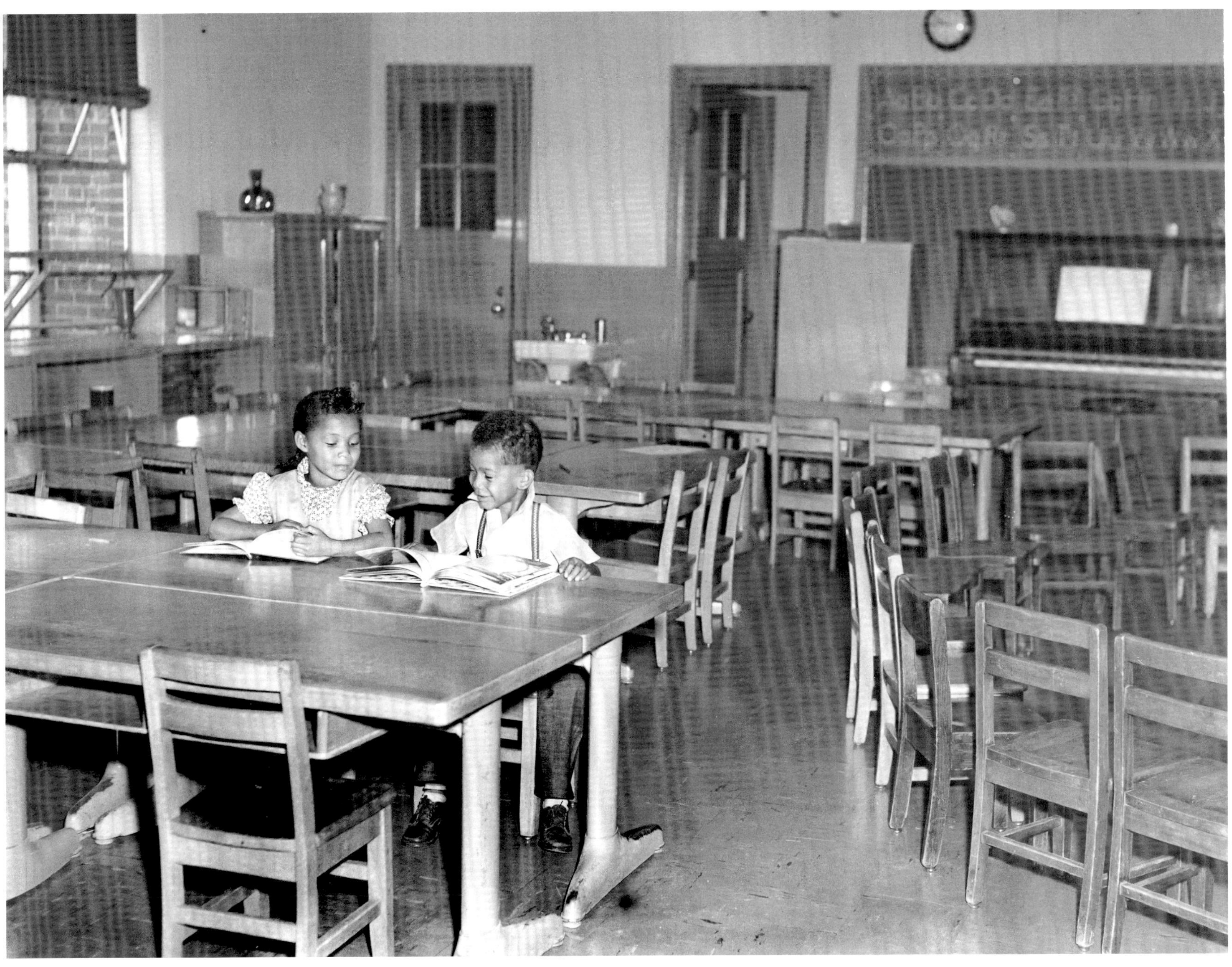

PLATE 17
Bill Goodman, *Nashville Banner*
SEPTEMBER 10, 1957
Linda McKinley and Charles Elbert Ridley were the only first graders at Fehr Elementary School in North Nashville on the day after the bombing of Hattie Cotton School.
Courtesy of the Nashville Public Library, Special Collections
Printed in the paper on September 10, 1957

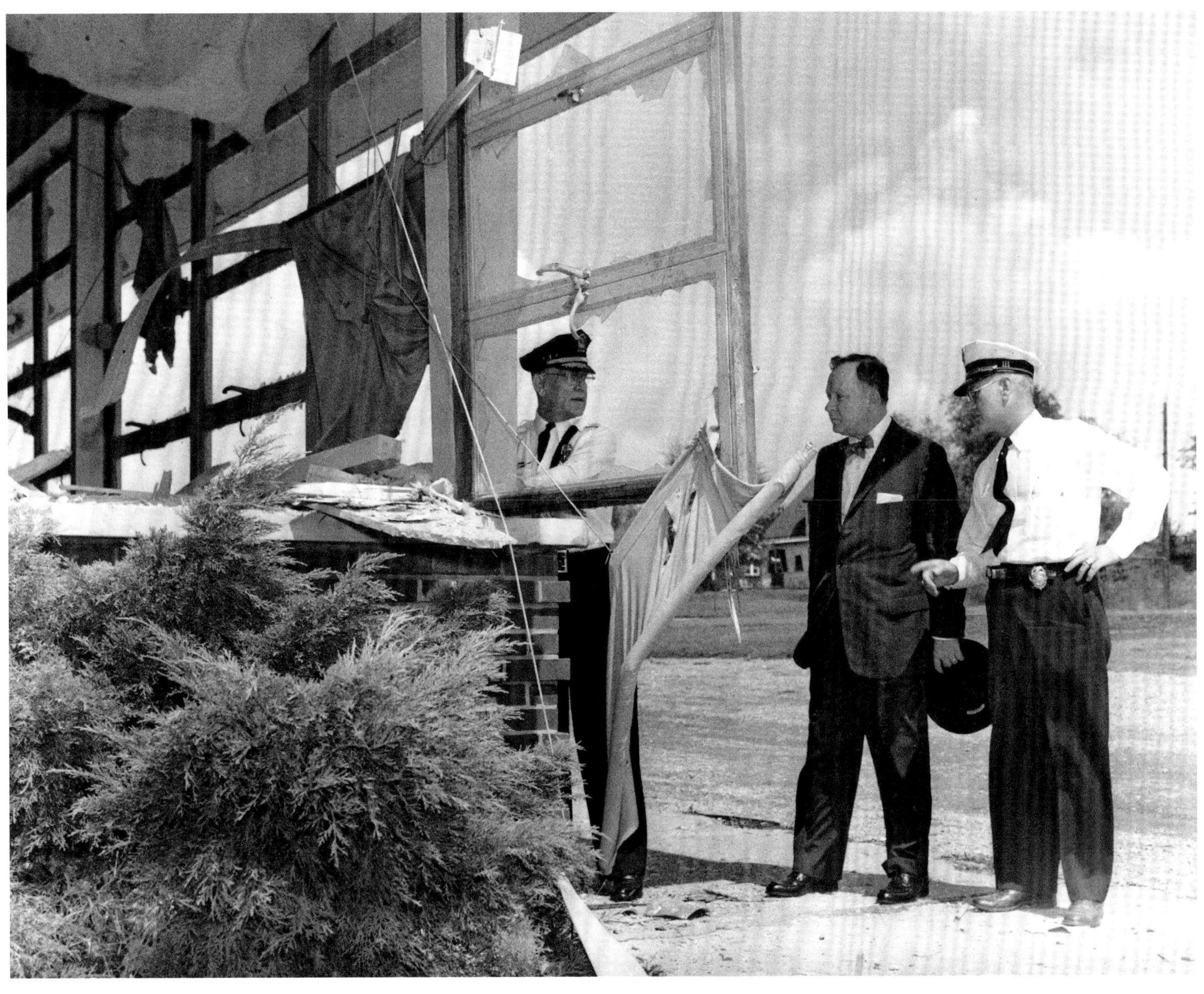

PLATE 18
Bill Goodman, *Nashville Banner*

SEPTEMBER 10, 1957

Police Chief Douglas Hosse, Mayor Ben West, and Fire Marshal Dan Hicks survey the ruins of Hattie Cotton School. At approximately 12:30 a.m. that morning, a dynamite blast destroyed the east wing of the school.
Courtesy of the Nashville Public Library, Special Collections

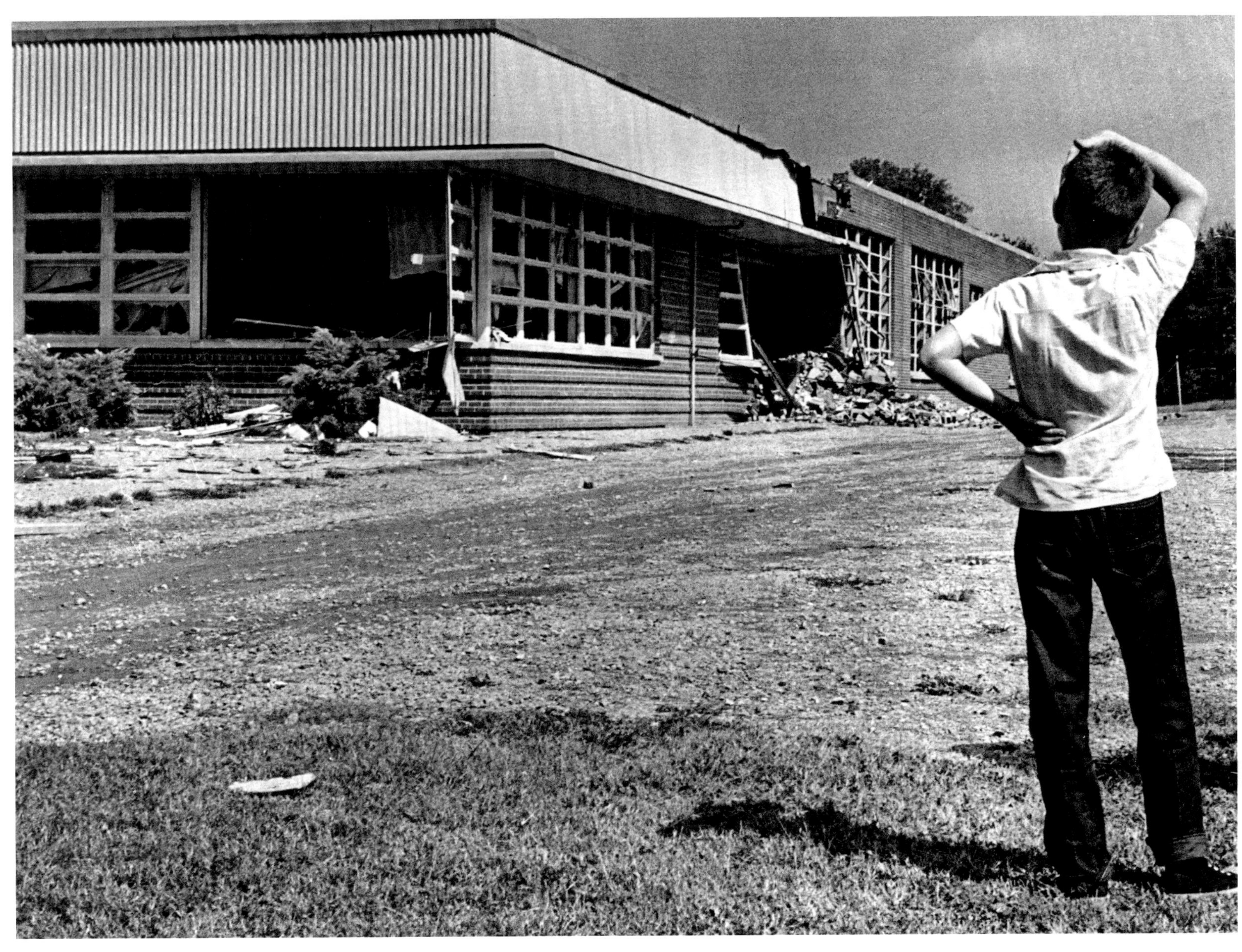

PLATE 19
Bill Preston, *The Tennessean*
SEPTEMBER 10, 1957
A perplexed little boy stands before the wreckage of Hattie Cotton School.
Courtesy of *The Tennessean*
Printed in the paper on September 11, 1957

PLATE 20

Staff photographer, *Nashville Banner*

SEPTEMBER 9 OR 10, 1957

A policeman patrols a brick sidewalk in a Nashville neighborhood near Glenn Elementary School. Mayor Ben West had vowed that no child would be hurt during the integration of the city's public schools. Courtesy of the Nashville Public Library, Special Collections

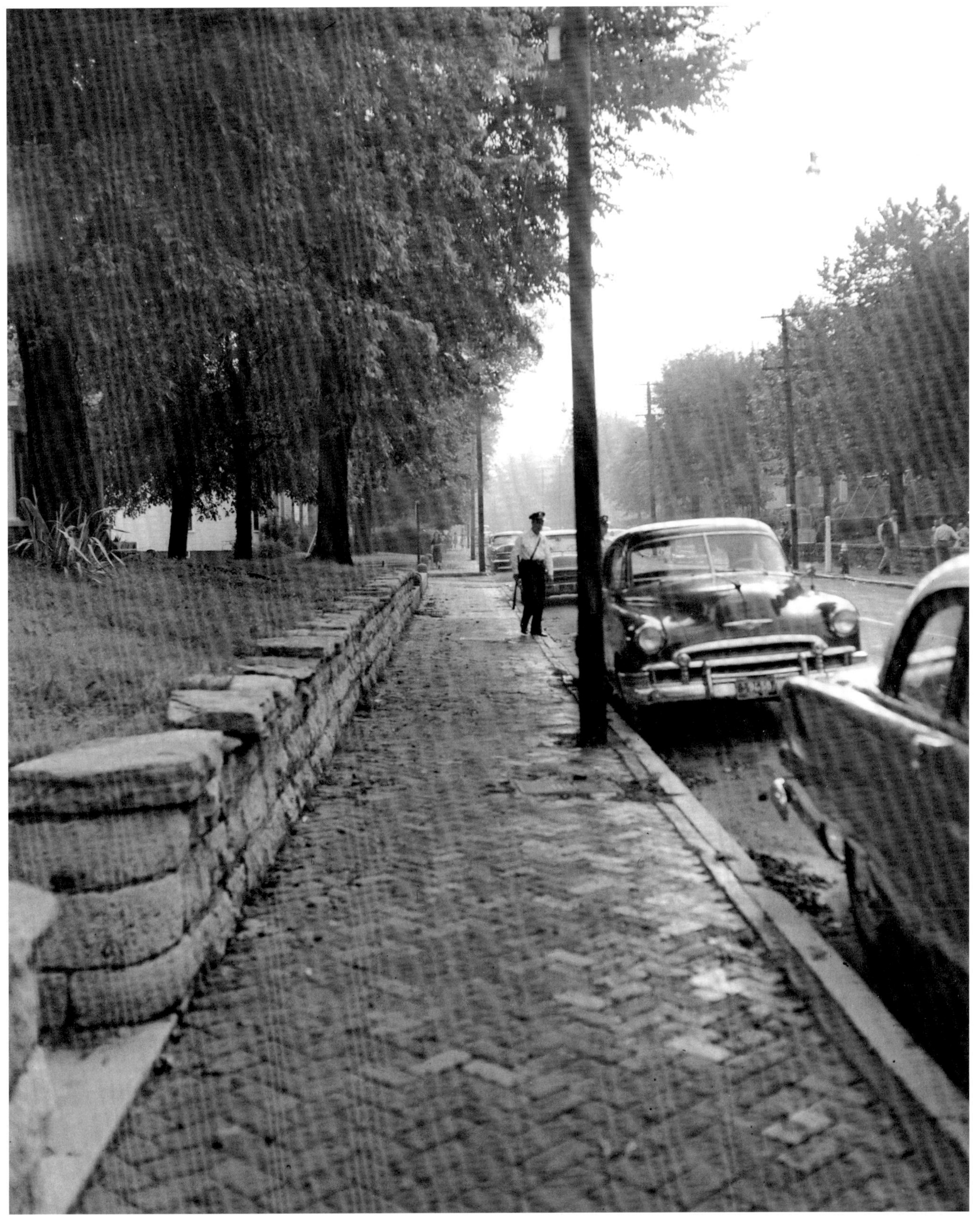

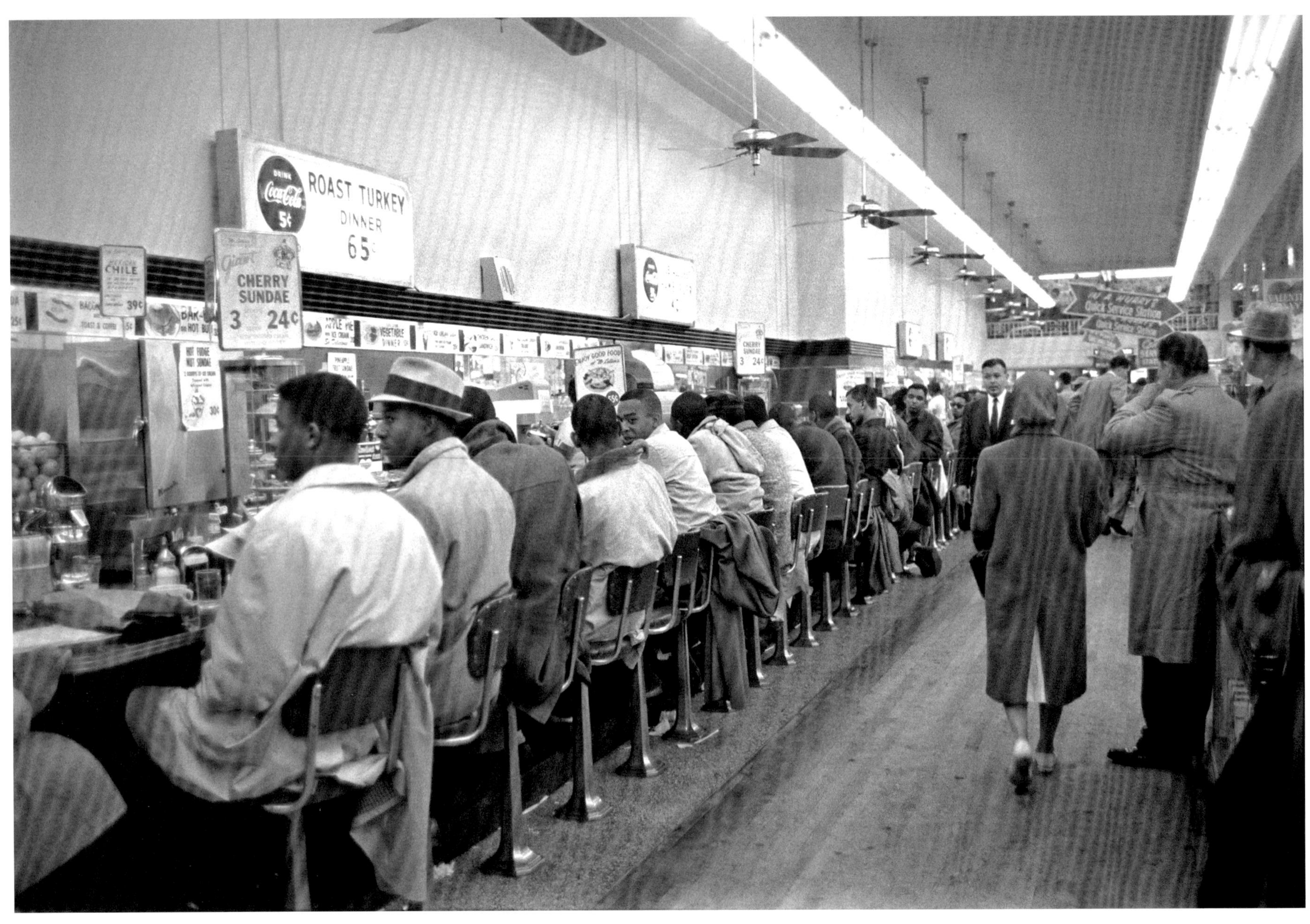

PLATE 21

Bill Goodman, *Nashville Banner*

FEBRUARY 13, 1960

The first large-scale, organized sit-in against segregated lunch counters took place in Nashville on February 13, 1960. More than one hundred protesters from American Baptist College, Fisk University, Meharry Medical College, and Tennessee A&I (now Tennessee State University) converged on downtown variety stores, including McLellan, seen here.

Courtesy of the Nashville Public Library, Special Collections

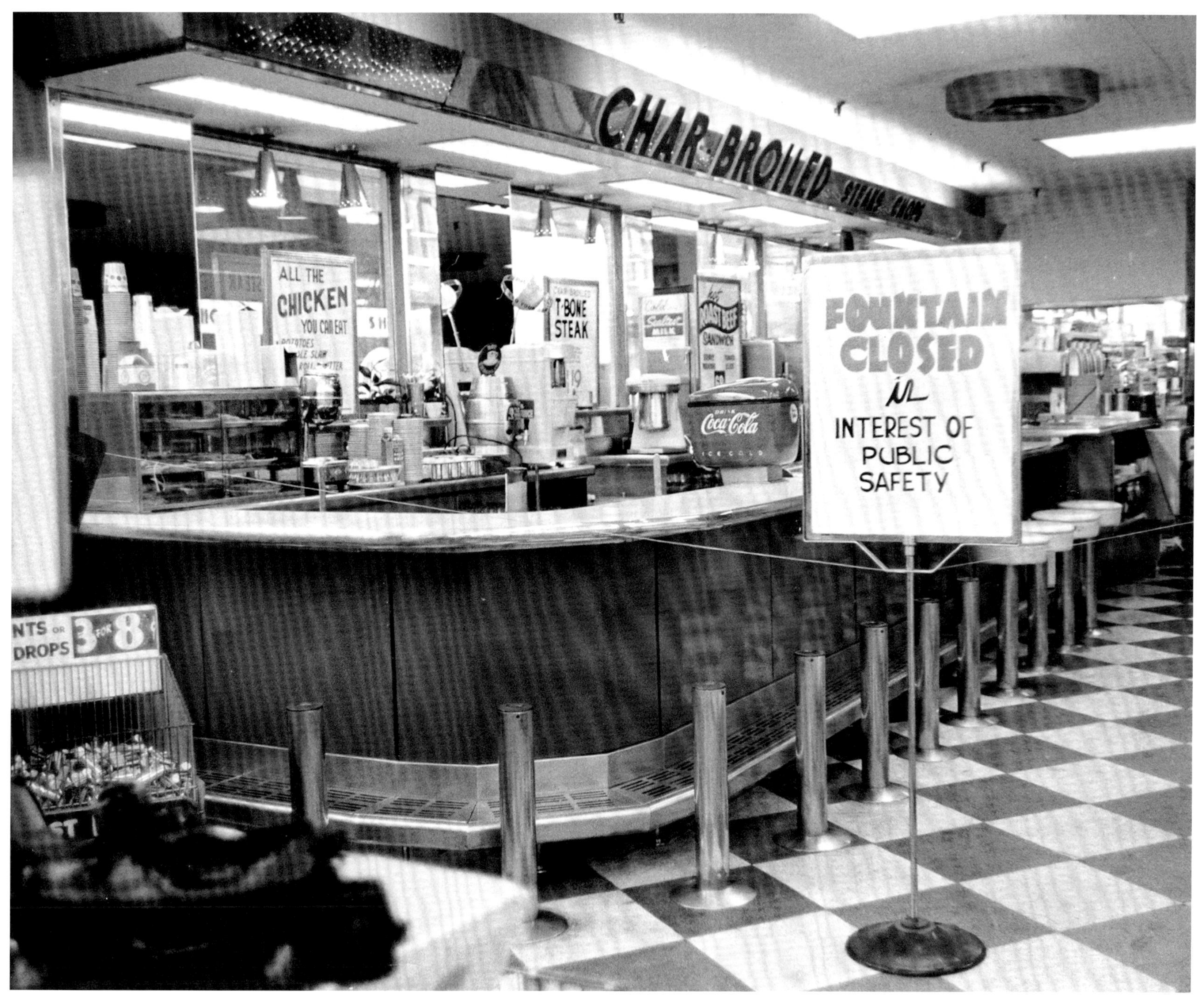

PLATE 22

Bill Goodman, *Nashville Banner*

FEBRUARY 27, 1960

Some store managers closed their lunch counters, like the one at Walgreens shown here, in response to the demonstrations. Courtesy of the Nashville Public Library, Special Collections

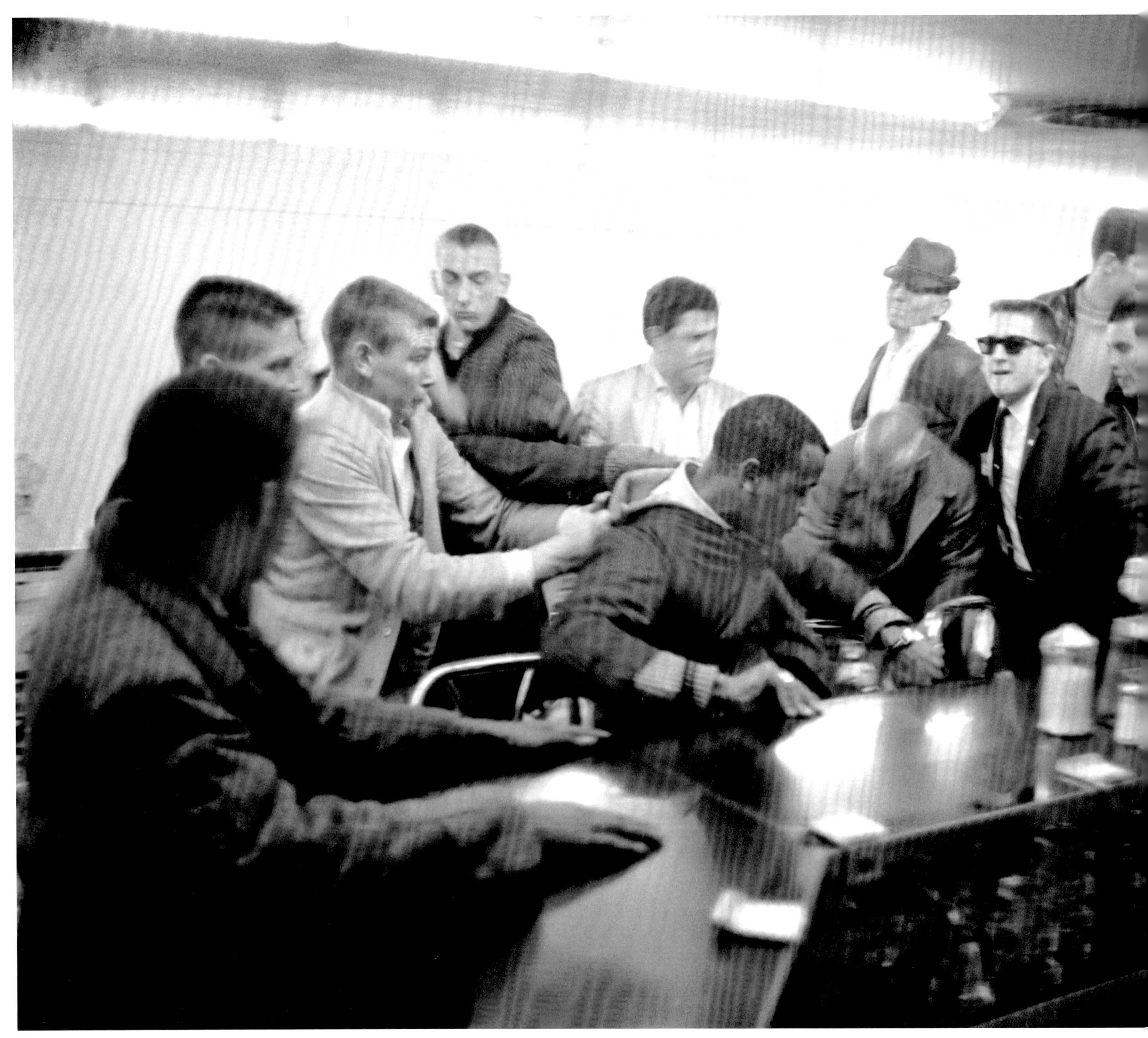

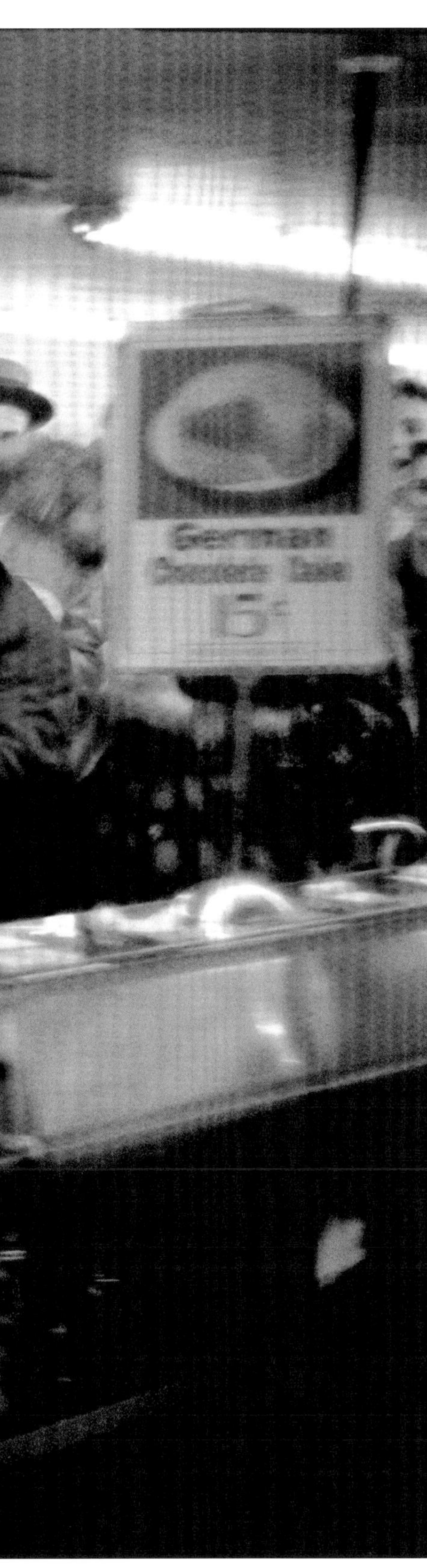

PLATE 23

Vic Cooley, *Nashville Banner*

FEBRUARY 27, 1960

Several men attempt to drag a nonviolent student sit-in demonstrator from his stool at the lunch counter in the upstairs section of Woolworth on Fifth Avenue North.

Courtesy of the Nashville Public Library, Special Collections

A very similar image was printed in the paper on February 29, 1960

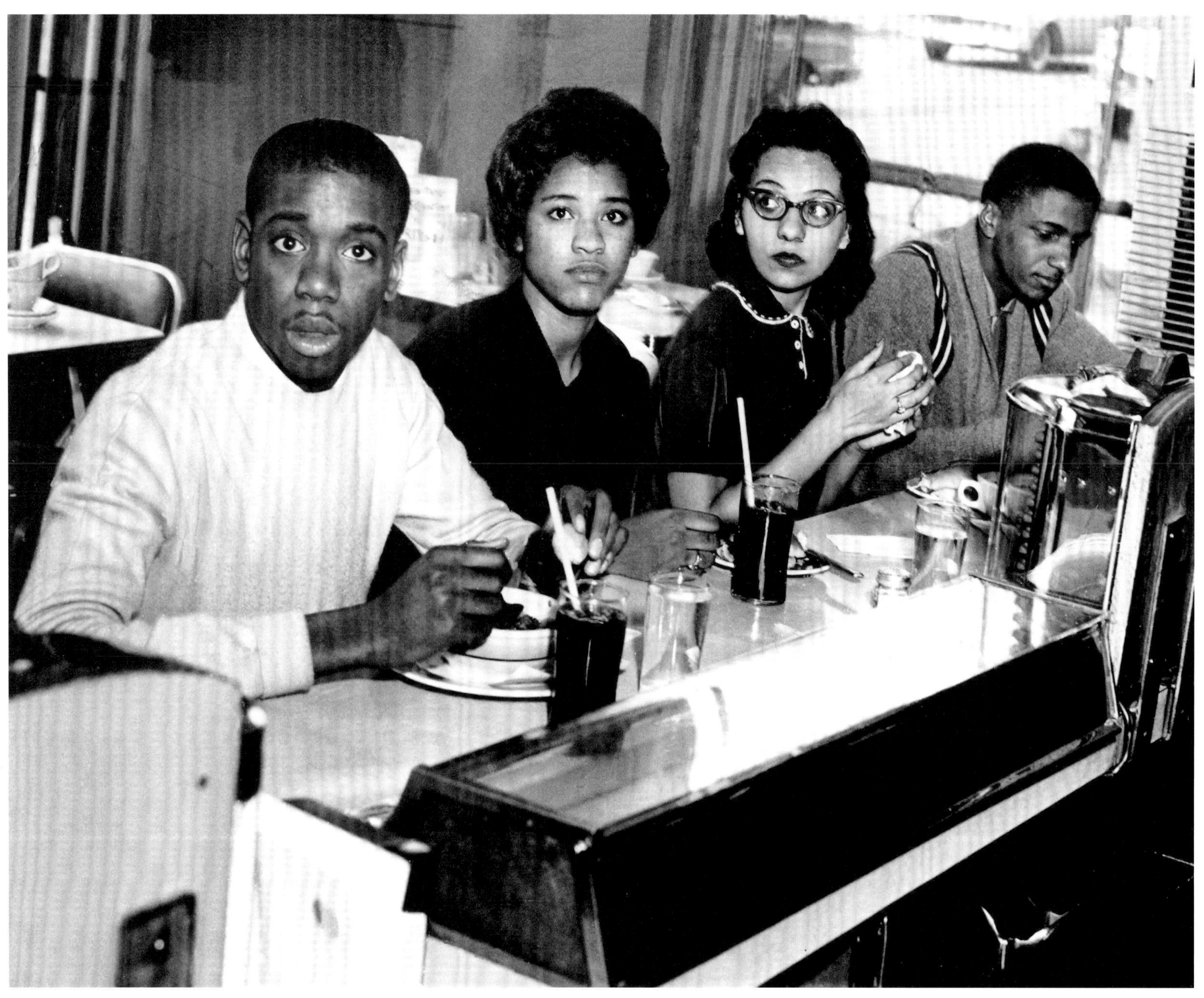

PLATE 24

Gerald Holly, *The Tennessean*

MARCH 16, 1960

Students Matthew Walker (left), Peggy Alexander, Diane Nash, and Stanley Hemphill are served at the lunch counter of the Post House Restaurant in the Nashville Greyhound bus terminal in response to the Interstate Commerce Commission ruling that banned segregated bus travel. Integration at lunch counters did not become widespread in Nashville until May 10, 1960.

Courtesy of *The Tennessean*

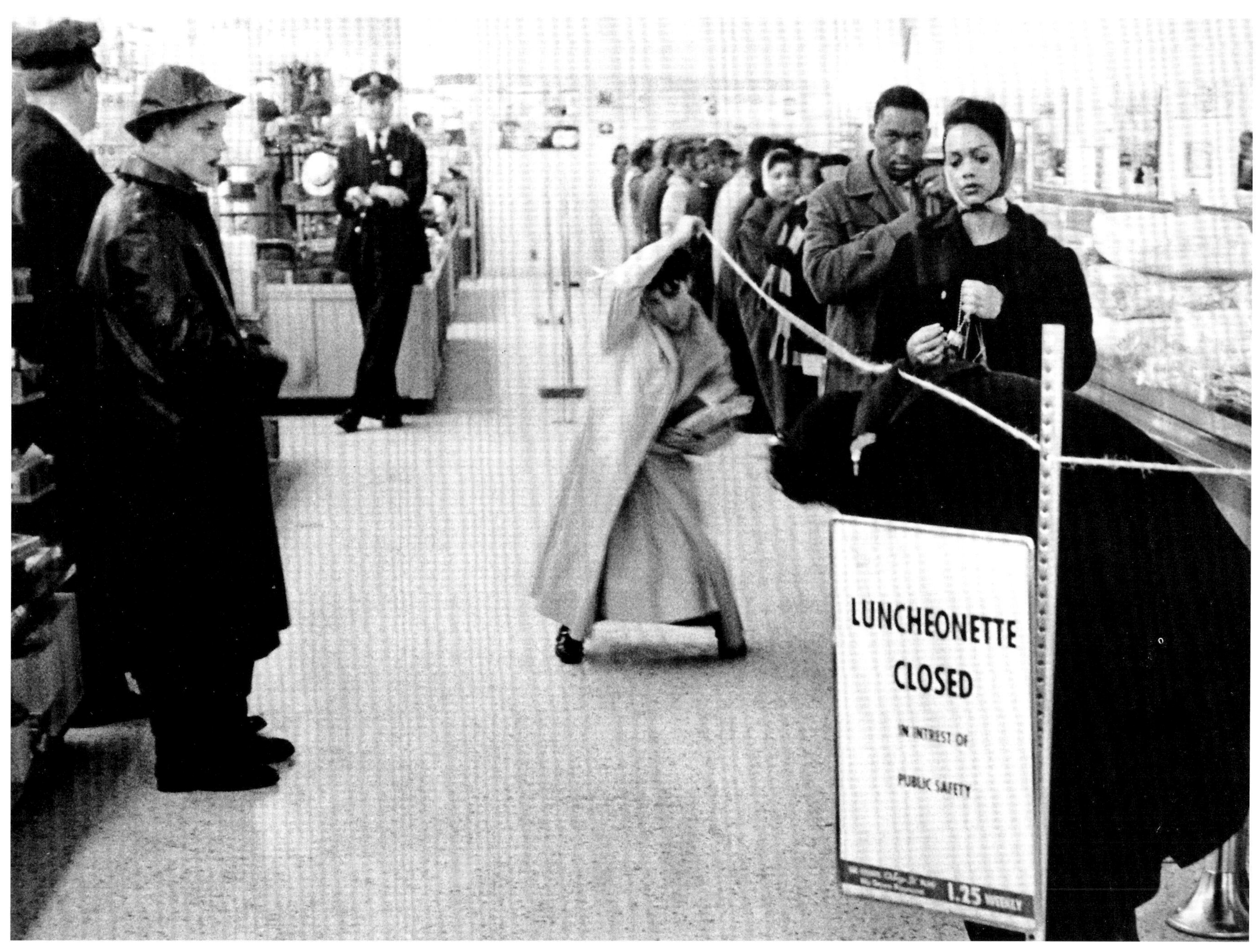

PLATE 25

Eldred Reaney, *The Tennessean*

MARCH 2, 1960

Tennessee A&I students Benny Grant (second from right), and Lucretia Collins (right), are among hundreds of demonstrators tramping through rain and slush to continue their sit-in campaign against lunch counter segregation.

Courtesy of *The Tennessean*

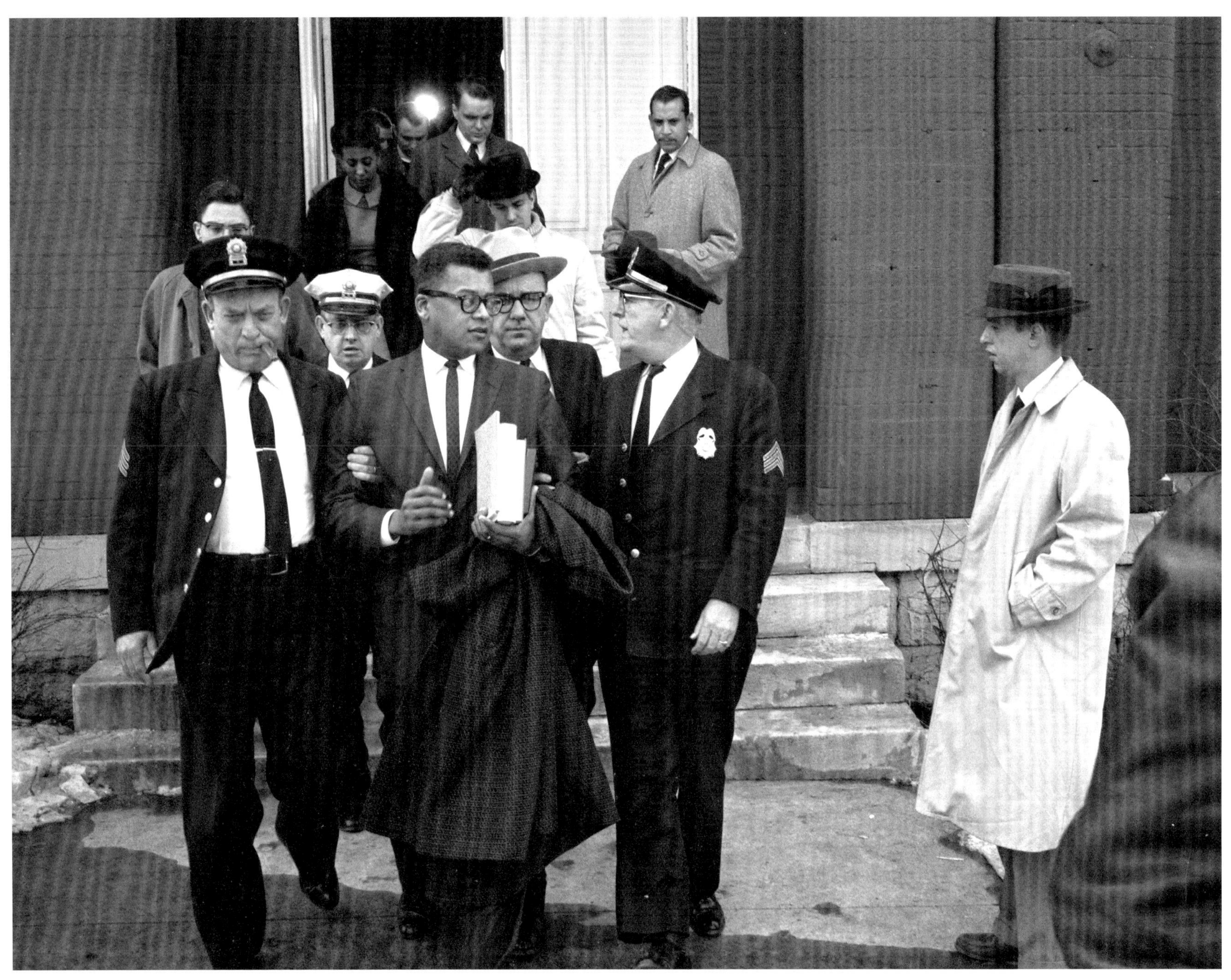

PLATE 26

Vic Cooley, *Nashville Banner*

MARCH 4, 1960

Four Nashville policemen arrive at First Baptist Church, Capitol Hill, to arrest James M. Lawson Jr. for conspiring to violate the state's trade and commerce law. He had been expelled from Vanderbilt University the day before for his participation in the sit-in movement. Courtesy of the Nashville Public Library, Special Collections

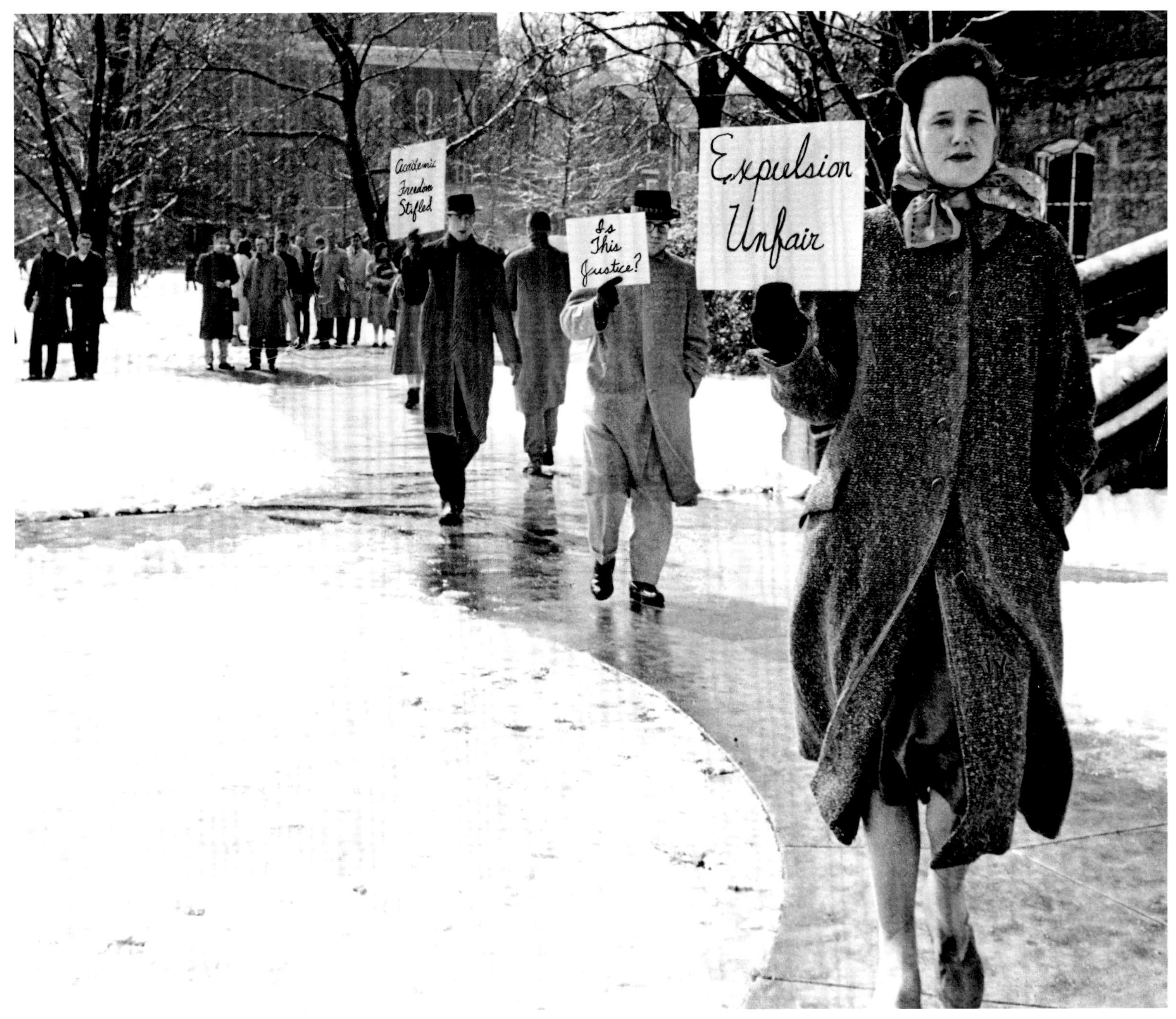

PLATE 27

Gerald Holly, *The Tennesseean*

MARCH 4, 1960

Picketers, most of them divinity school students at Vanderbilt University, march in front of Kirkland Hall protesting the expulsion of Lawson for his part in recent lunch-counter desegregation demonstrations.

Courtesy of *The Tennessean*

Printed in the paper on March 5, 1960

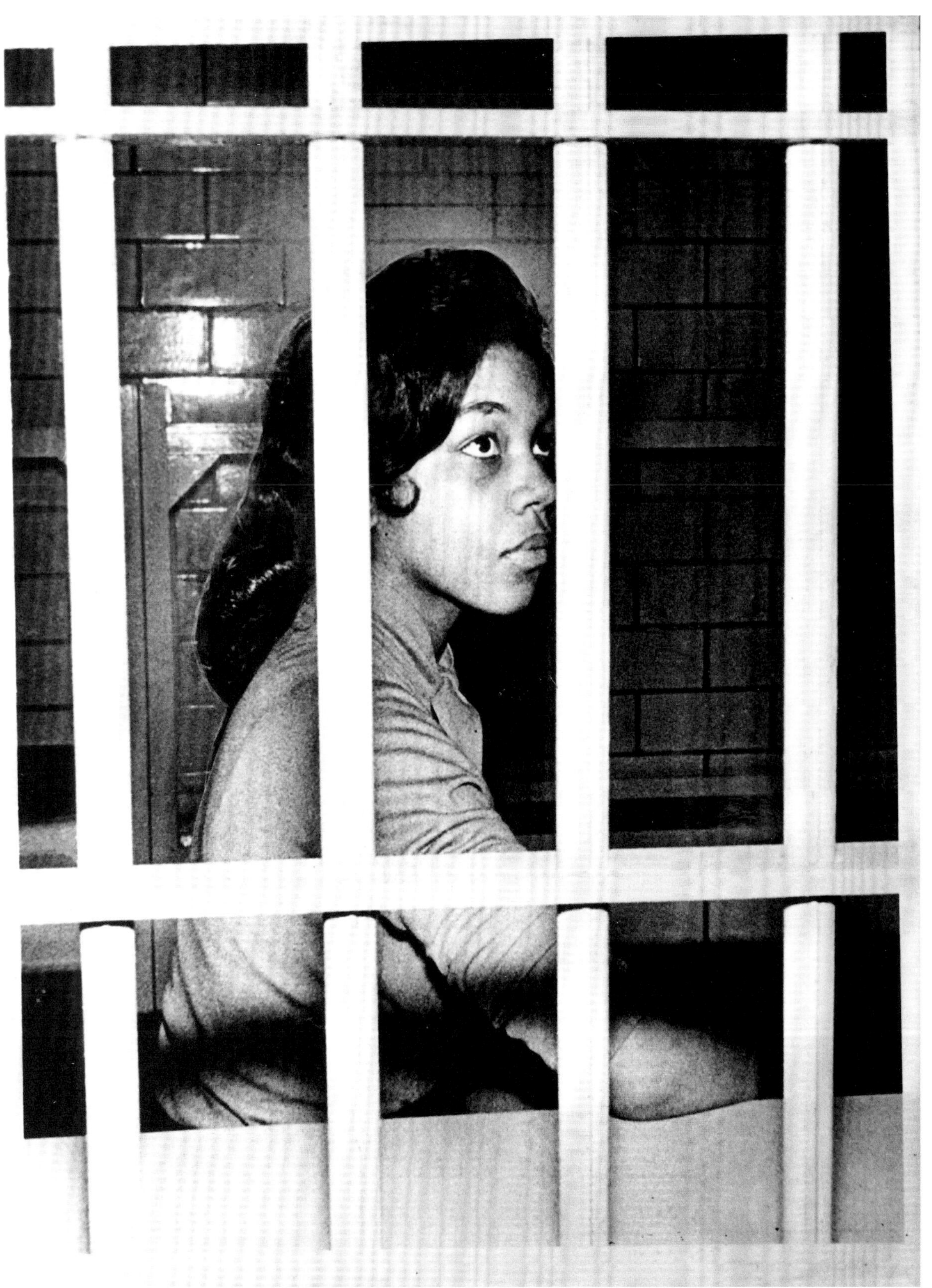

PLATE 28

Jimmy Ellis, *The Tennessean*

MARCH 25, 1960

Jean Wynona Fleming, a Fisk University student, is behind bars in a Nashville city jail after her arrest at a downtown Moon-McGrath drugstore lunch counter.

Courtesy of *The Tennessean*

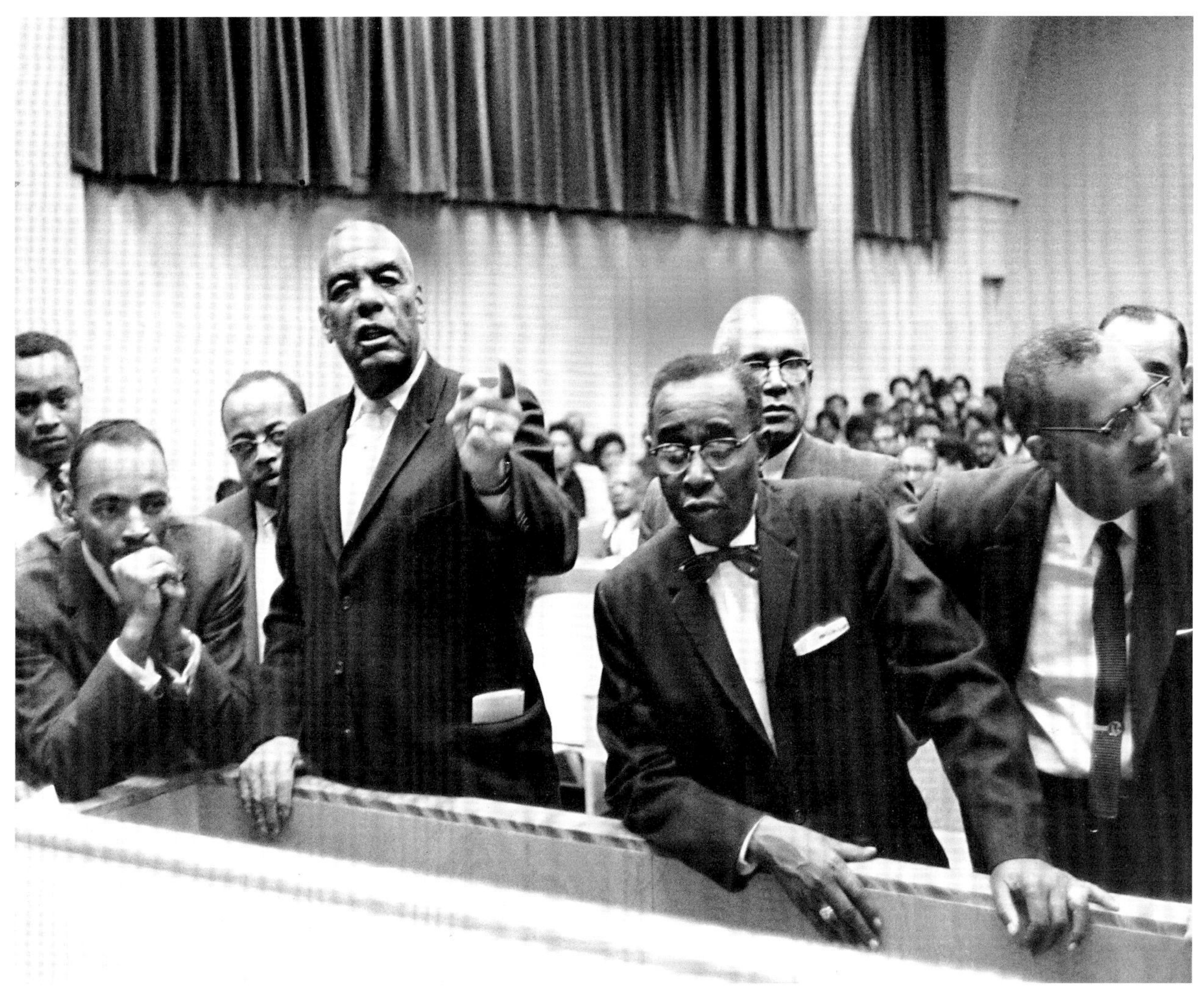

PLATE 29

Vic Cooley, *Nashville Banner*

MARCH 2, 1960

Along with Z. Alexander Looby (not pictured), these attorneys were the spearheads of the defense for the student demonstrators: from left, Adolpho A. Birch, Robert E. Lillard, Coyness I. Ennix Sr., and Avon Williams Jr.

Courtesy of the Nashville Public Library, Special Collections

Printed in the paper on March 2, 1960

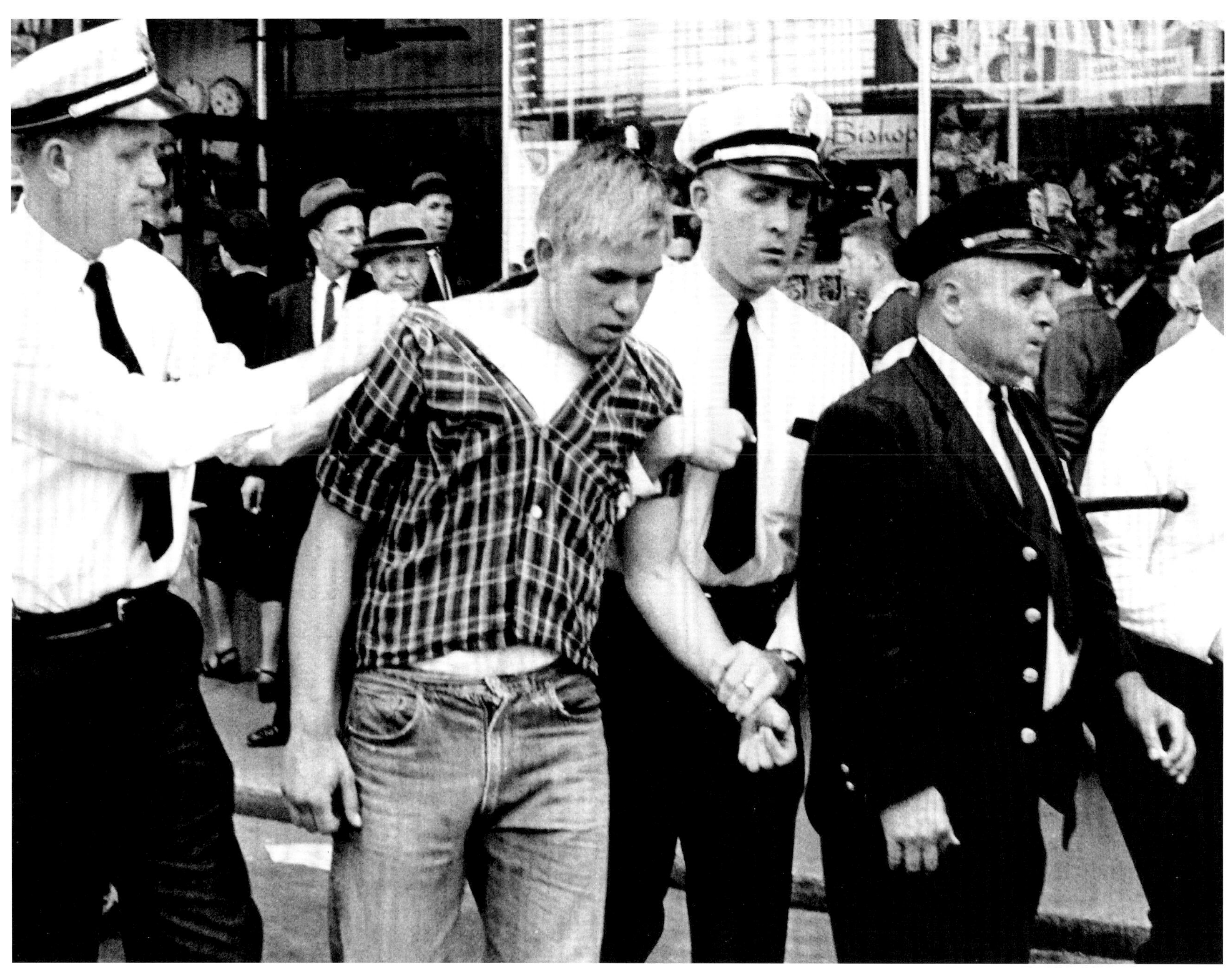

PLATE 30

Gerald Holly, *The Tennessean*

APRIL 12, 1960

Robert Glennon, seventeen (second from left), is led to a police car moments after Nashville police arrested him for attacking Marion Barry, a Fisk University sit-in demonstrator. Traffic Officer Fred Cobb (left) holds onto Glennon after catching him with a flying tackle, getting a hand from Traffic Officer Earl Cullum (second from right) and Patrolman M. Q. Dickens. Courtesy of *The Tennessean*

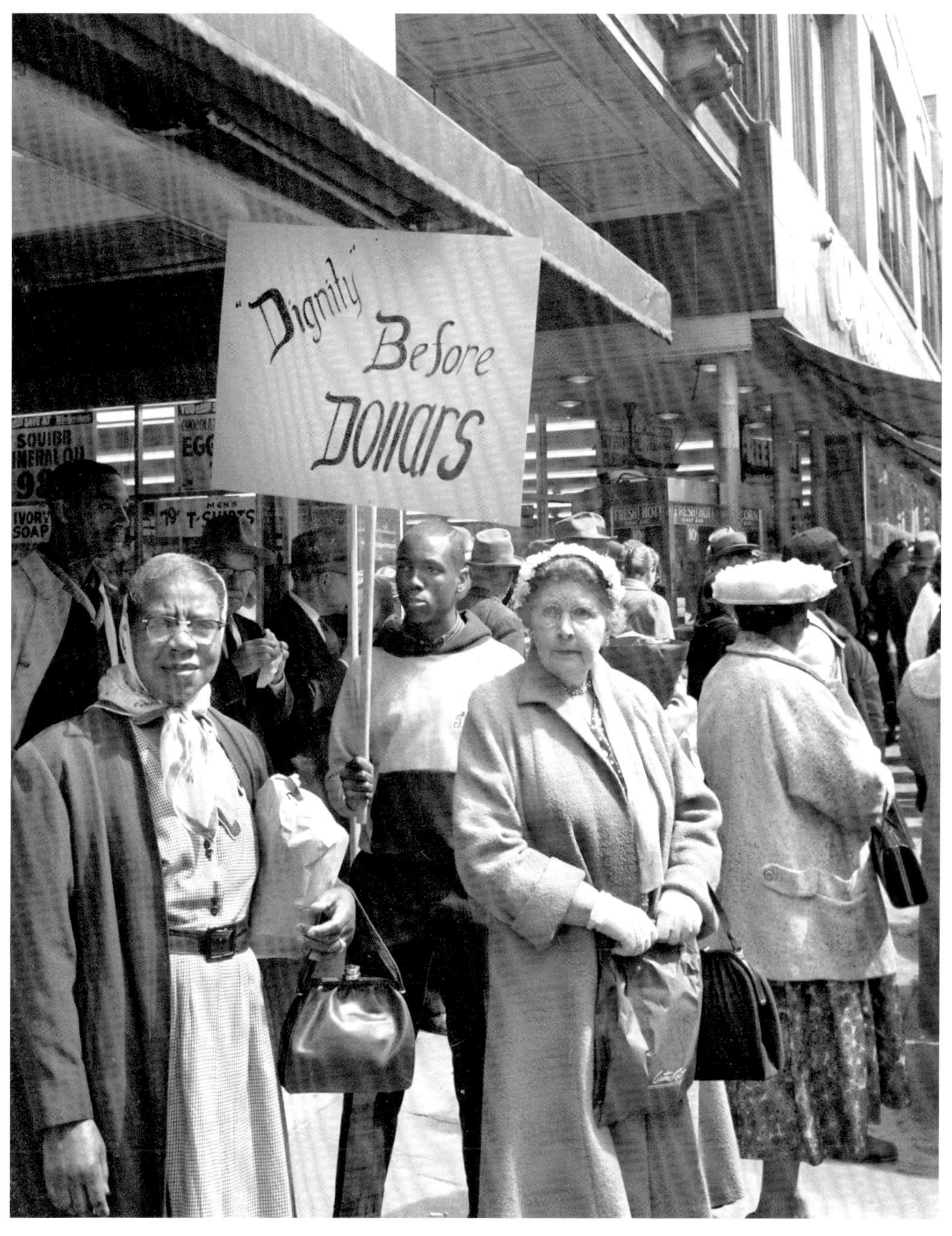

PLATE 31

Vic Cooley, *Nashville Banner*

APRIL 11, 1960

Shoppers stand at the entrance of the Nashville Arcade business center as a demonstrator holds a sign in support of the economic boycott of downtown stores. The boycott, which coincided with the pre-Easter shopping season, lasted seven weeks.

Courtesy of the Nashville Public Library, Special Collections

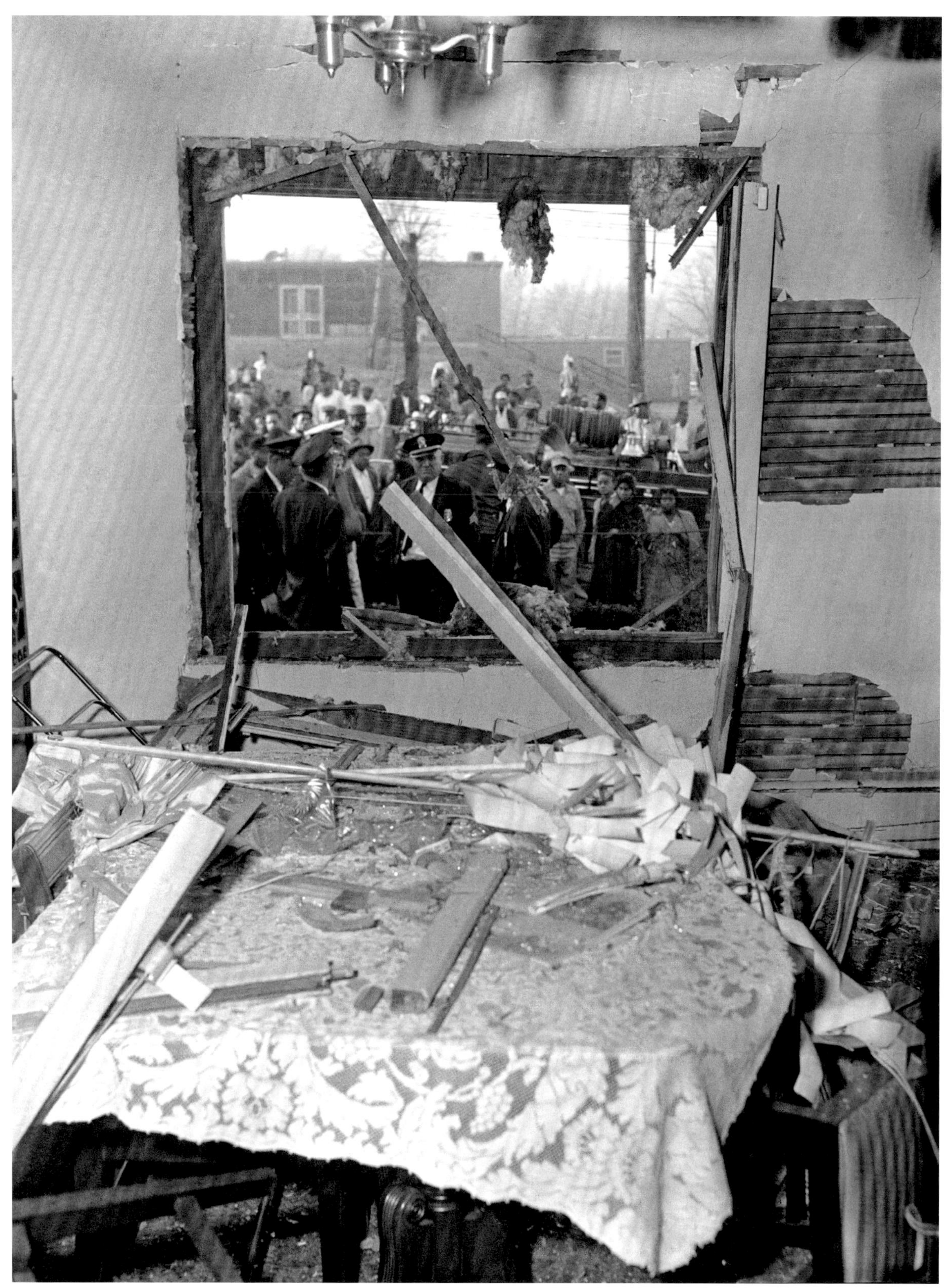

PLATE 32

Bob Ray, *Nashville Banner*

APRIL 19, 1960

Officials and neighbors observe the damage to the house of Z. Alexander Looby, a civil rights attorney and Nashville City Council member. Looby and his wife, Grafta (Mosby) Looby survived the early dawn bombing, though it destroyed their home.

Courtesy of the Nashville Public Library, Special Collections

A similar image was printed in the paper on April 19, 1960

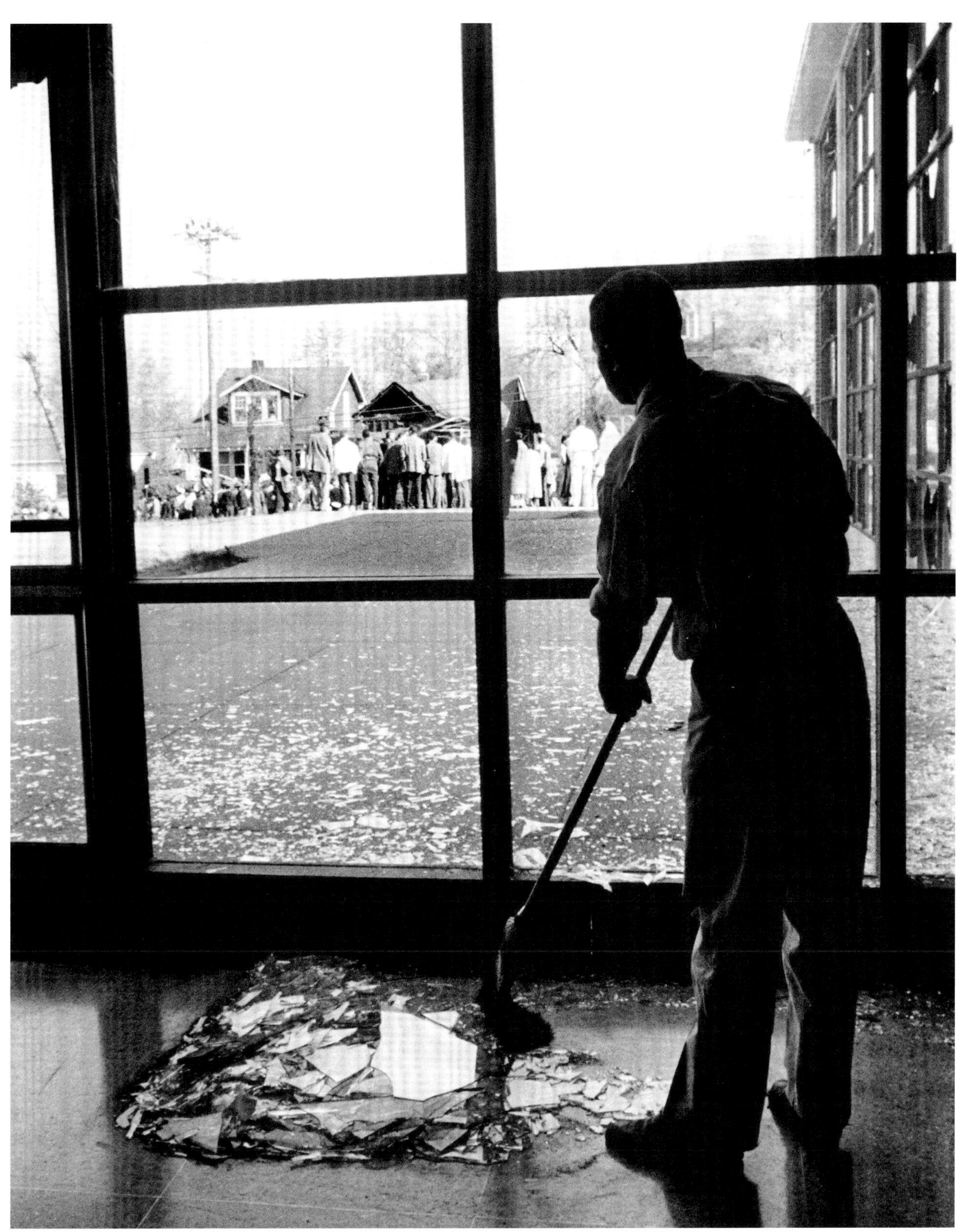

PLATE 33

Joe Rudis, *The Tennessean*

APRIL 19, 1960

Silhouetted against disaster, John Thomas Martin wields his broom, sweeping up the fragments of glass from shattered windows in the Meharry Medical College alumni building. The bombing of the Looby home across the street shattered 147 windows at the college.

Courtesy of *The Tennessean*

Printed in the paper on April 20, 1960

PLATE 34

Eldred Reaney, *The Tennessean*

APRIL 19, 1960

As many as four thousand people marched from the campus of Tennessee A&I to the office of Mayor Ben West in the courthouse building to protest the bombing of Grafta and Z. Alexander Looby's home. Here, a line of demonstrators snakes down James Robertson Boulevard.

Courtesy of *The Tennessean*

Printed in the paper on April 20, 1960

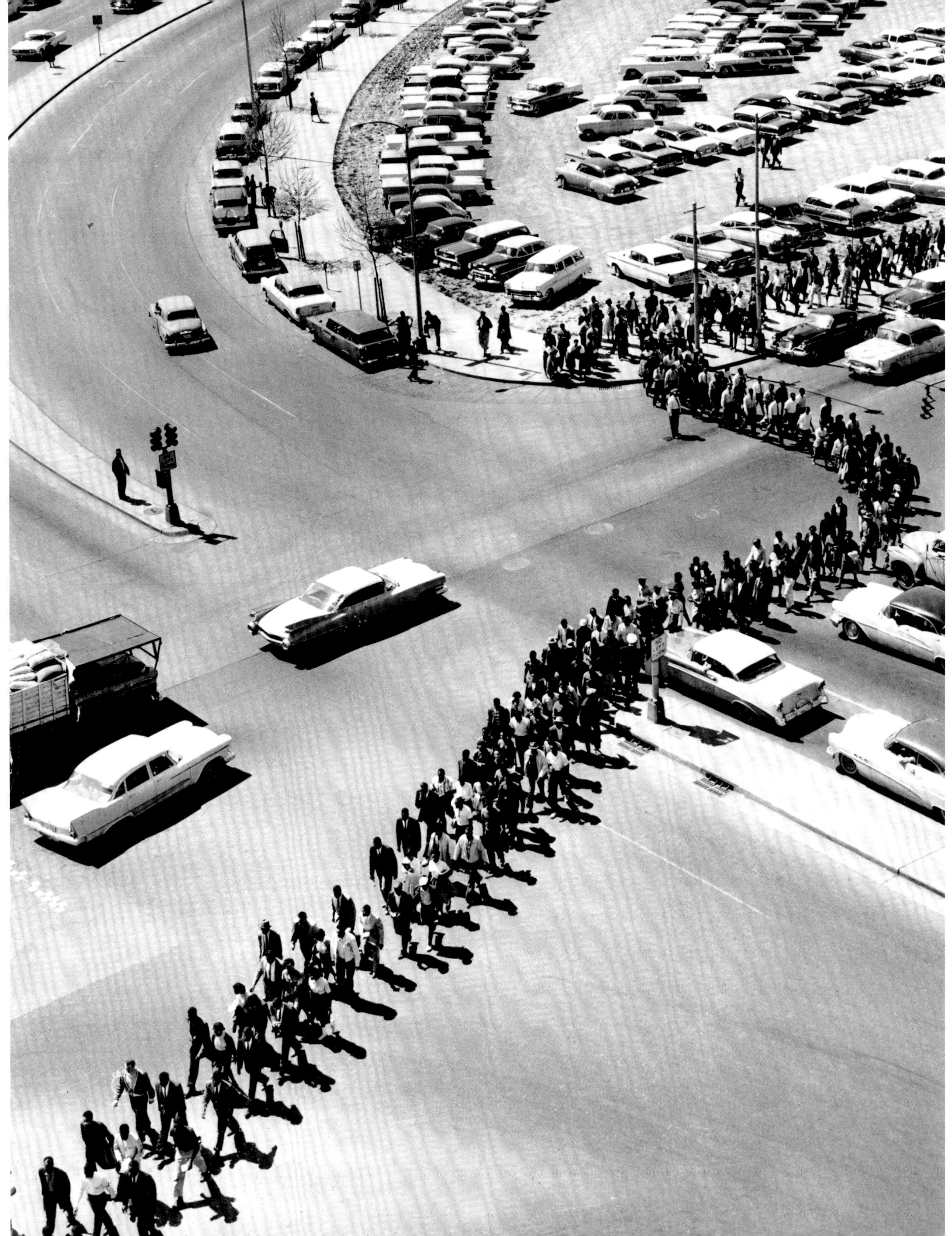

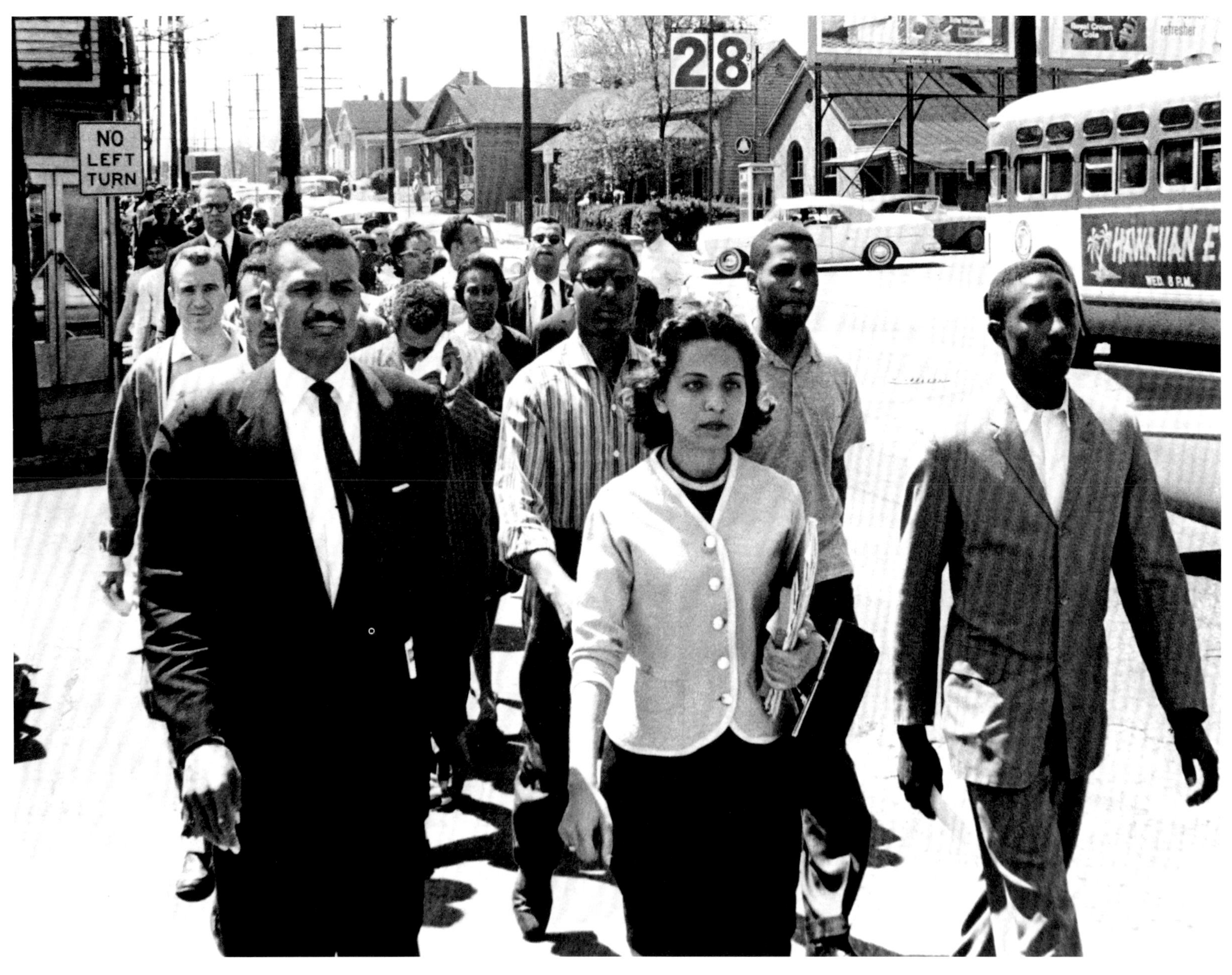

PLATE 35

Jack Corn, *The Tennessean*

APRIL 19, 1960

Demonstrators march down Jefferson Street on the day of the Looby bombing. In the first row are Rev. C. T. Vivian (left), Diane Nash of Fisk, and Bernard Lafayette of American Baptist Seminary. In the second row are Kenneth Frazier and Curtis Murphy of Tennessee A&I and Rodney Powell of Meharry. Using his handkerchief in the third row is Rev. James Lawson.

Courtesy of *The Tennessean*

Printed in the paper on April 20, 1960

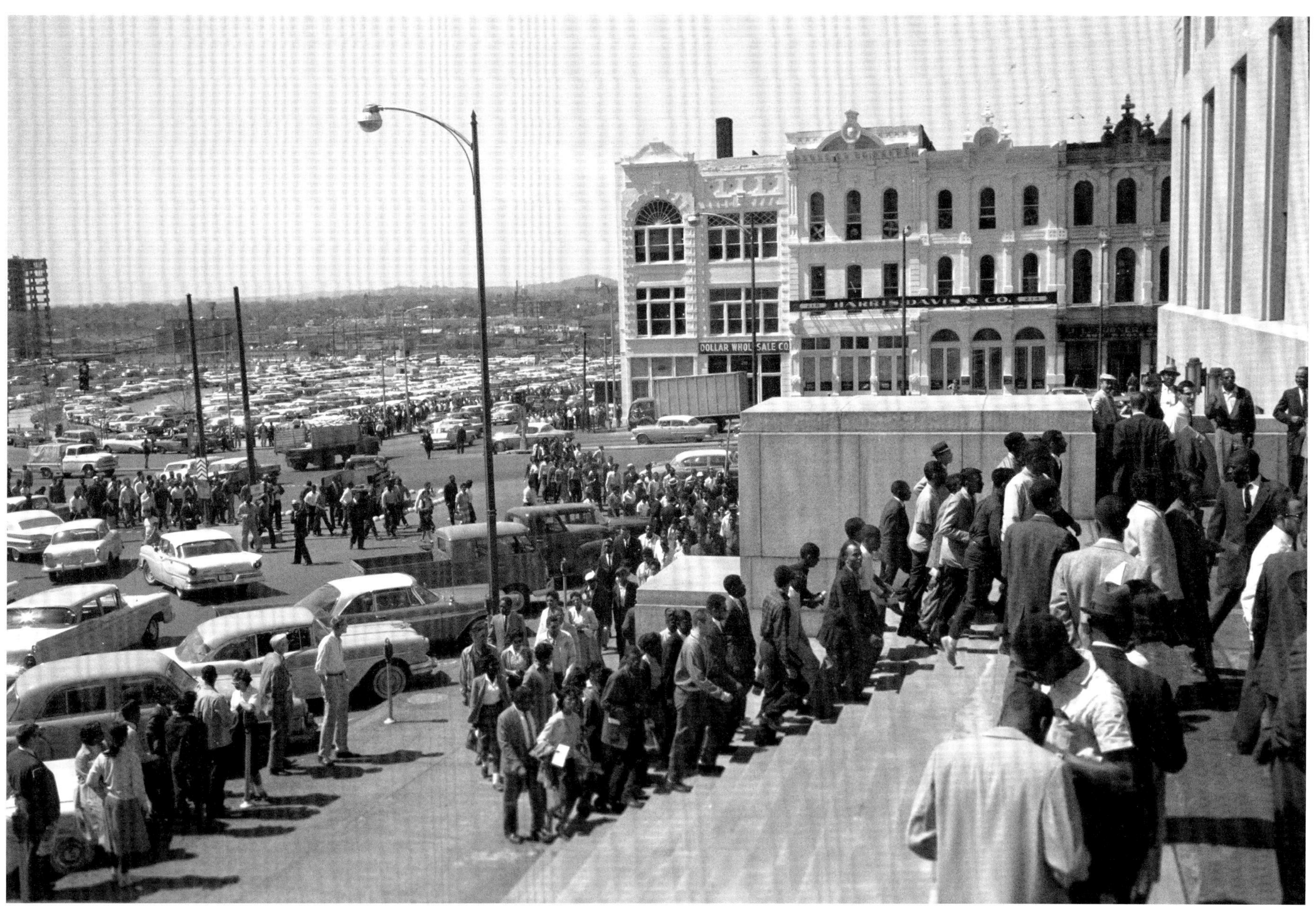

PLATE 36

Vic Cooley, *Nashville Banner*

APRIL 19, 1960

The protesters marched three abreast in a line stretching across ten blocks until they reached the courthouse steps.
Courtesy of the Nashville Public Library, Special Collections

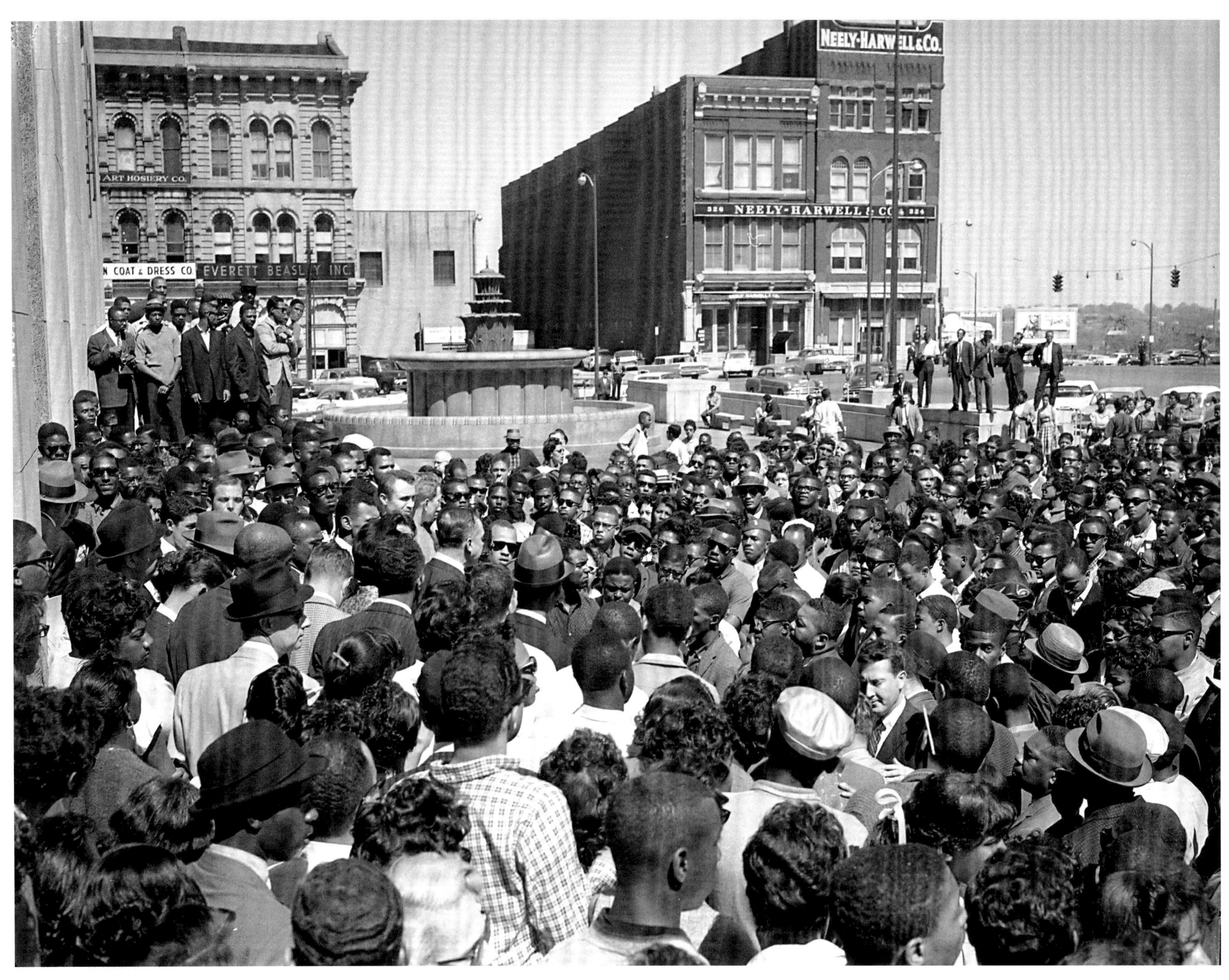

PLATE 37

Don Foster, *Nashville Banner*

APRIL 19, 1960

Silent marchers gather near the fountain in the courthouse plaza and wait to hear what Mayor West will say.
Courtesy of the Nashville Public Library, Special Collections

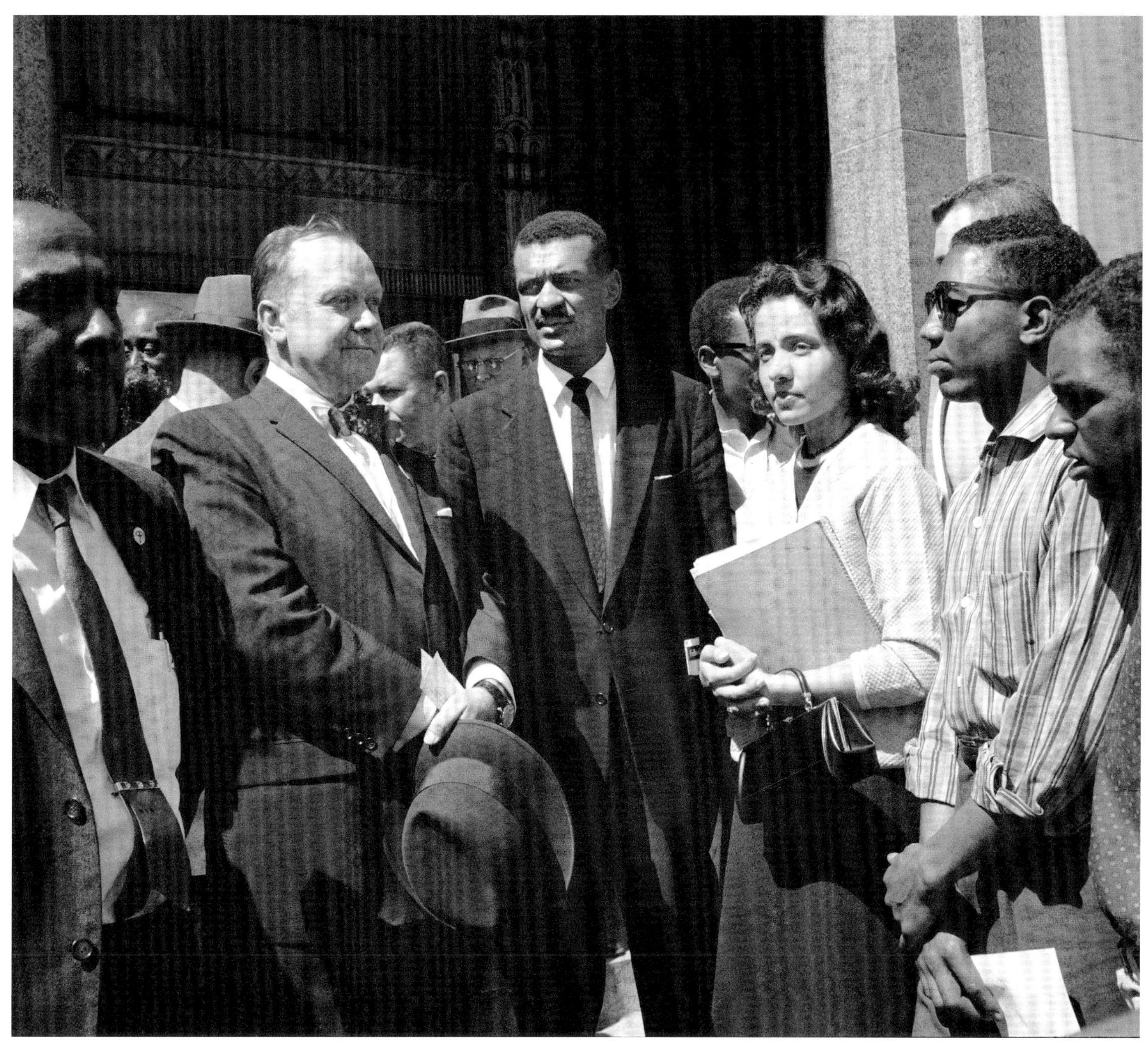

PLATE 38

Vic Cooley, *Nashville Banner*

APRIL 19, 1960

Mayor West meets with Rev. C. T. Vivian and Diane Nash. During the confrontation, Nash asked the mayor, “Do you feel it is wrong to discriminate against a person solely on the basis of their race or color?” Mayor West replied, “Yes.”

Courtesy of the Nashville Public Library, Special Collections

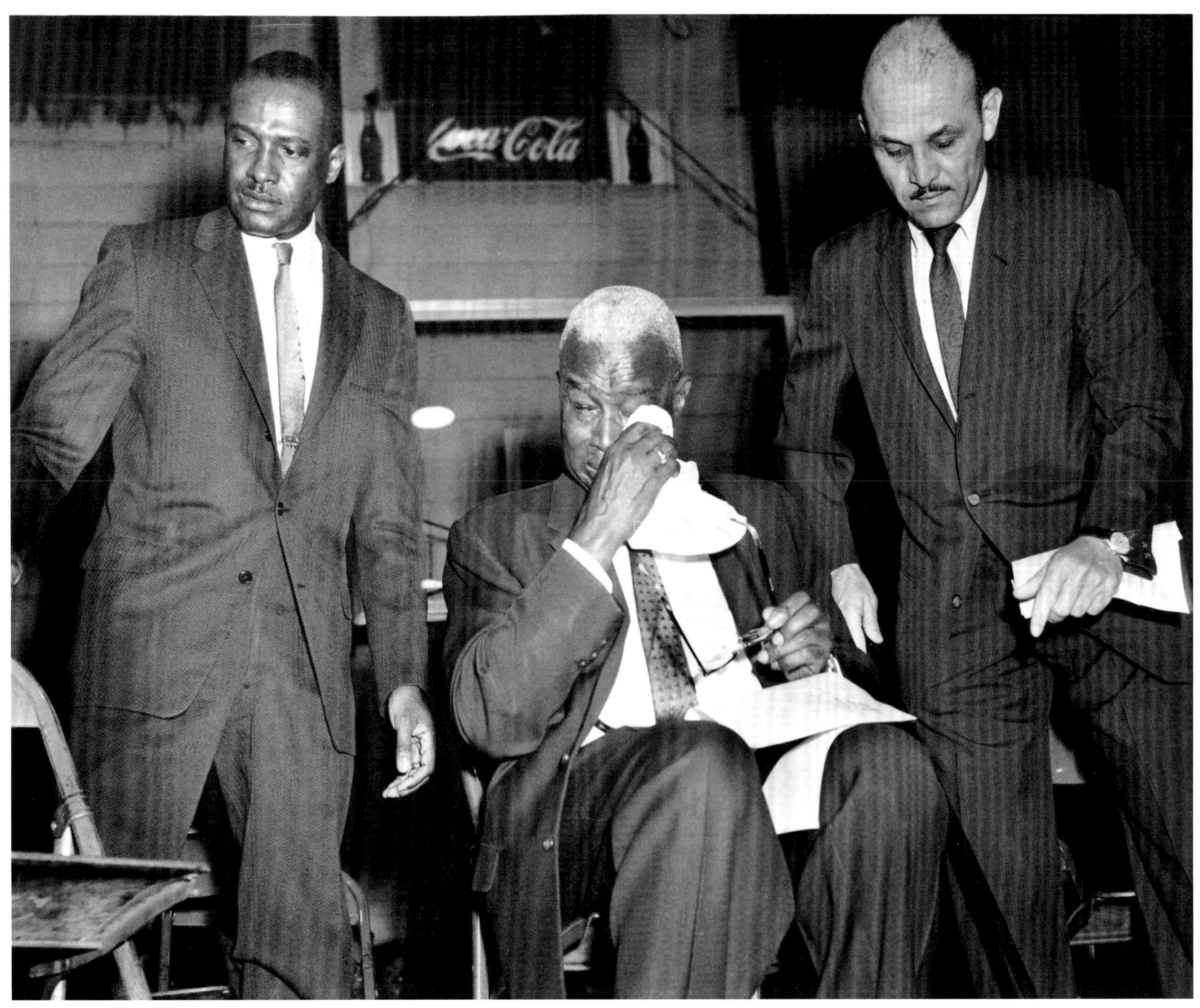

PLATE 39

Jack Gunter, *Nashville Banner*

APRIL 20, 1960

The day after the bombing of his home, Attorney Z. Alexander Looby became emotional after an audience of four thousand people at Fisk University paid tribute to his tireless work for justice in Nashville.

Courtesy of Nashville Public Library, Special Collections

Very similar images were printed in both papers on April 21

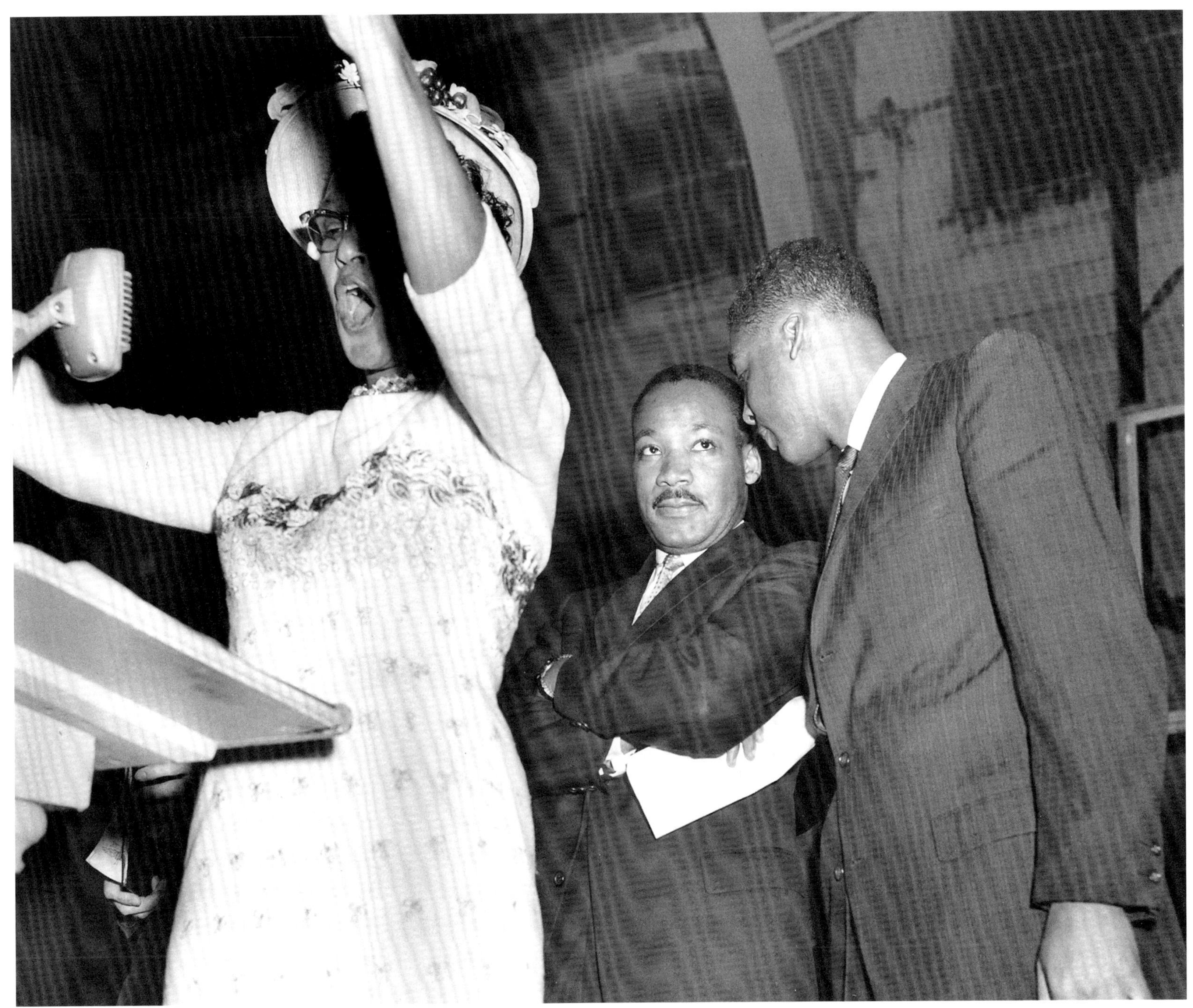

PLATE 40
Jack Gunter, *Nashville Banner*
APRIL 20, 1960
Rev. Kelly Miller Smith speaks to Dr. Martin Luther King Jr. as King waits to address the audience. In appreciation of the recent nonviolent demonstrations, King said, "I came to Nashville not to bring inspiration, but to gain inspiration from the great movement that has taken place in this community."
Courtesy of the Nashville Public Library, Special Collections

PLATE 41

Jack Gunter, *Nashville Banner*

APRIL 20, 1960

Guy Carawan (center), credited with helping make "We Shall Overcome" an anthem of the civil rights movement, performs during the gathering at Fisk University. John Lewis (right) is one of the student leaders on the stage.

Courtesy of the Nashville Public Library, Special Collections

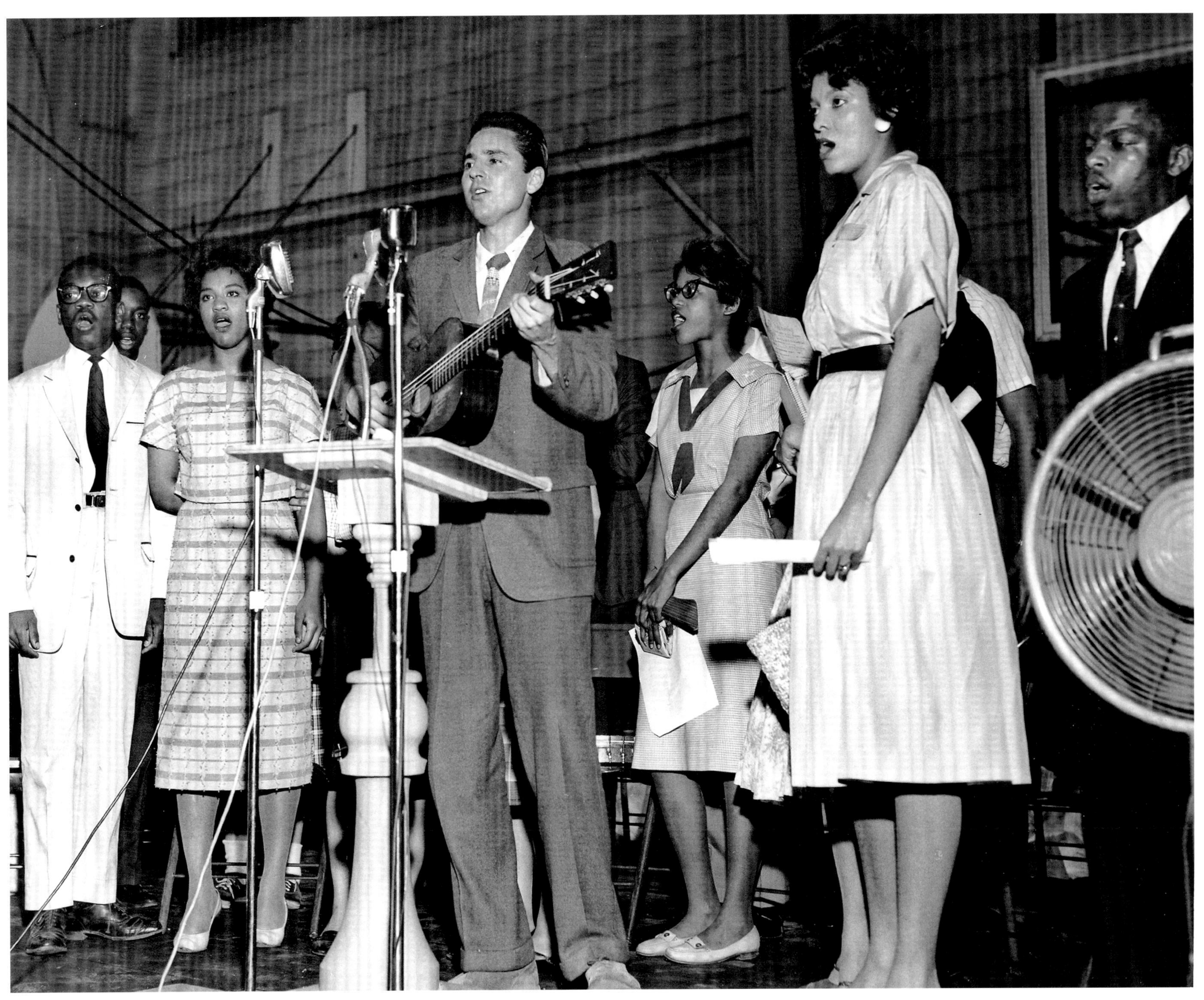

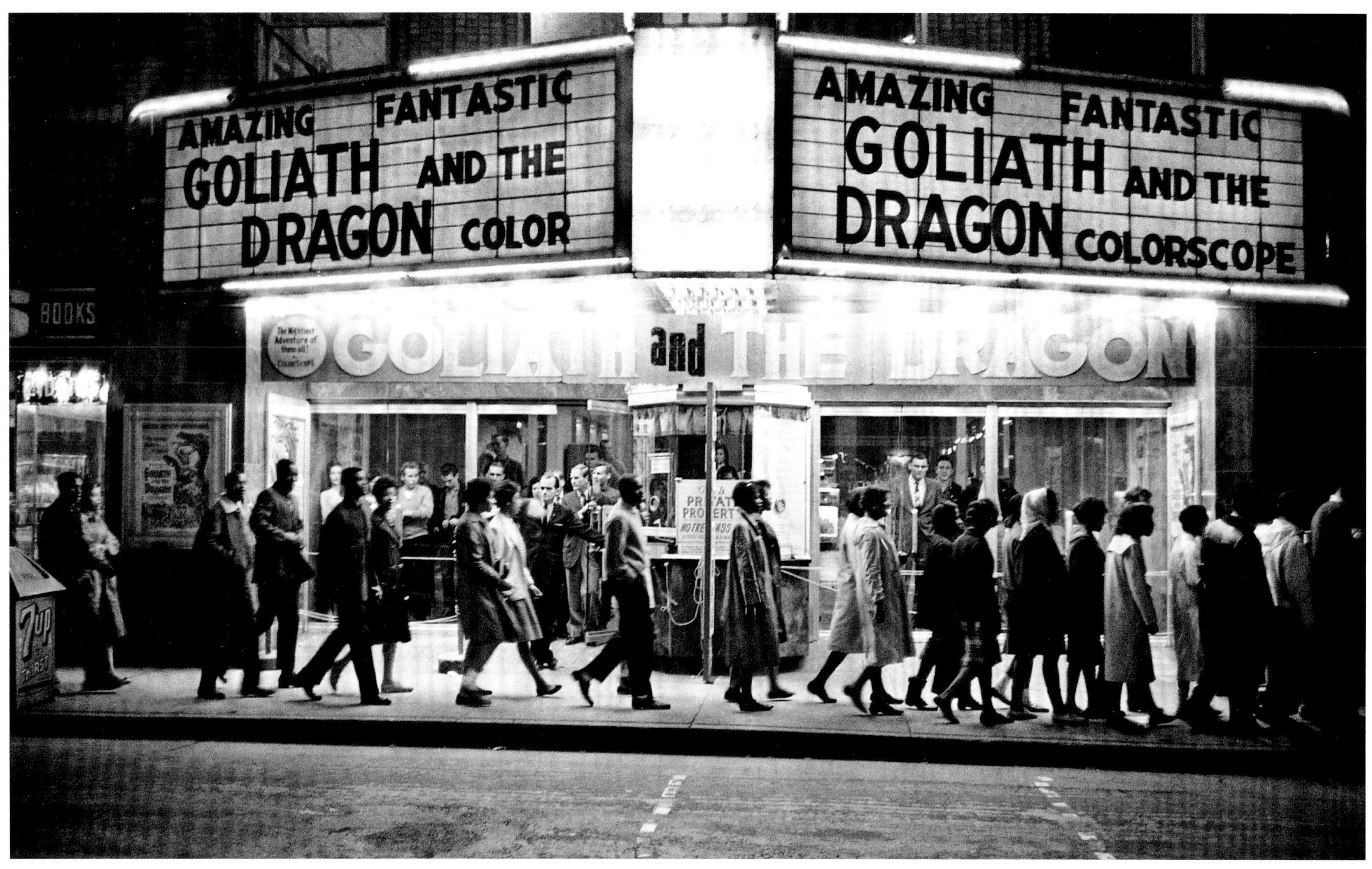

PLATE 42

Gerald Holly, *The Tennessean*

FEBRUARY 24, 1961

Rocks and eggs were thrown at some 123 anti-segregation demonstrators as they marched through downtown Nashville during a seventy-five-minute stand-in at four Church Street theaters, including the Paramount seen here. A band of about seventy white boys pitched the rocks and eggs, but no one was reported seriously hurt. Courtesy of *The Tennessean*

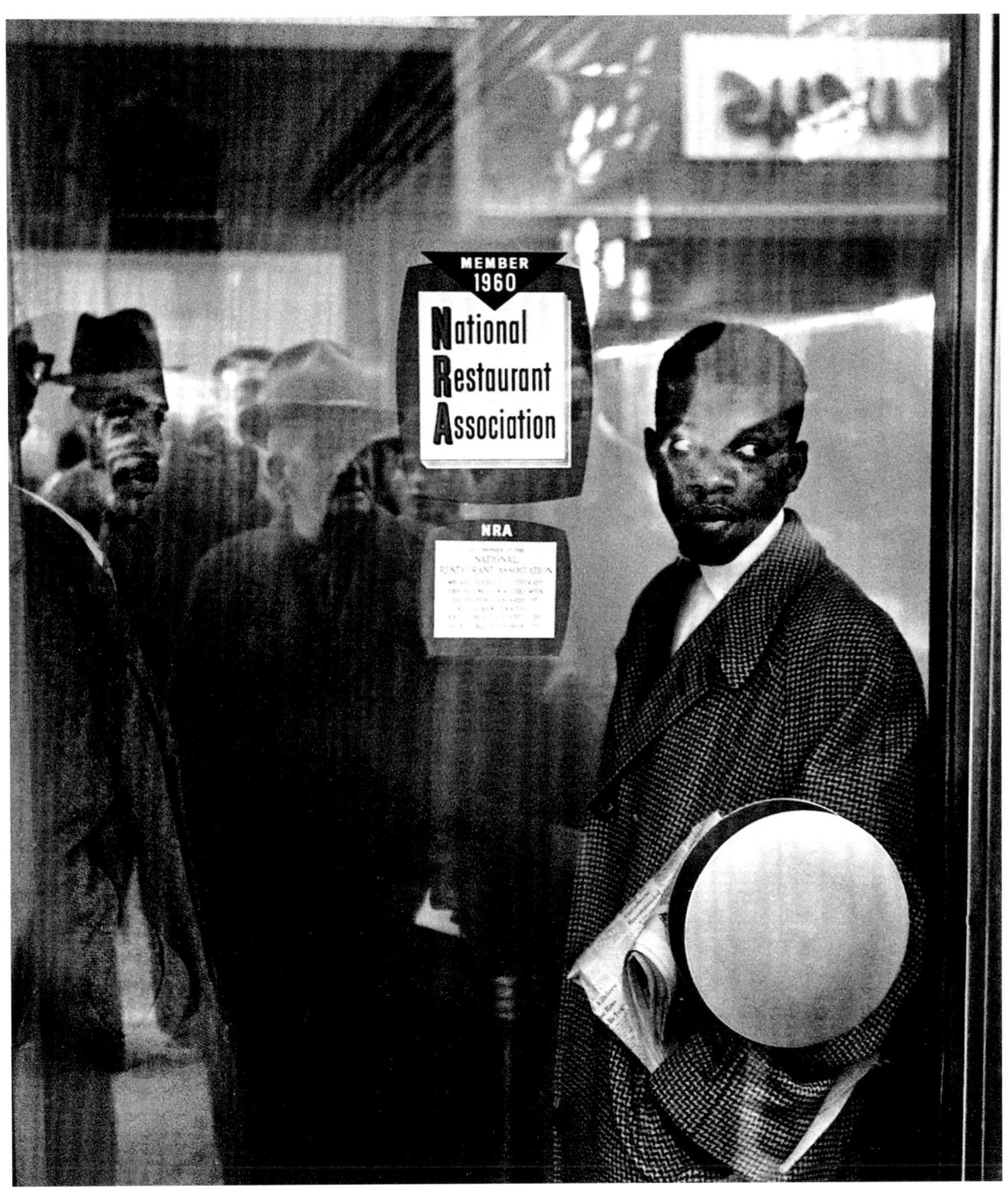

PLATE 43

Jack Corn, *The Tennessean*

NOVEMBER 10, 1960

Student demonstrators James Bevel (left) and John Lewis (right) stand inside the Krystal restaurant at 204 Fifth Avenue North after the manager turned on a fumigating machine to disrupt their sit-in. The pair remained inside the restaurant for half an hour while a dense cloud of nontoxic insect spray filled it.

Courtesy of *The Tennessean*

A very similar image was printed in the paper on November 11, 1960

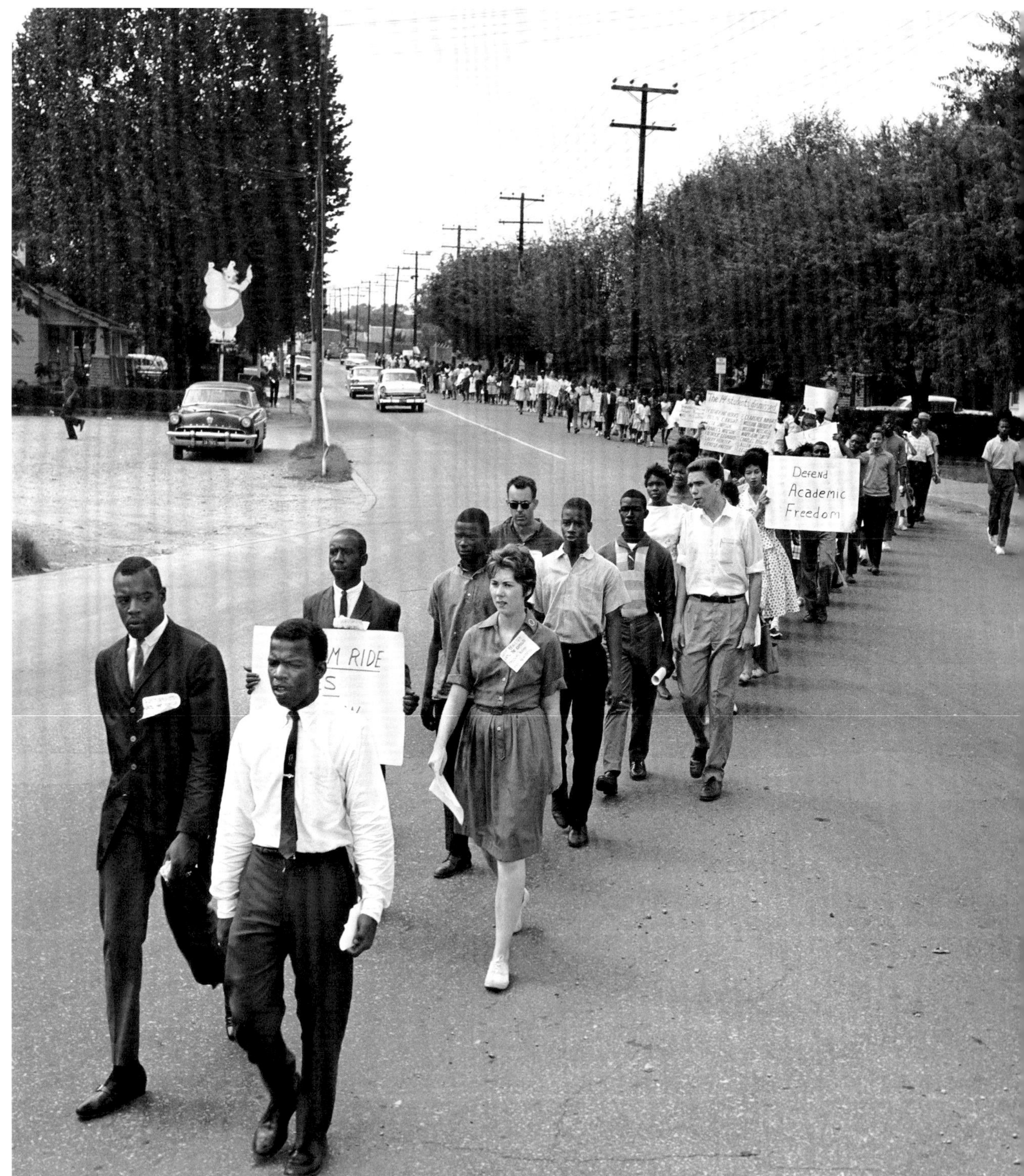

PLATE 44

Paul Schleicher, *Nashville Banner*

SEPTEMBER 14, 1961

Led by John Lewis (front), approximately two hundred students sing hymns and march from Tennessee A&I toward the capitol to protest the dismissal of fourteen Freedom Riders from the university. Members of the Nashville student movement played significant roles in the continuation of the interstate bus trip through the Alabama and Mississippi in May of 1961.

Courtesy of the Nashville Public Library, Special Collections

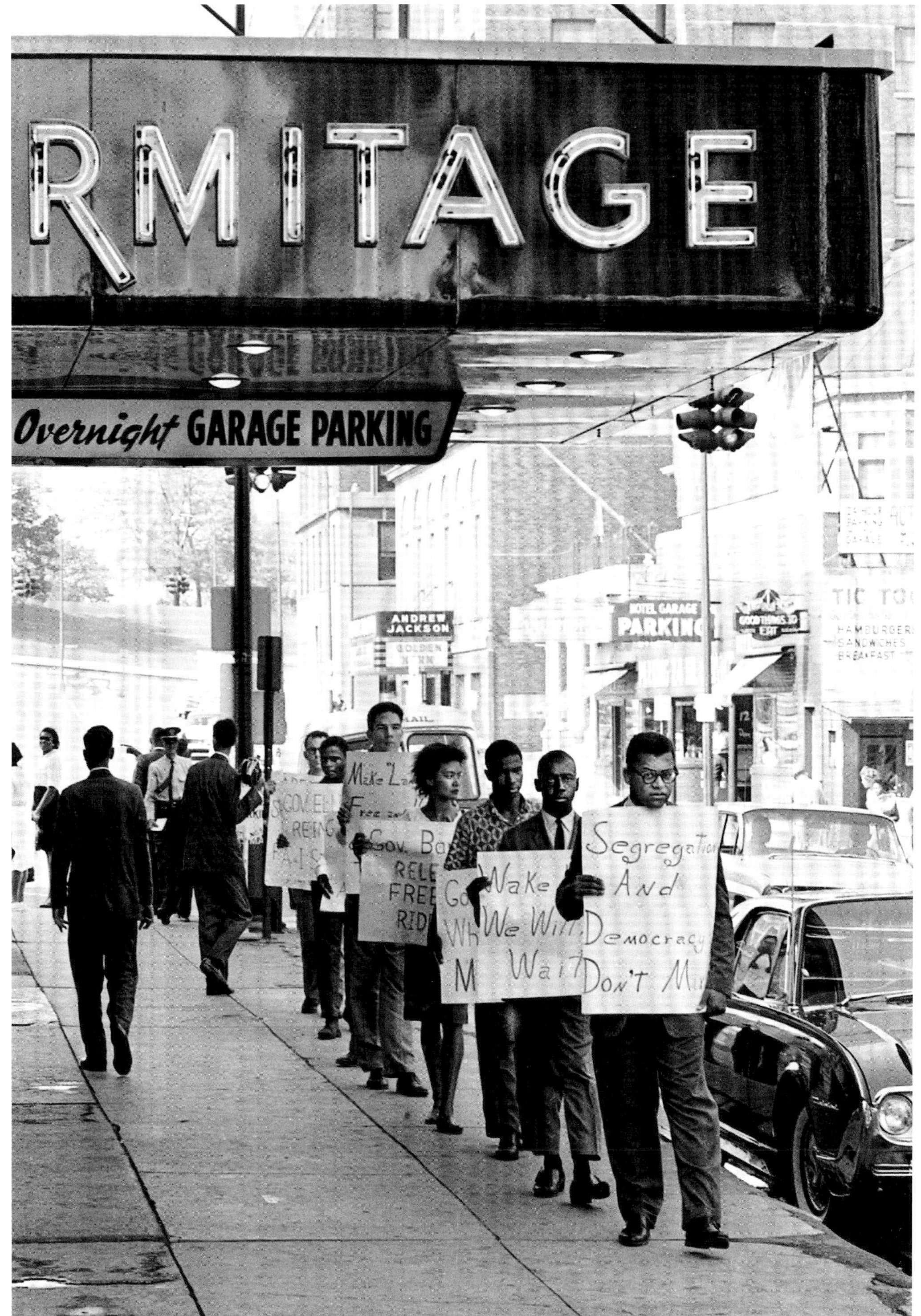

PLATE 45

Harold Lowe Jr., *The Tennessean*

SEPTEMBER 25, 1961

A small group of protesters picket in front of the Hermitage Hotel in downtown Nashville, where Tennessee Governor Buford Ellington is attending a conference. The group, including James Lawson (front), is seeking reinstatement of the fourteen Freedom Riders dismissed from Tennessee A&I in June. Courtesy of *The Tennessean*

PLATE 46

Eldred Reaney, *The Tennessean*

AUGUST 7, 1961

Demonstrators sing in front of the Nashville Police Department as they protest what they call police brutality in a racial clash two nights earlier. They criticized "inadequate" police protection and called for qualified black personnel to "replace incompetent officers on the police force."

Courtesy of *The Tennessean*

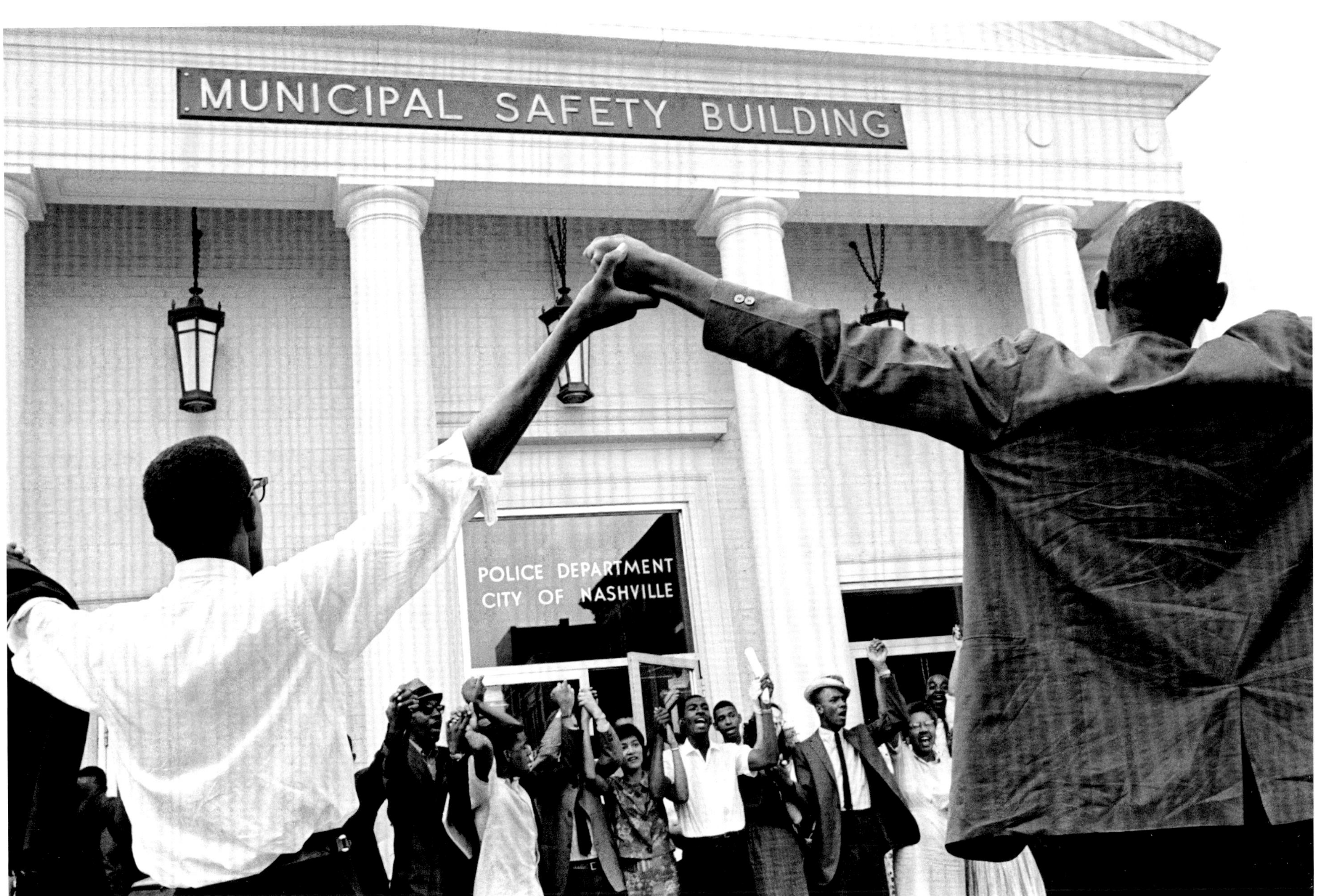
MUNICIPAL SAFETY BUILDING
POLICE DEPARTMENT
CITY OF NASHVILLE

PLATE 47

Bill Preston, *The Tennessean*

FEBRUARY 24, 1963

A group of about sixty black and white demonstrators, including Rev. Kelly Miller Smith (third man from the left), leaves the First Baptist Church, Capitol Hill, at Eighth Avenue North. They marched two and a half blocks to protest the segregation policy of the YMCA building.

Courtesy of *The Tennessean*

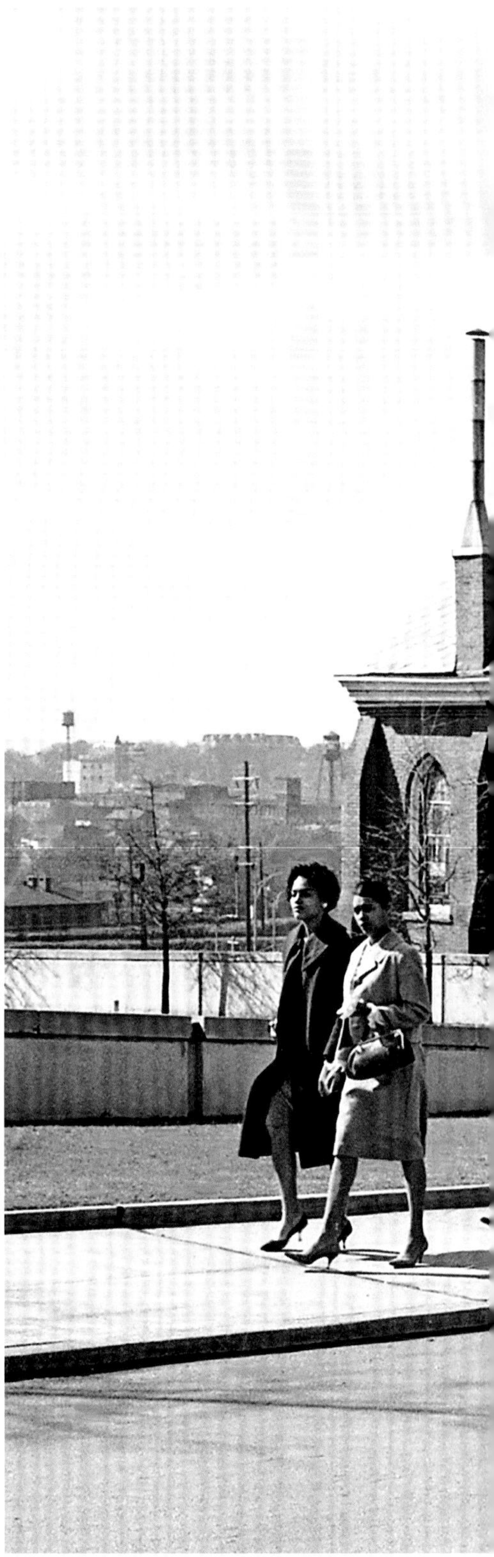

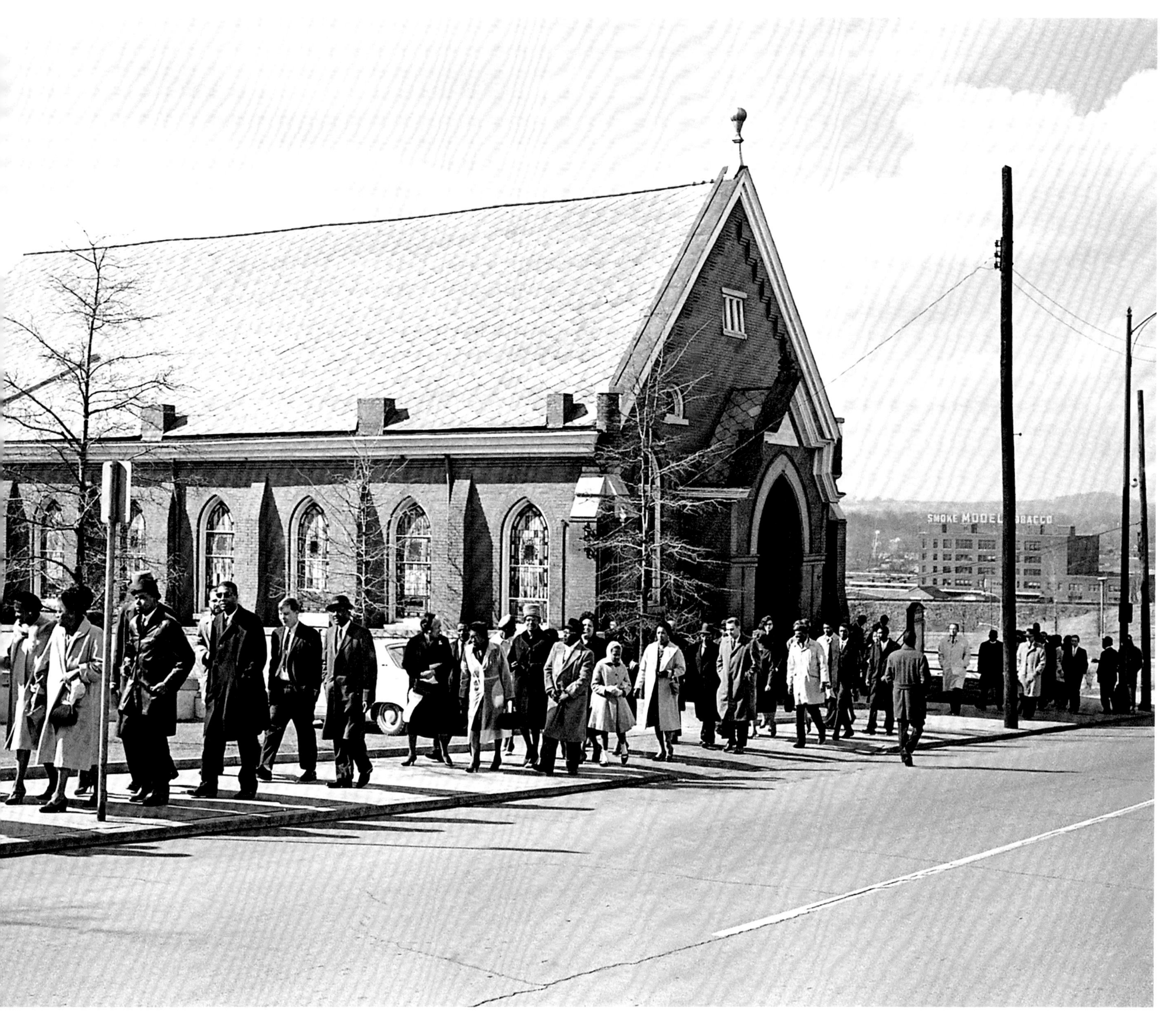
SMOKE MODEL

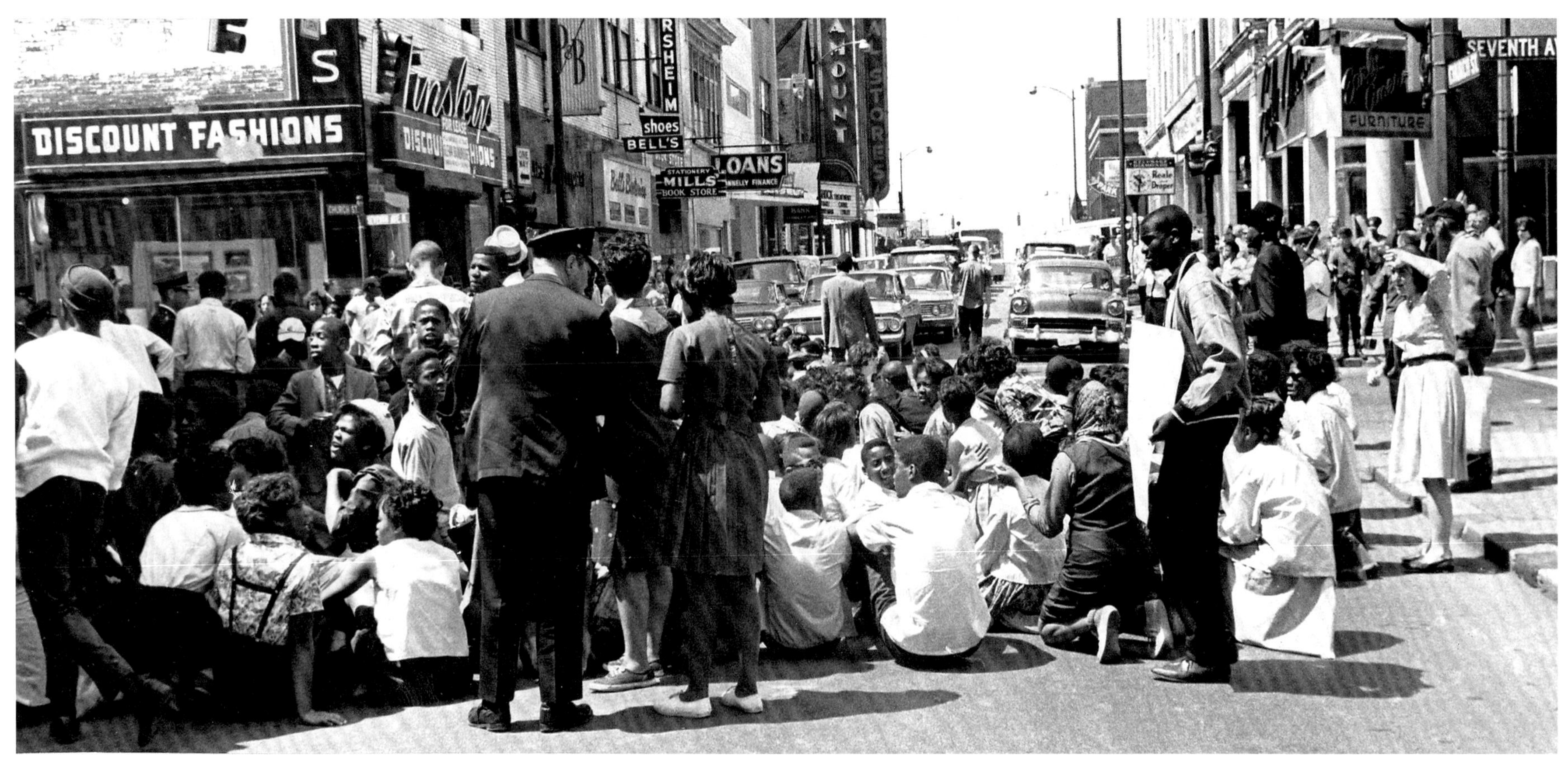

PLATE 48

Vic Cooley, *Nashville Banner*

APRIL 28, 1964

Students seal off downtown Nashville by sitting and lying in the street (a method known as a "lie-in") at the corner of Church Street and Seventh Avenue North in protest of many businesses' continued segregation policies.

Courtesy of the Nashville Public Library, Special Collections

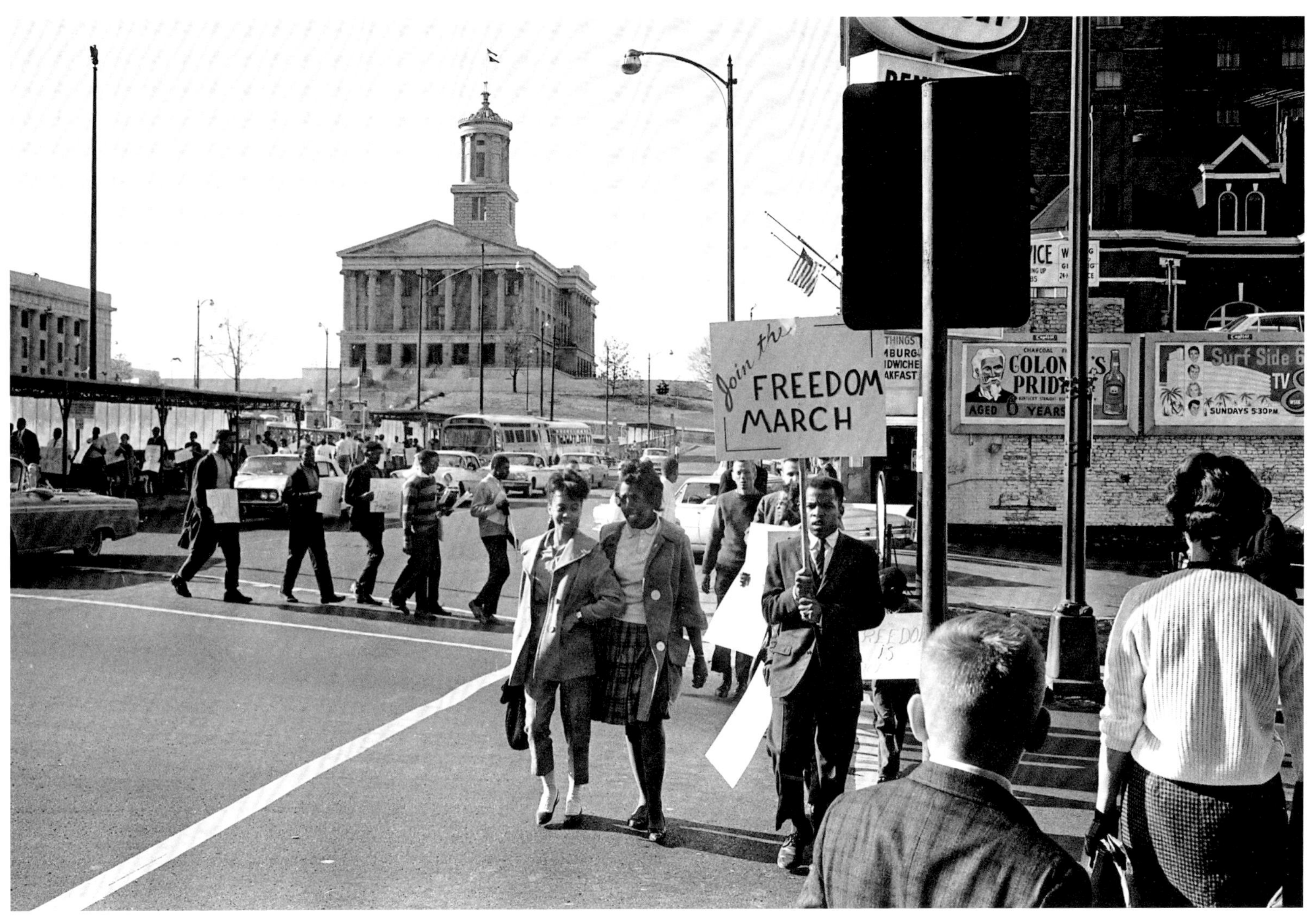

PLATE 49

Frank Empson, *The Tennessean*

MARCH 23, 1963

Demonstrators march in the shadow of the state capital to protest racial discrimination in Nashville with a "Freedom March." The group was led by John Lewis, chairman of the Student Central Committee of the Nashville Christian Leadership Council, sponsors of the movement.

Courtesy of *The Tennessean*

A very similar image was printed in the paper on March 24, 1963

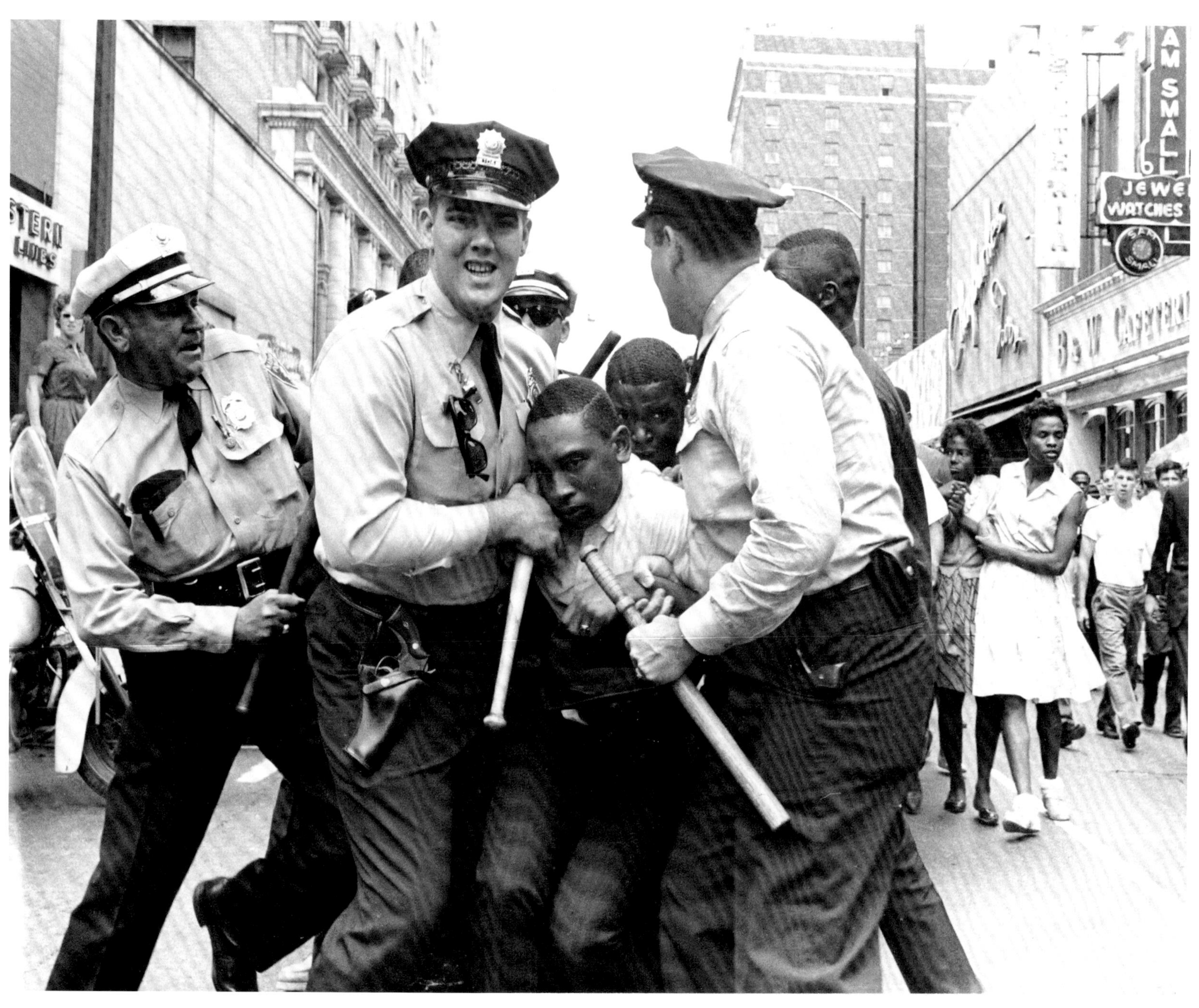

PLATE 50

Jack Gunter, *Nashville Banner*

MAY 10, 1963

Nashville students demonstrate in solidarity with protesters in Birmingham, Alabama, who had been assaulted by police dogs and water hoses days earlier. Local police made multiple arrests.

Courtesy of the Nashville Public Library, Special Collections

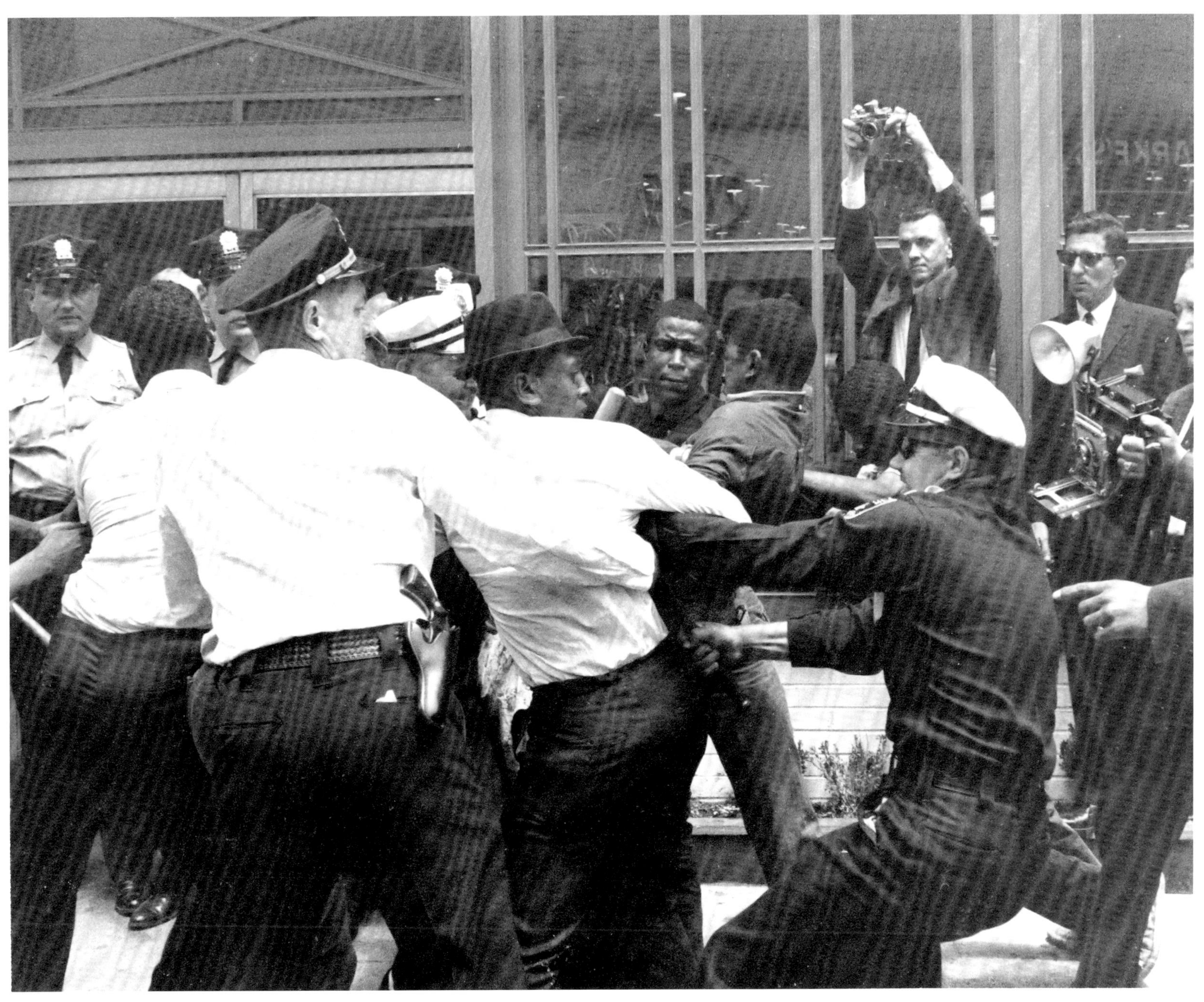

PLATE 51

Bill Goodman, *Nashville Banner*

MAY 10, 1963

Tensions between police and protestors are strong. Bill Goodman captured fellow *Banner* photographer Jack Gunter covering the demonstrations on Sixth Avenue North. A sunglasses-wearing reporter stands nearby.

Courtesy of the Nashville Public Library, Special Collections

PLATE 52

Harold Lowe Jr., *The Tennessean*

MAY 11, 1963

Louis Miller, sixteen, one of two African Americans arrested on charges of throwing a brick that broke a car windshield, being put into the police van at First Baptist Church, Capitol Hill. Miller would be sent to juvenile detention. The photographer at right is Milton McClurkan, who worked for the City.

Courtesy of *The Tennessean*

Printed in the paper on May 12, 1964

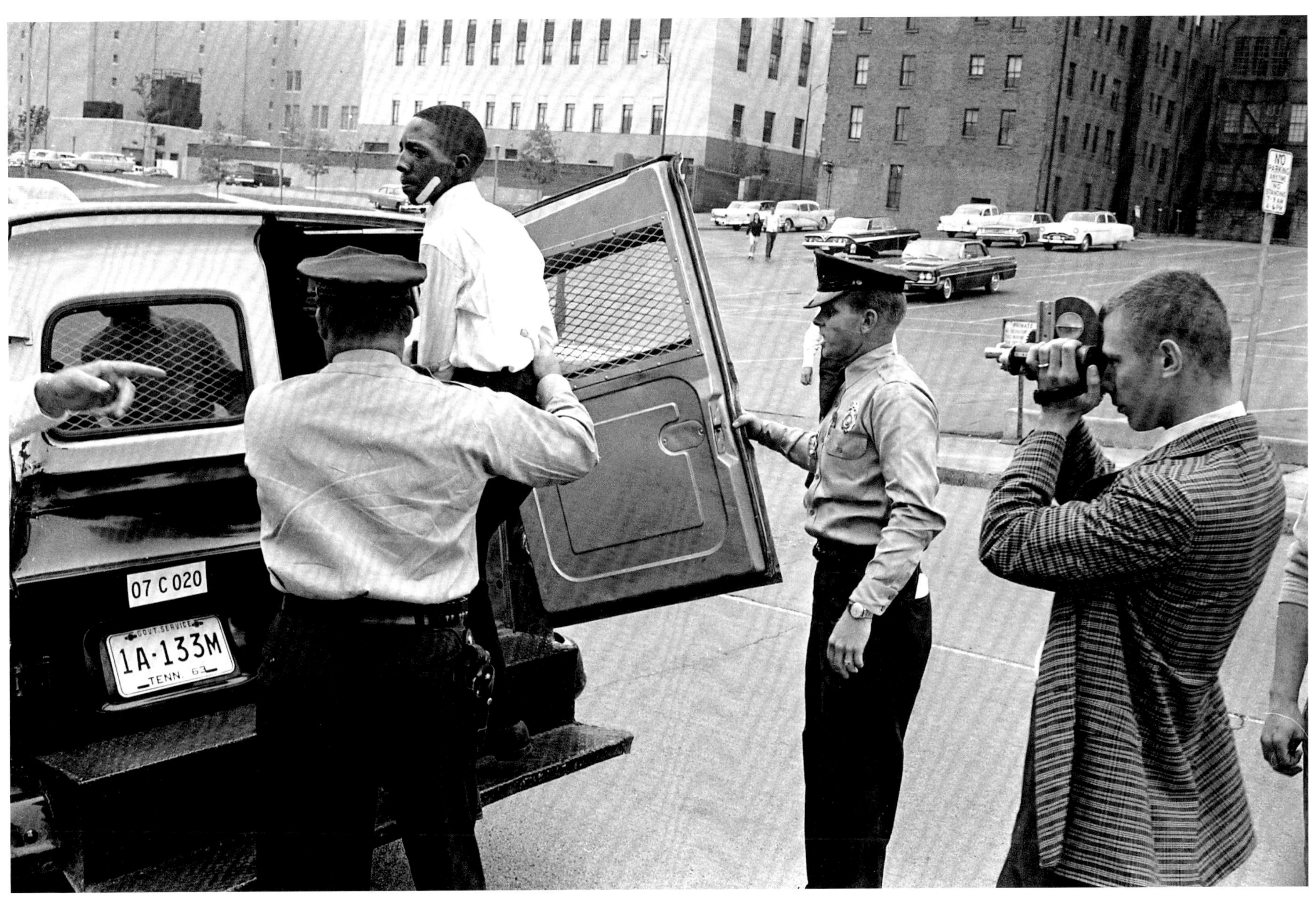
07 C 020
GOVT. SERVICE
1A·133M
TENN. 63

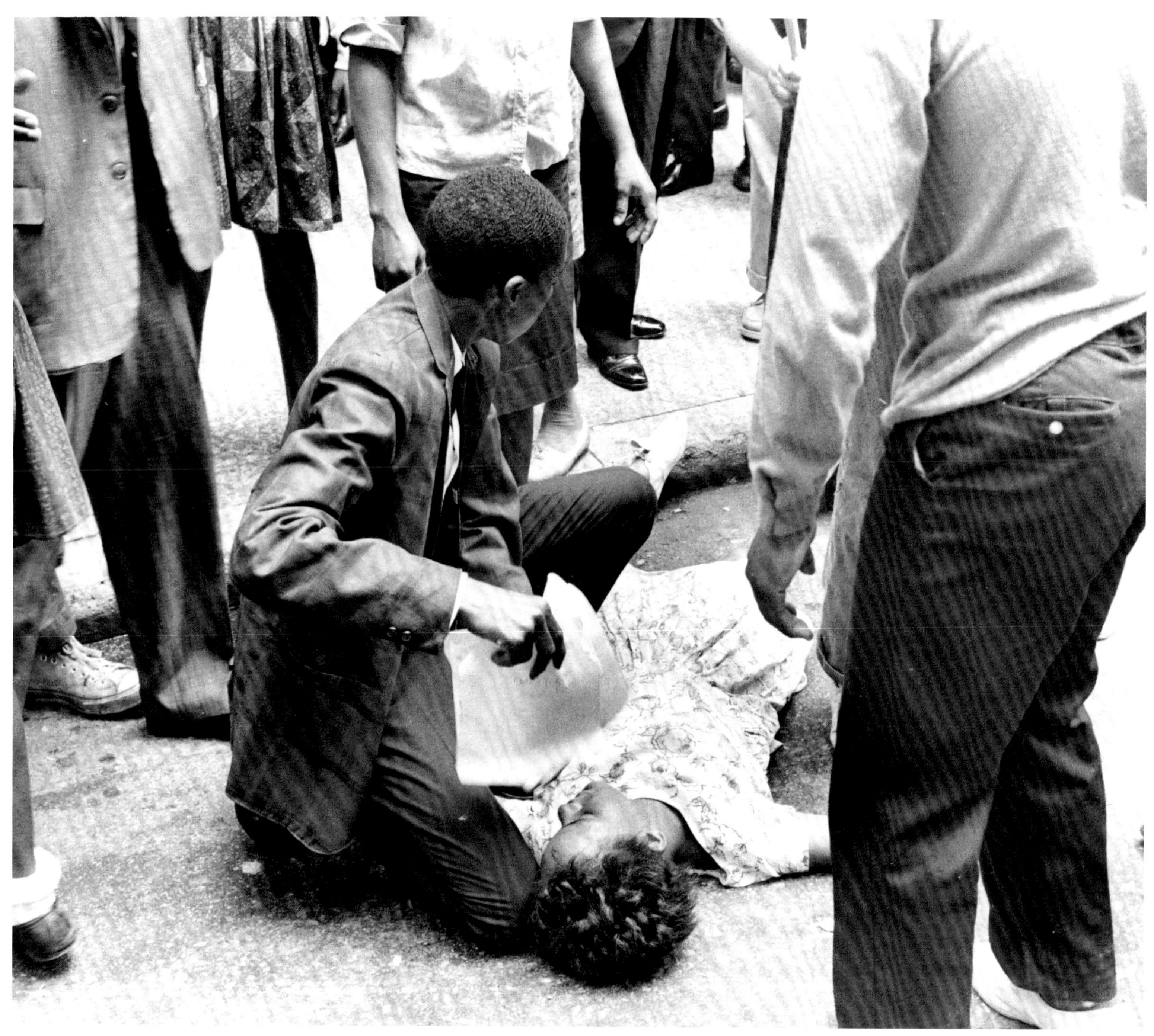

PLATE 53

Jack Gunter, *Nashville Banner*

MAY 10, 1963

Wharton Junior High School freshman Ewingella Bigham, fifteen, lies unconscious in the street shortly after she was injured during a near-riot between white youths and black demonstrators.

Courtesy of the Nashville Public Library, Special Collections

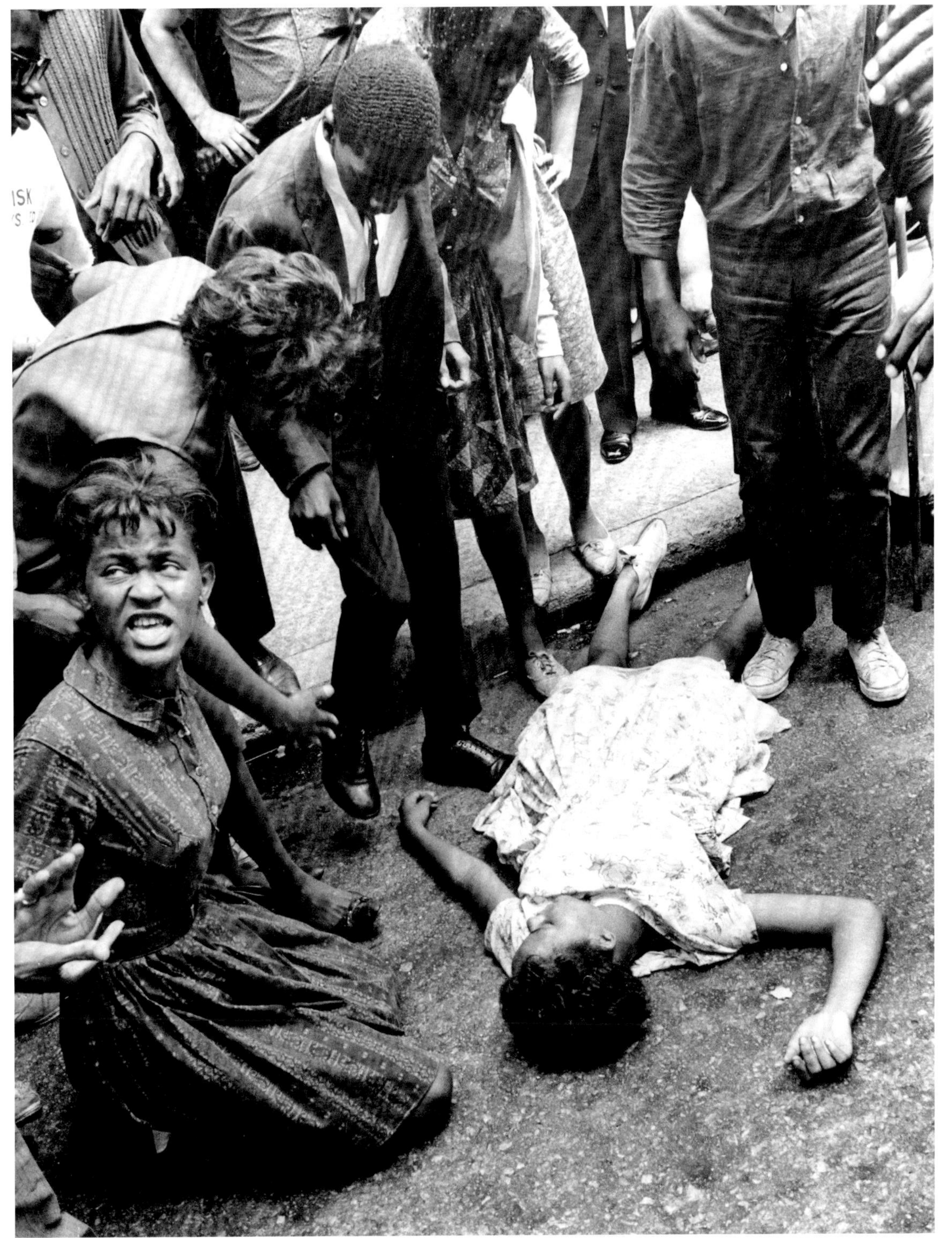

PLATE 54

Harold Lowe Jr., *The Tennessean*

MAY 10, 1963

This photograph of the same scene taken by Jack Gunter includes Bigham's sister, kneeling at left. She said the girl had been struck with a patrolman's billy stick.

Courtesy of *The Tennessean*

Printed in the paper on May 11, 1963

PLATE 55

Jack Gunter, *Nashville Banner*

MAY 10, 1963

Injured young demonstrator Ewingella Bigham is carried off by fellow protester Joe Goldthreate.

Courtesy of the Nashville Public Library, Special Collections

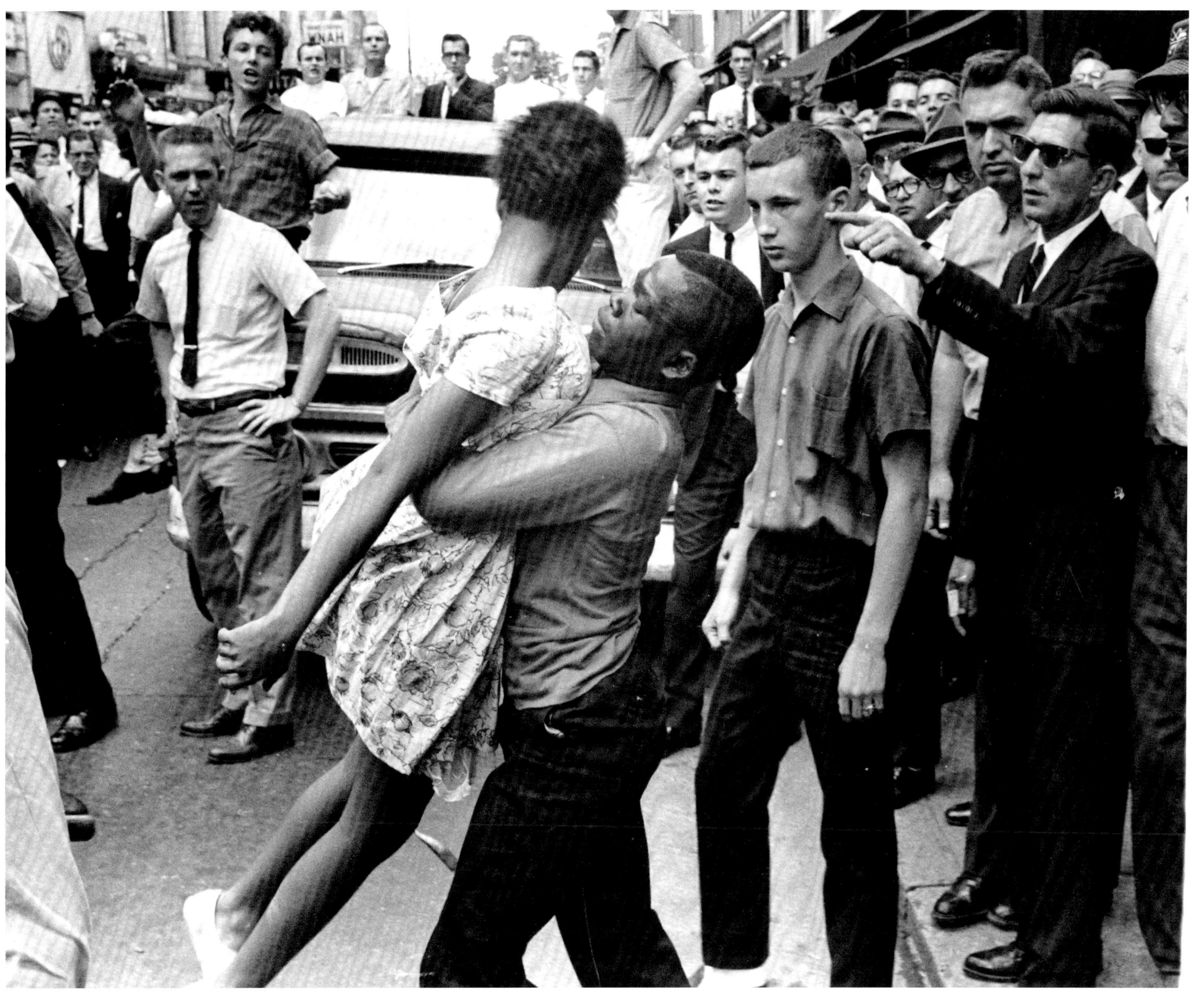
WNAH

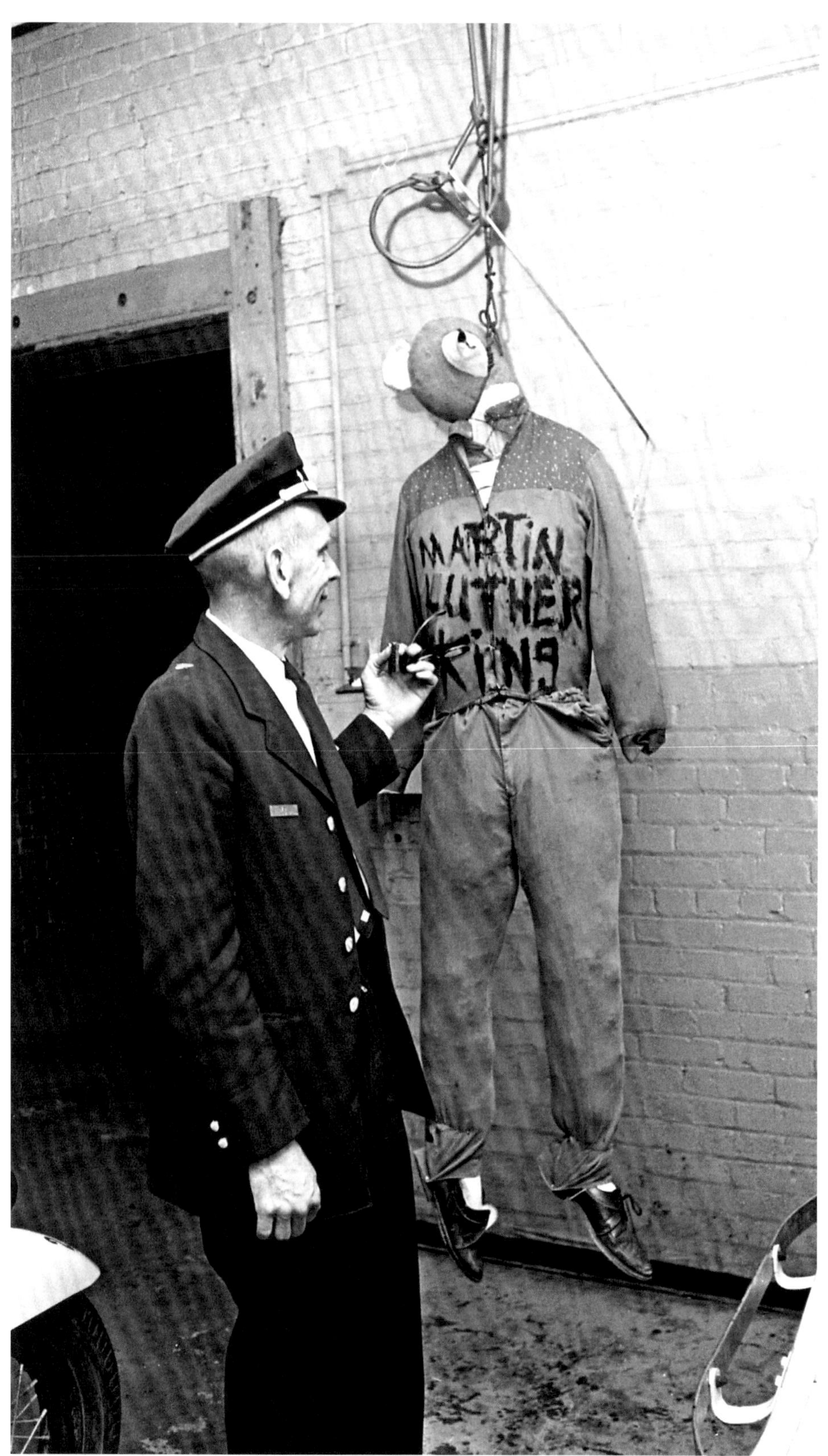

PLATE 56

Harold Lowe Jr., *The Tennessean*

APRIL 13, 1963

An effigy of Dr. Martin Luther King Jr. hangs in the rear of Metro Nashville Police headquarters. The effigy was first found hanging from the railroad overpass on Murfreesboro Road, where two officers cut it down and threw it in the dumpster at headquarters. Someone there found it and put it up again.

Courtesy of *The Tennessean*

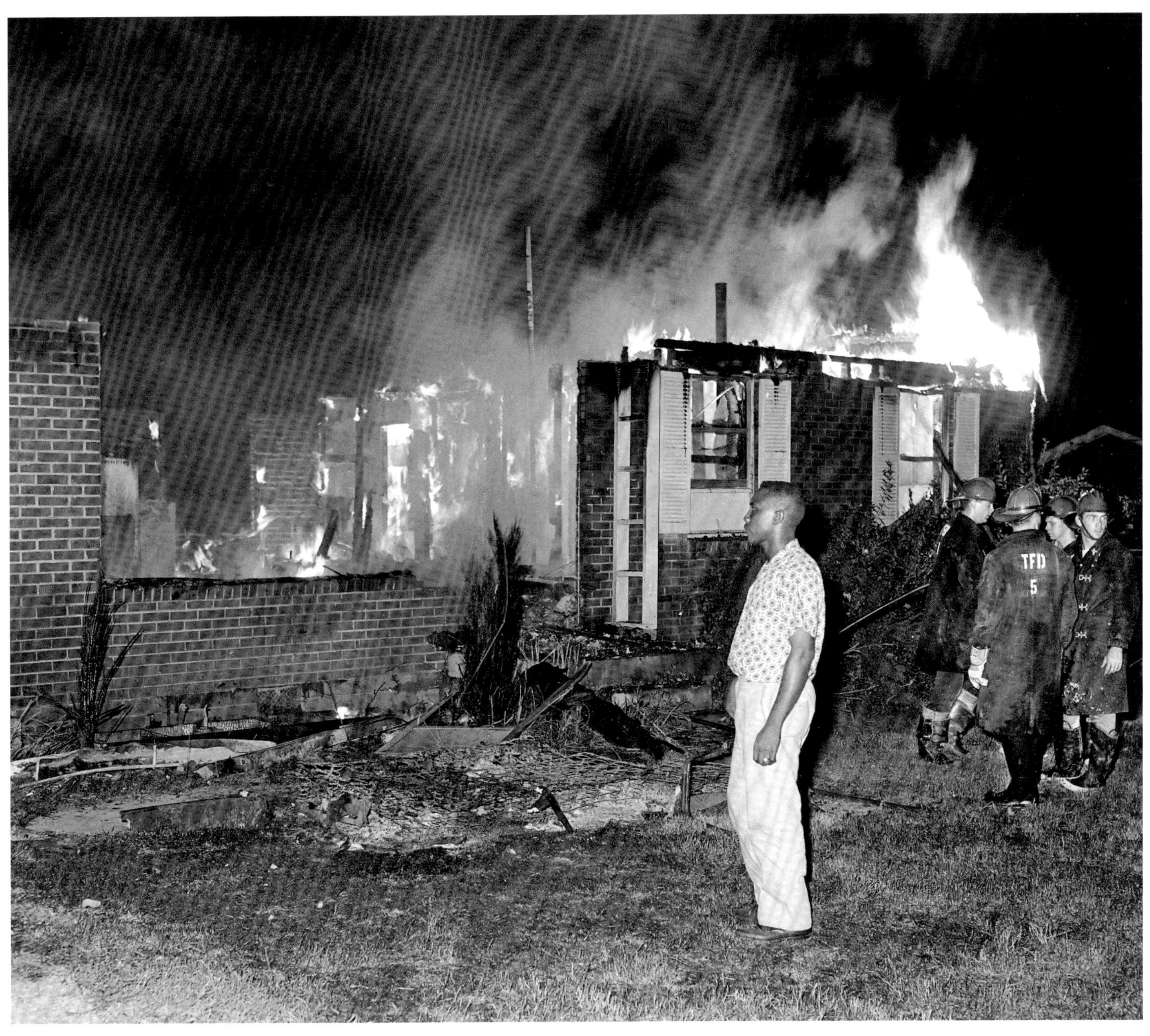

PLATE 57
Bill Preston, *The Tennessean*

AUGUST 7, 1962

Tusculum firemen (right) stand by to protect buildings on either side of the burning home of Rev. Cephus C. Coleman (center), an African American minister. His house, in the predominantly white neighborhood of Tusculum near Nolensville Road, was destroyed by the third blaze to break out that night.
Courtesy of *The Tennessean*
A very similar image was printed in the paper on April 8, 1962

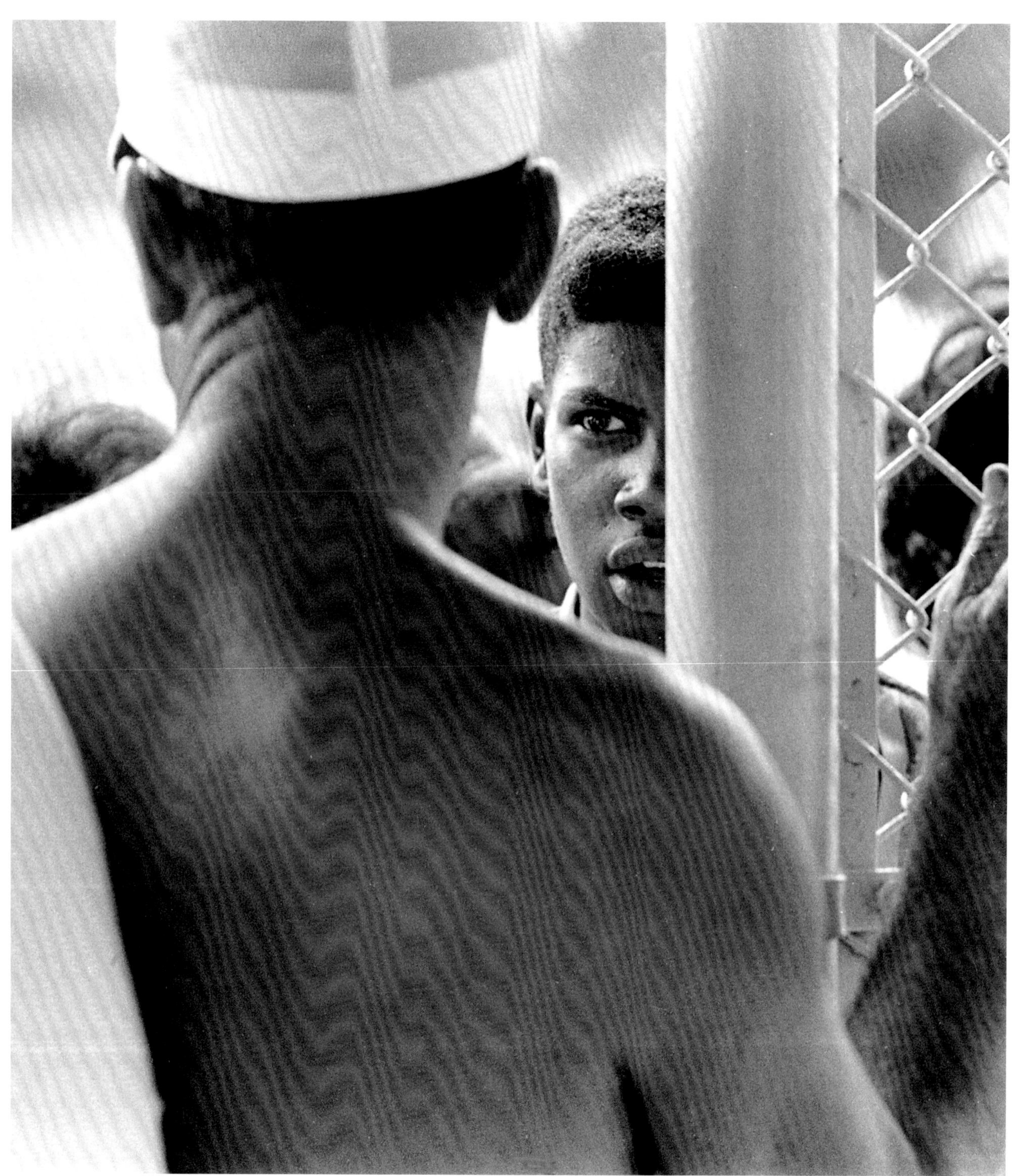

PLATE 58

Gerald Holly, *The Tennessean*

JUNE 19, 1963

A demonstrator is blocked by an official and not allowed in to the Cascade Plunge Swimming Club at the State Fairgrounds. Courtesy of *The Tennessean*

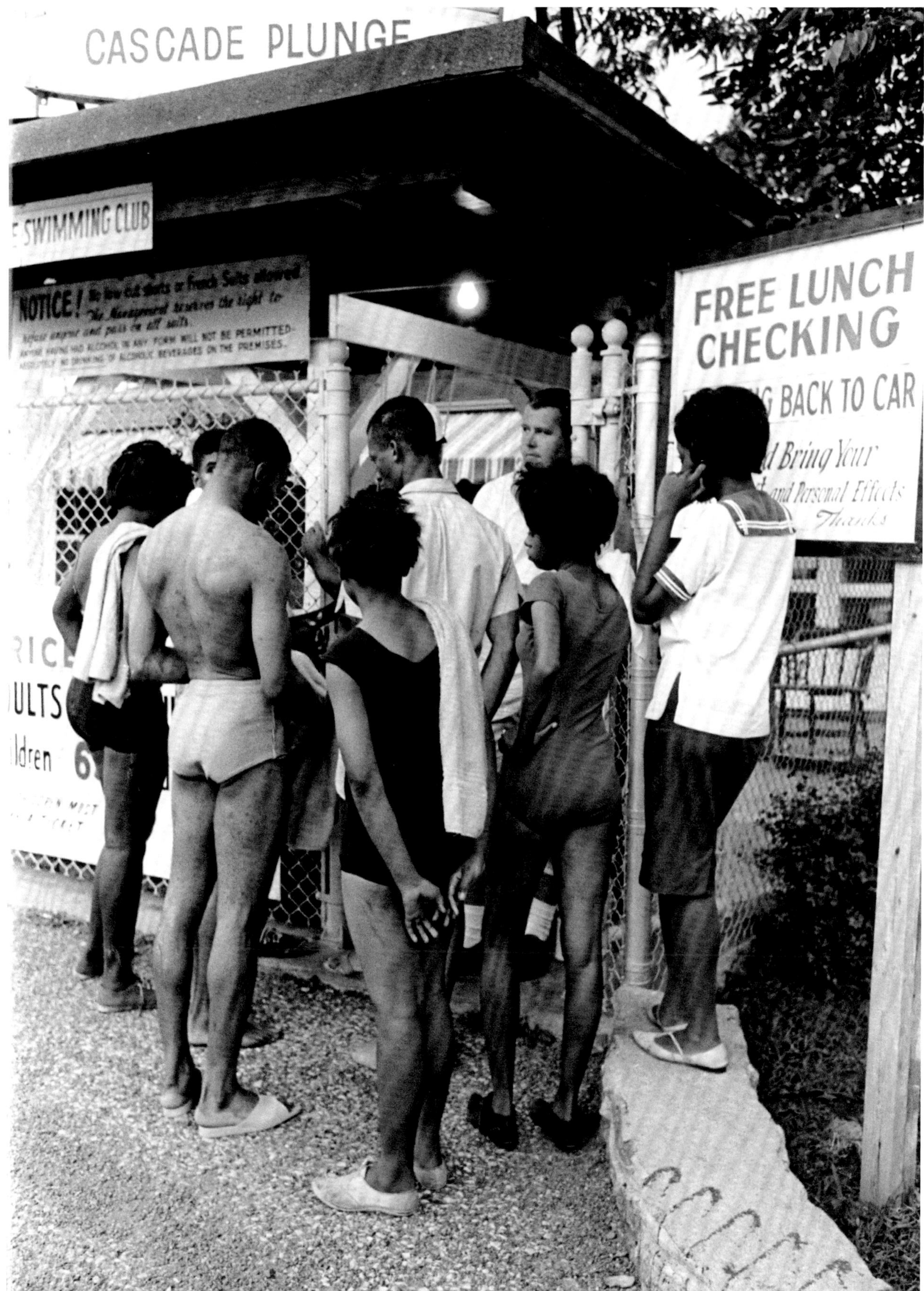

PLATE 59

Gerald Holly, *The Tennessean*

JUNE 19, 1963

Demonstrators, some wearing bathing suits, attempt to enter the Cascade Plunge Swimming Club, a segregated pool.

Courtesy of *The Tennessean*

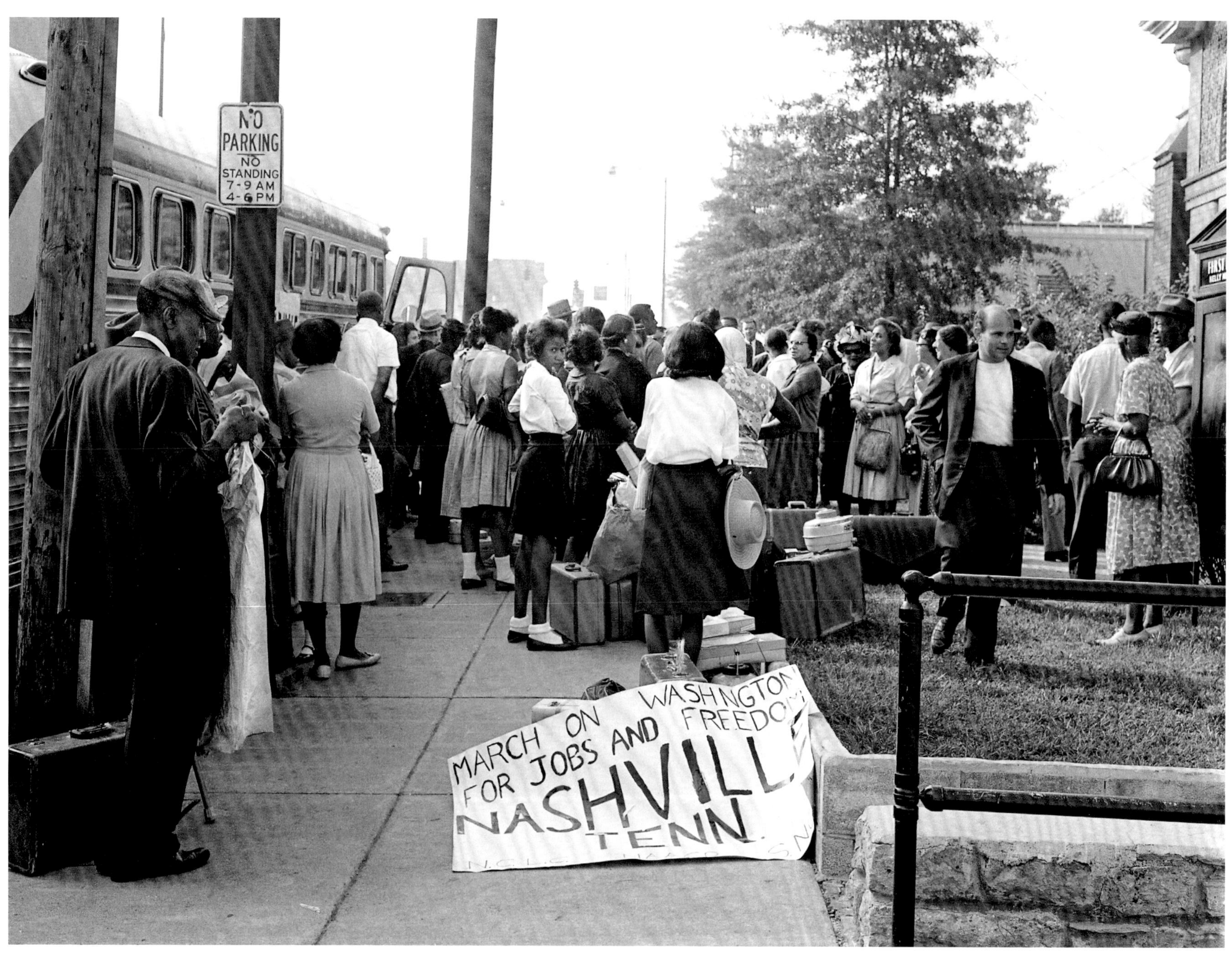

PLATE 60

Bill Preston, *The Tennessean*

AUGUST 27, 1963

A group of black and white Nashvillians board buses at First Baptist Church, Capitol Hill, for the March on Washington for Jobs and Freedom. They were among the two hundred thousand people at the Lincoln Memorial who heard Dr. Martin Luther King Jr.'s "I Have a Dream" speech.

Courtesy of *The Tennessean*

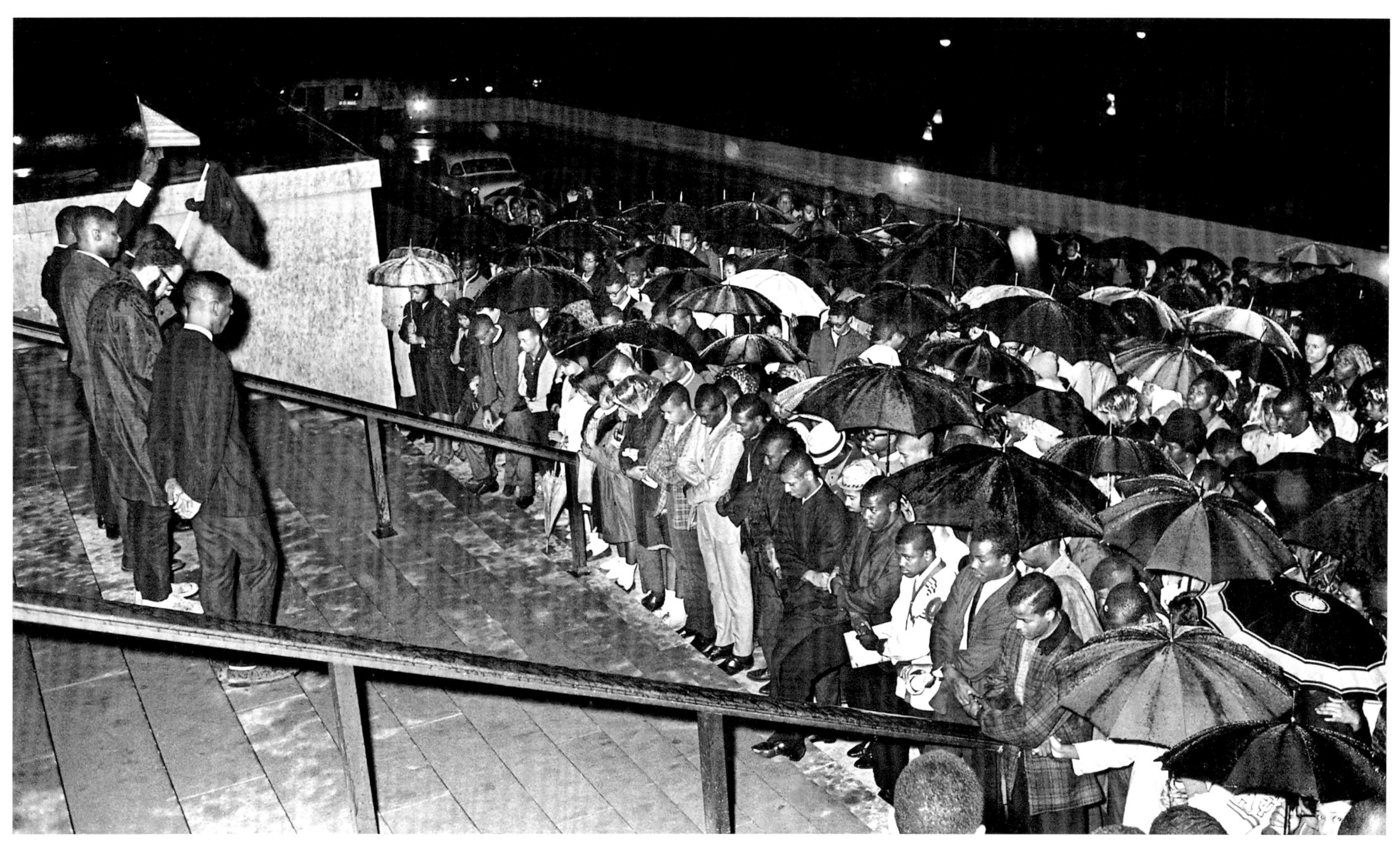

PLATE 61

Jack Corn, *The Tennessean*

NOVEMBER 22, 1963

Several hundred African Americans, grief-stricken at the assassination that afternoon of the man many revered as their greatest champion, stood in pelting rain on the steps of the state capitol in Nashville and silently prayed for the late President John F. Kennedy.

Courtesy of *The Tennessean*

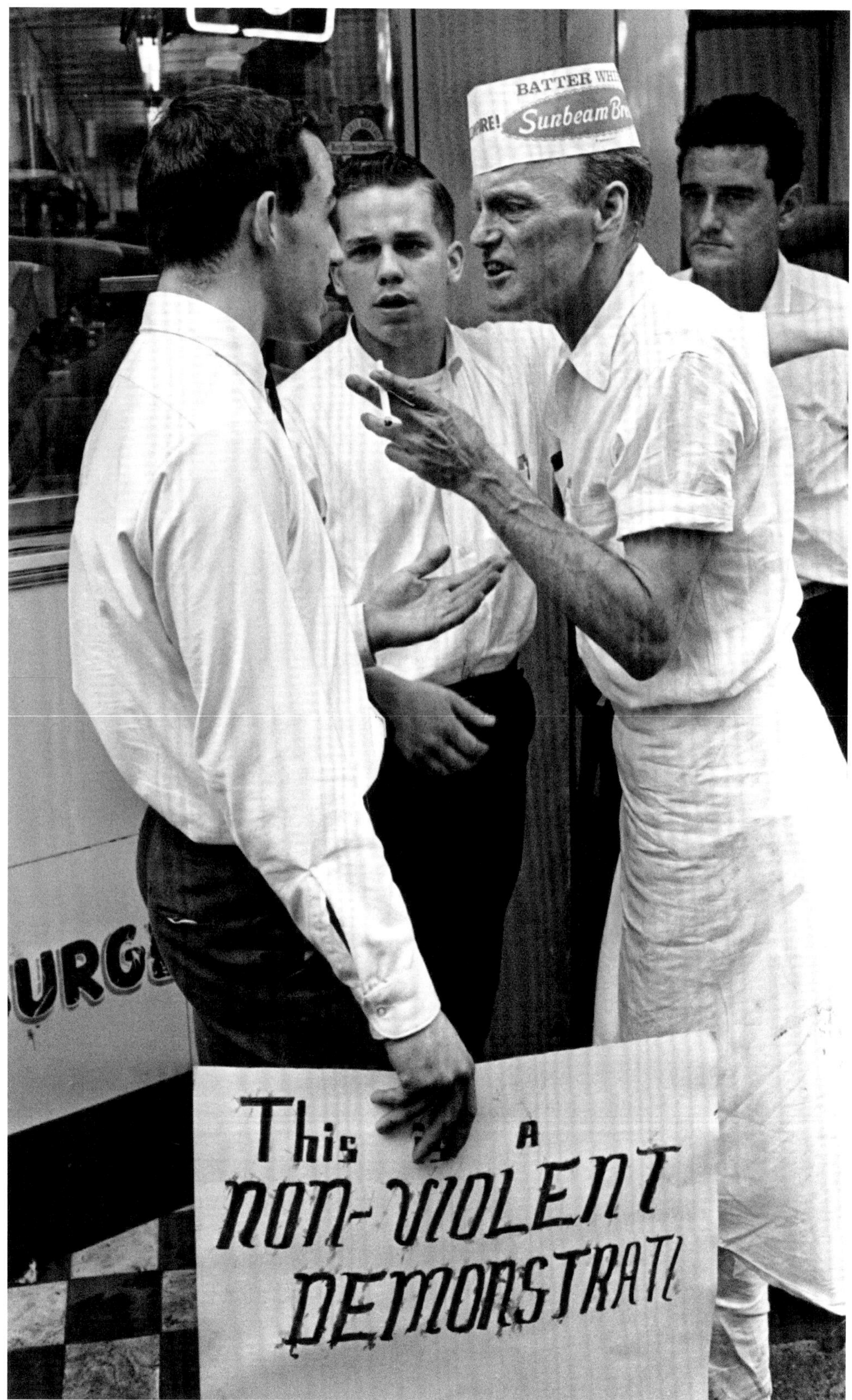

PLATE 62

Jack Corn, *The Tennessean*

APRIL 27, 1964

Archie Allen (left), a Scarritt College for Christian Workers student and civil rights demonstrator, talks with employees of the Tic Toc Restaurant on downtown Church Street. Moments later, Allen was attacked by the employees and knocked down to the sidewalk.

Courtesy of *The Tennessean*

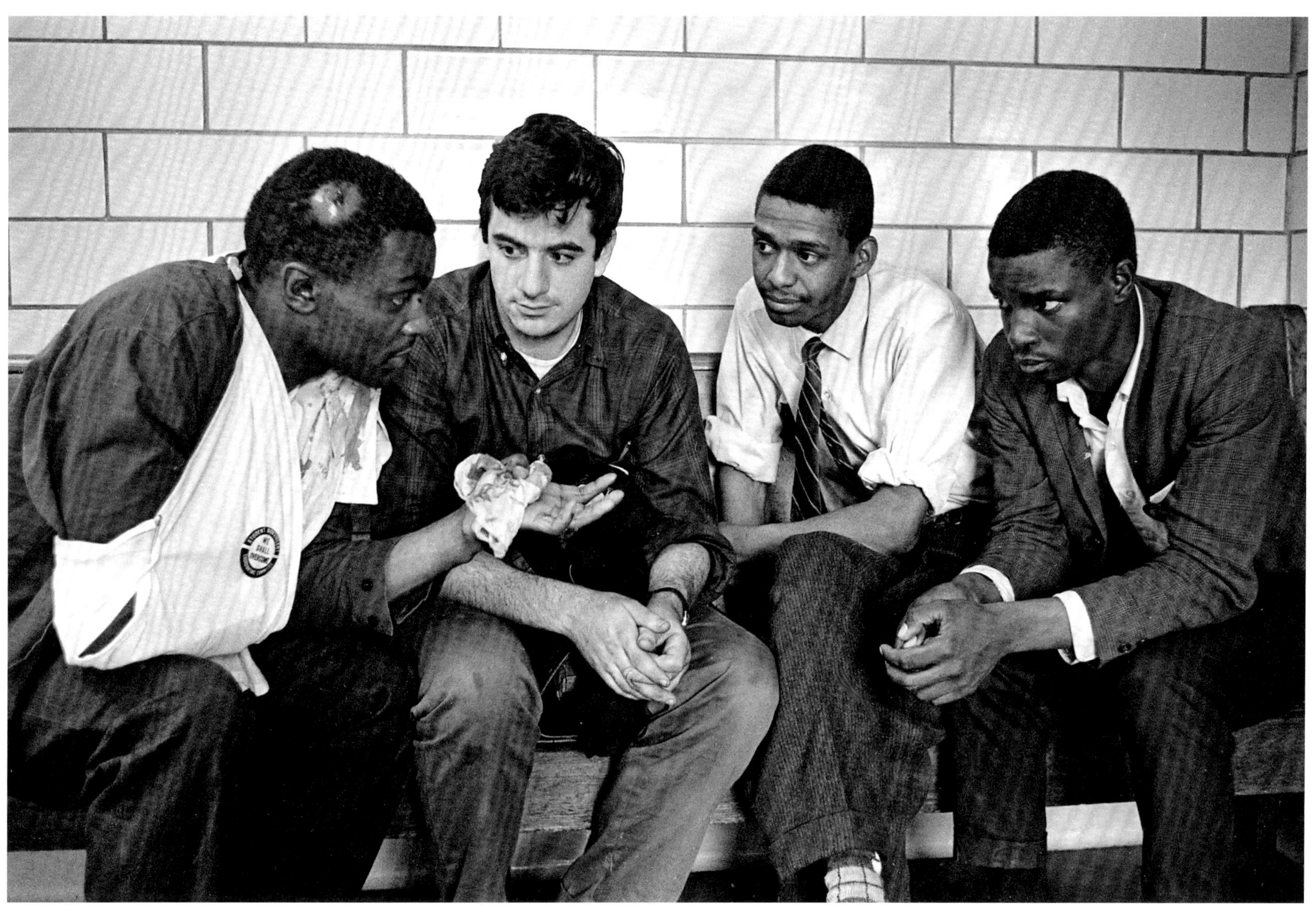

PLATE 63

Jack Corn, *The Tennessean*

APRIL 27, 1964

Civil rights demonstrators sit in Metro Nashville jail while waiting to make bond. They are Lester McKinnie (left), one of the leaders; Allen Wolfe, a Vanderbilt student; William T. Barbee, a Scarritt student; and Frederick Leonard, a student at Tennessee A&I. McKinnie had been subdued by police and was treated for injuries at General Hospital.

Courtesy of *The Tennessean*

Printed in the paper on April 28, 1964

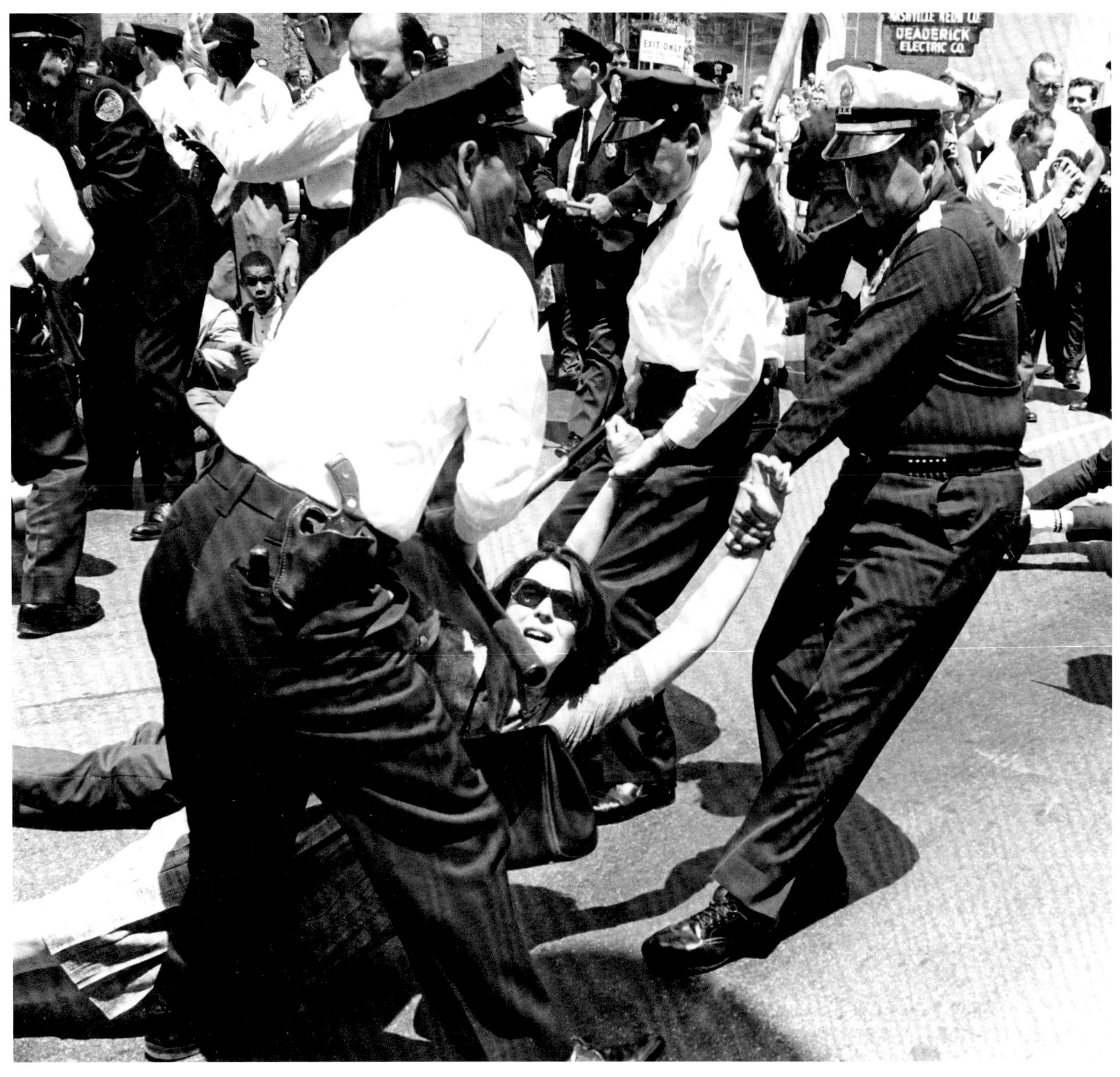

PLATE 64

Harold Lowe Jr., *The Tennessean*

APRIL 29, 1964

A civil rights protester gets dragged out of the middle of West End Avenue in front of Morrison's Cafeteria. The mass arrests came on the third straight day of anti-segregation demonstrations. Courtesy of *The Tennessean*

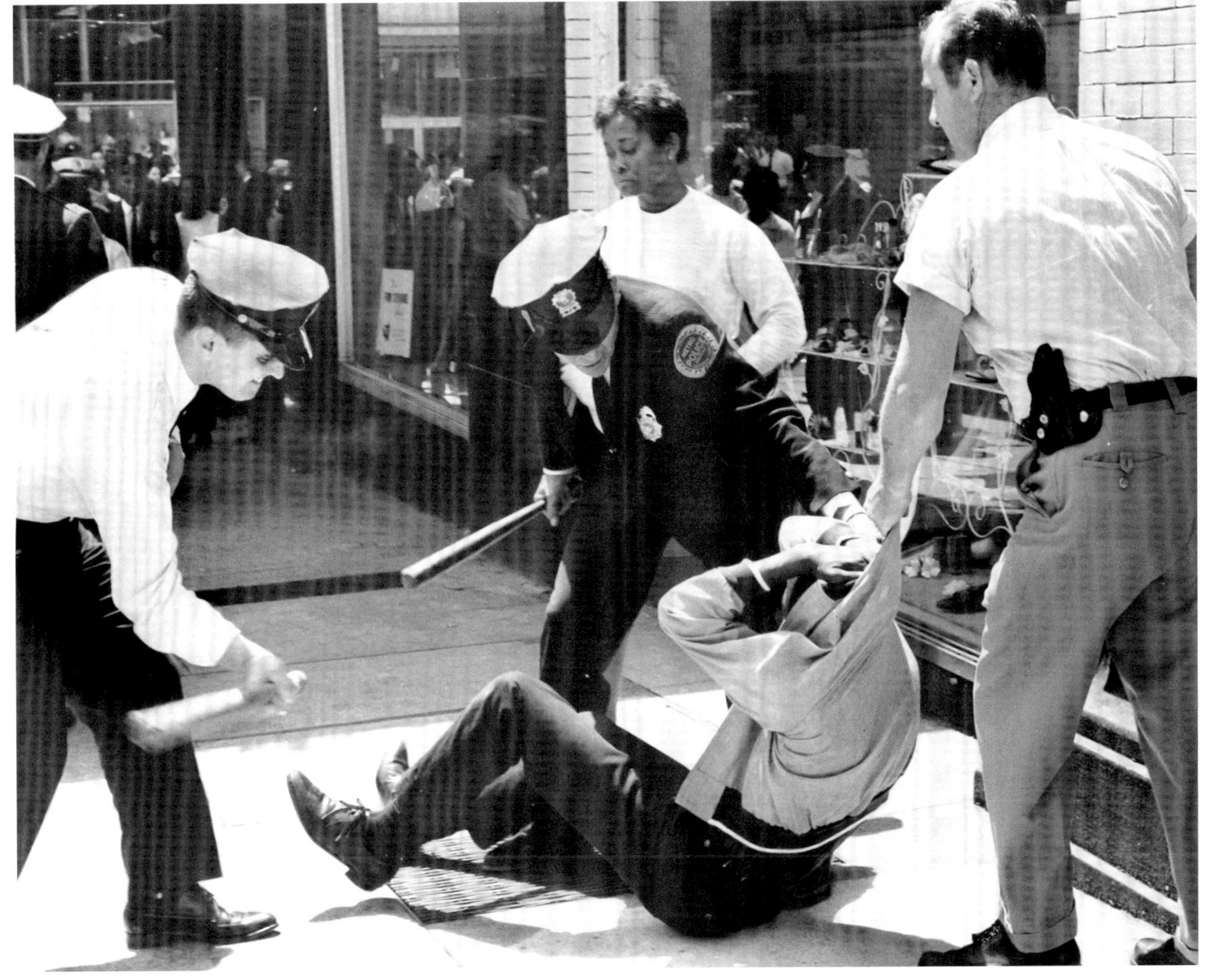

PLATE 65

Bill Goodman, *Nashville Banner*

APRIL 27, 1964

Police swing billy clubs in an effort to make a protester "lying-in" on the sidewalk stand up.

Courtesy of the Nashville Public Library, Special Collections

Printed in the paper on April 28, 1964

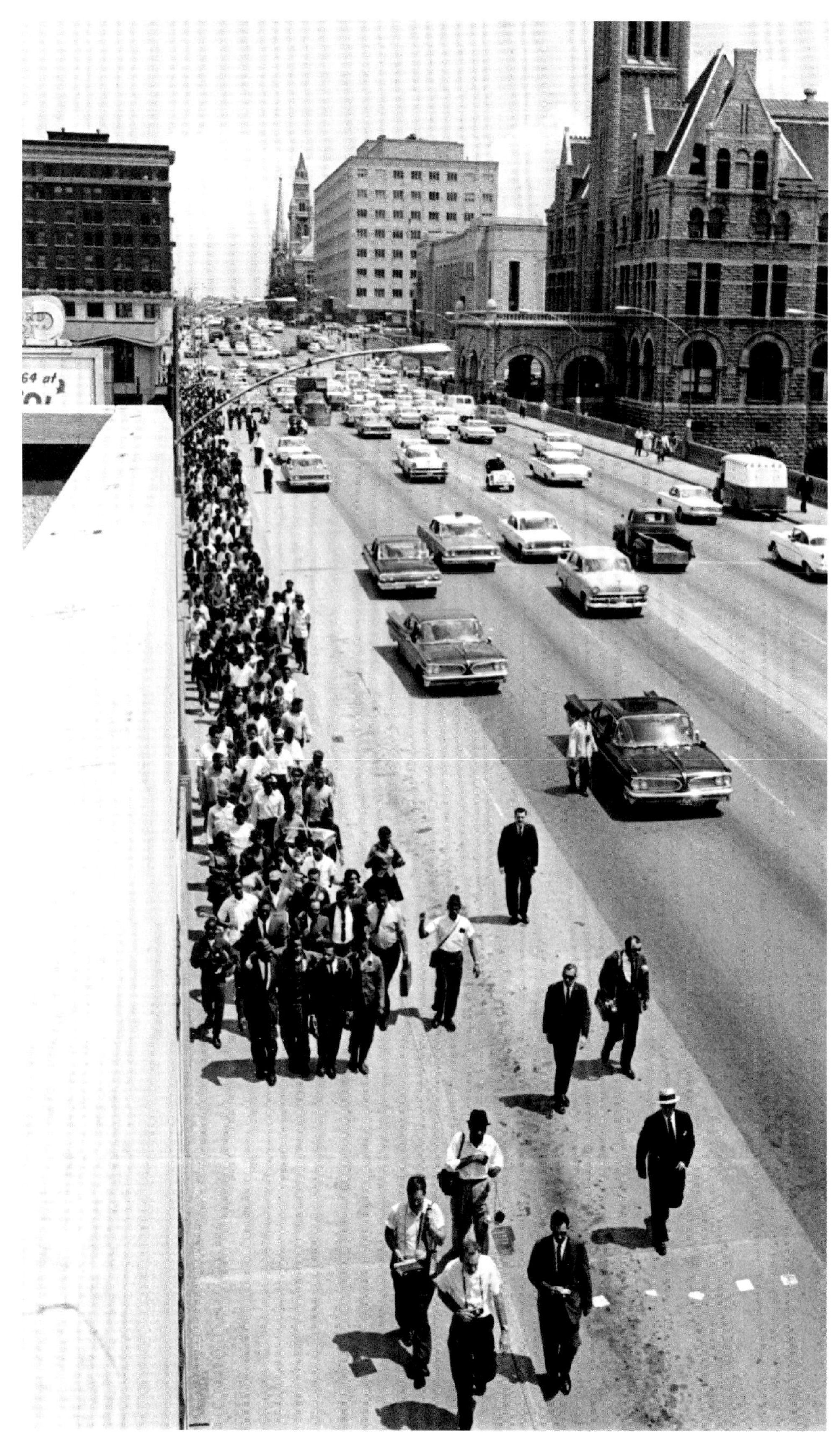

PLATE 66

Joe Rudis, *The Tennessean*

APRIL 29, 1964

Led by John Lewis, national chairman of the Student Nonviolent Coordinating Committee (SNCC), more than three hundred demonstrators march up Broadway toward Morrison's Cafeteria at West End Avenue. There, the marchers began to sit down in the middle of the street.

Courtesy of *The Tennessean*

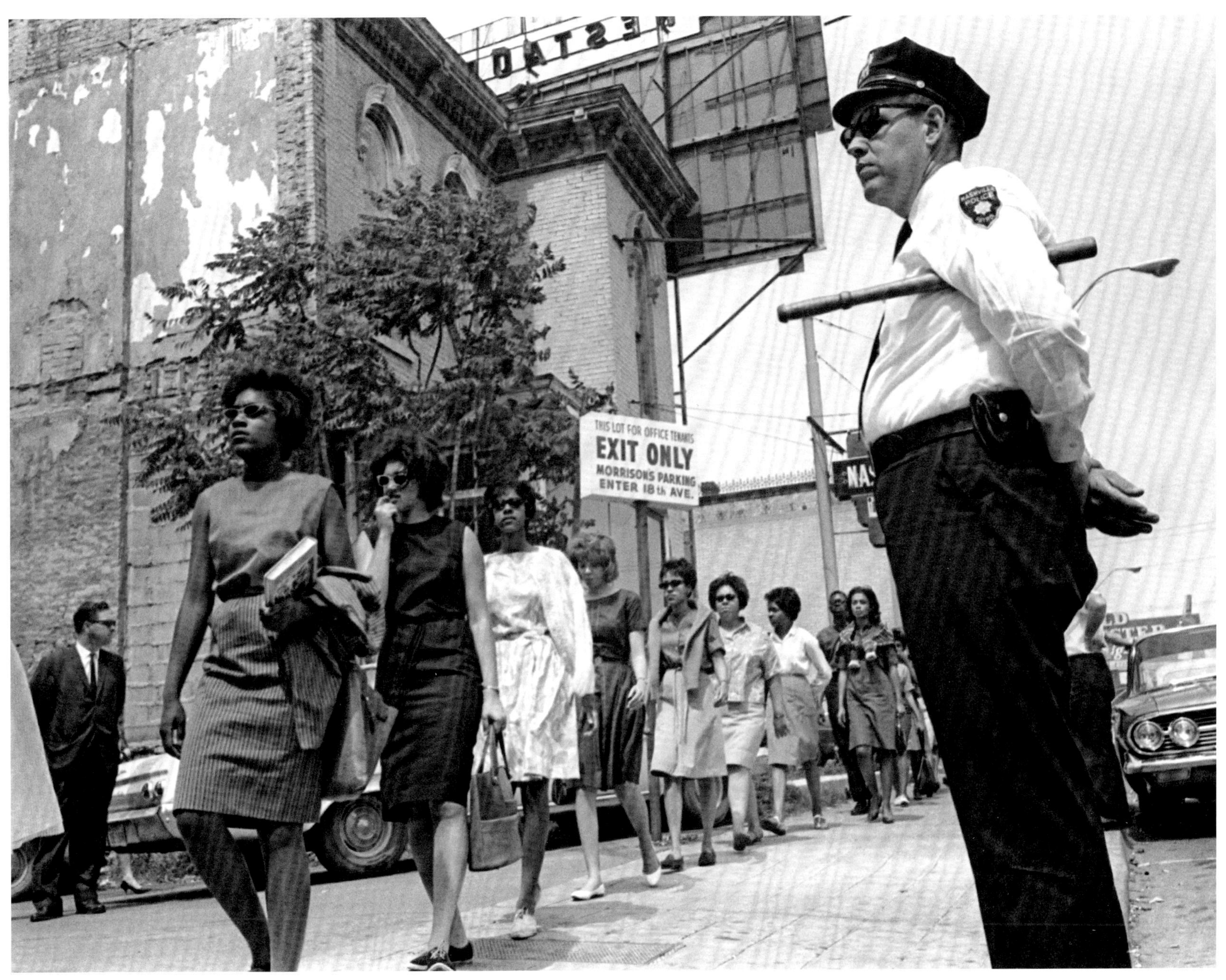

PLATE 67

Joe Rudis, *The Tennessean*

MAY 8, 1964

Under the watchful eyes of a Metro Nashville police officer, a group of high-school-age students march to Morrison's Cafeteria after a demonstration at the Metro Nashville jail to protest the arrest of college students earlier in the week. Courtesy of *The Tennessean*

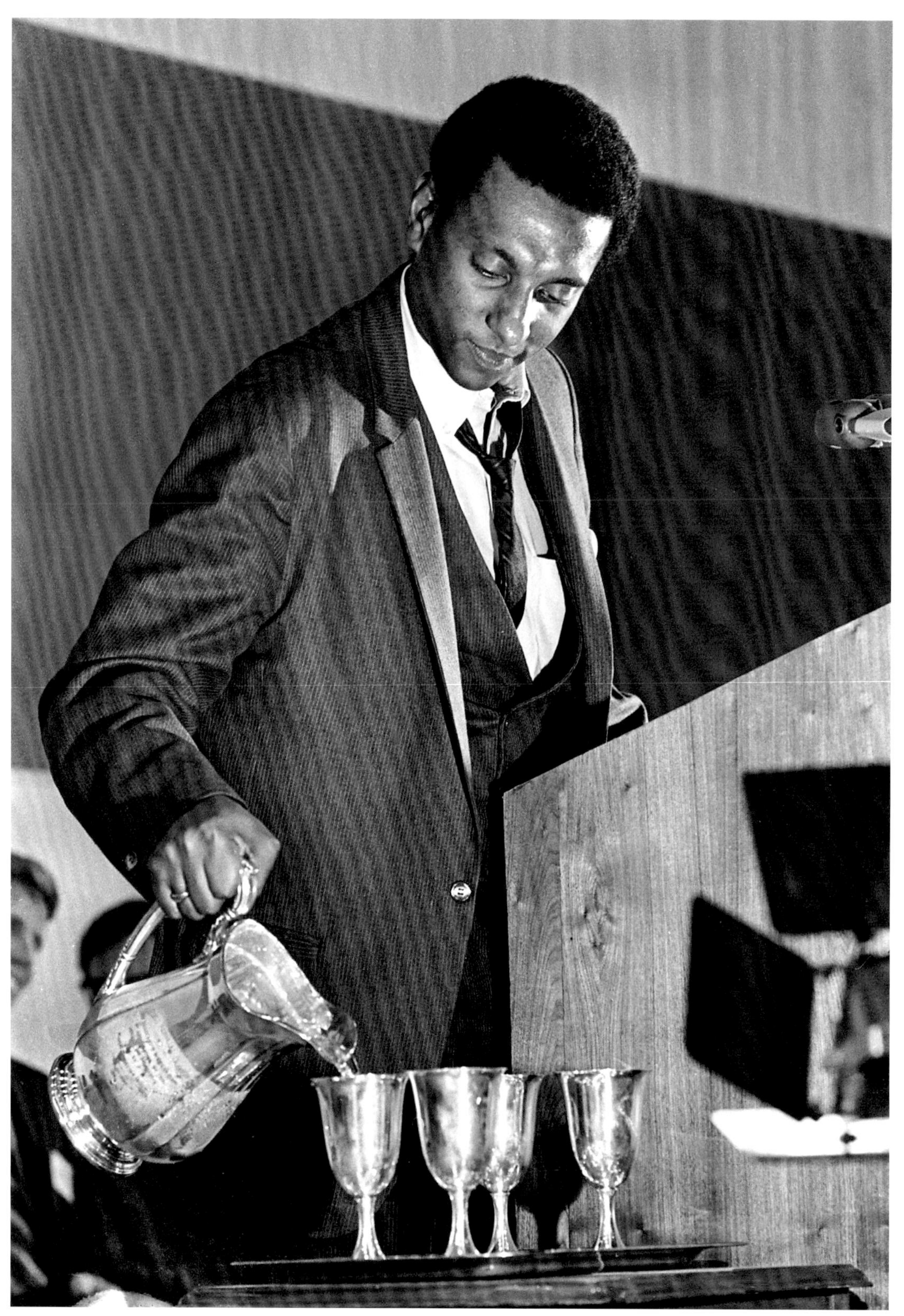

PLATE 68

Dale Ernsberger, *The Tennessean*

APRIL 8, 1967

Stokely Carmichael, black power advocate and recently elected leader of the increasingly militant SNCC, pours himself a glass of water before speaking during the Impact Symposium at Vanderbilt University.

Courtesy of *The Tennessean*

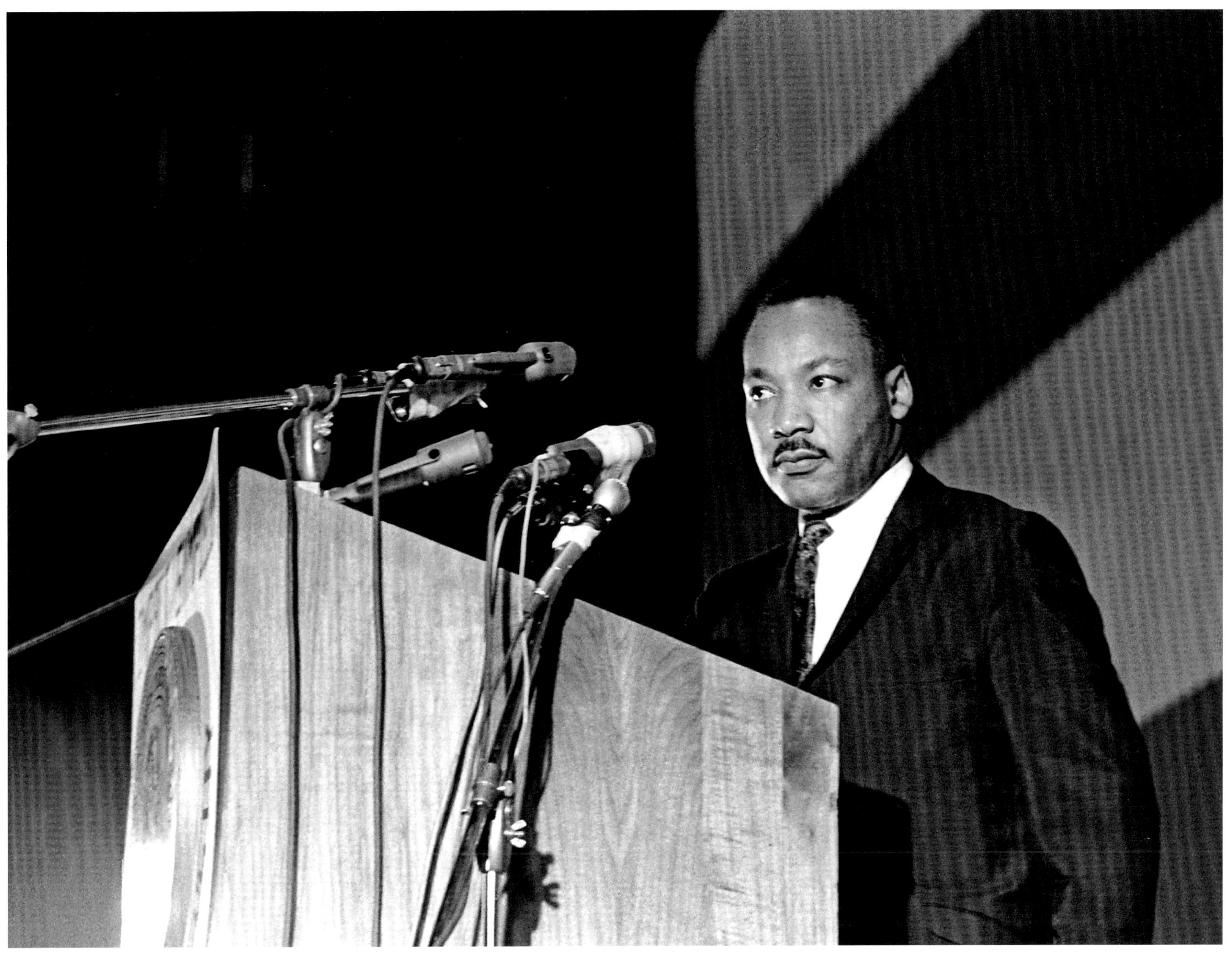

PLATE 69

Jimmy Ellis, *The Tennessean*

APRIL 7, 1967

In a speech during Impact Symposium at Vanderbilt's Memorial Gym, Dr. Martin Luther King Jr. says he remains convinced that the best route to a true integration is nonviolence. Courtesy of *The Tennessean*

PLATE 70

J. T. Phillips, *The Tennessean*

APRIL 8, 1967

An estimated crowd of 4,500, filling the north side of Vanderbilt University's Memorial Gym, listen to Stokely Carmichael's speech on the last day of the Impact Symposium.
Courtesy of *The Tennessean*

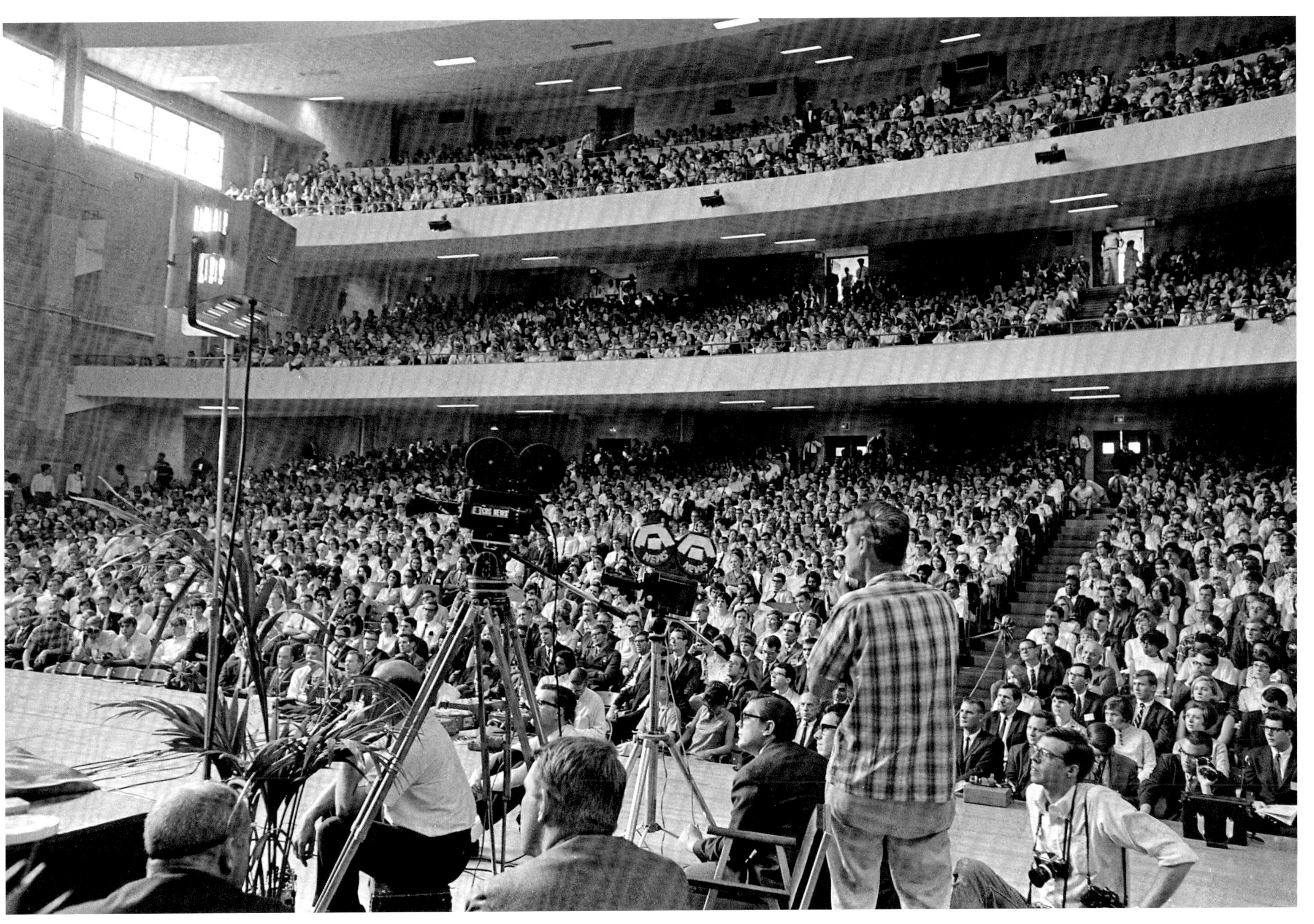
CBS NEWS

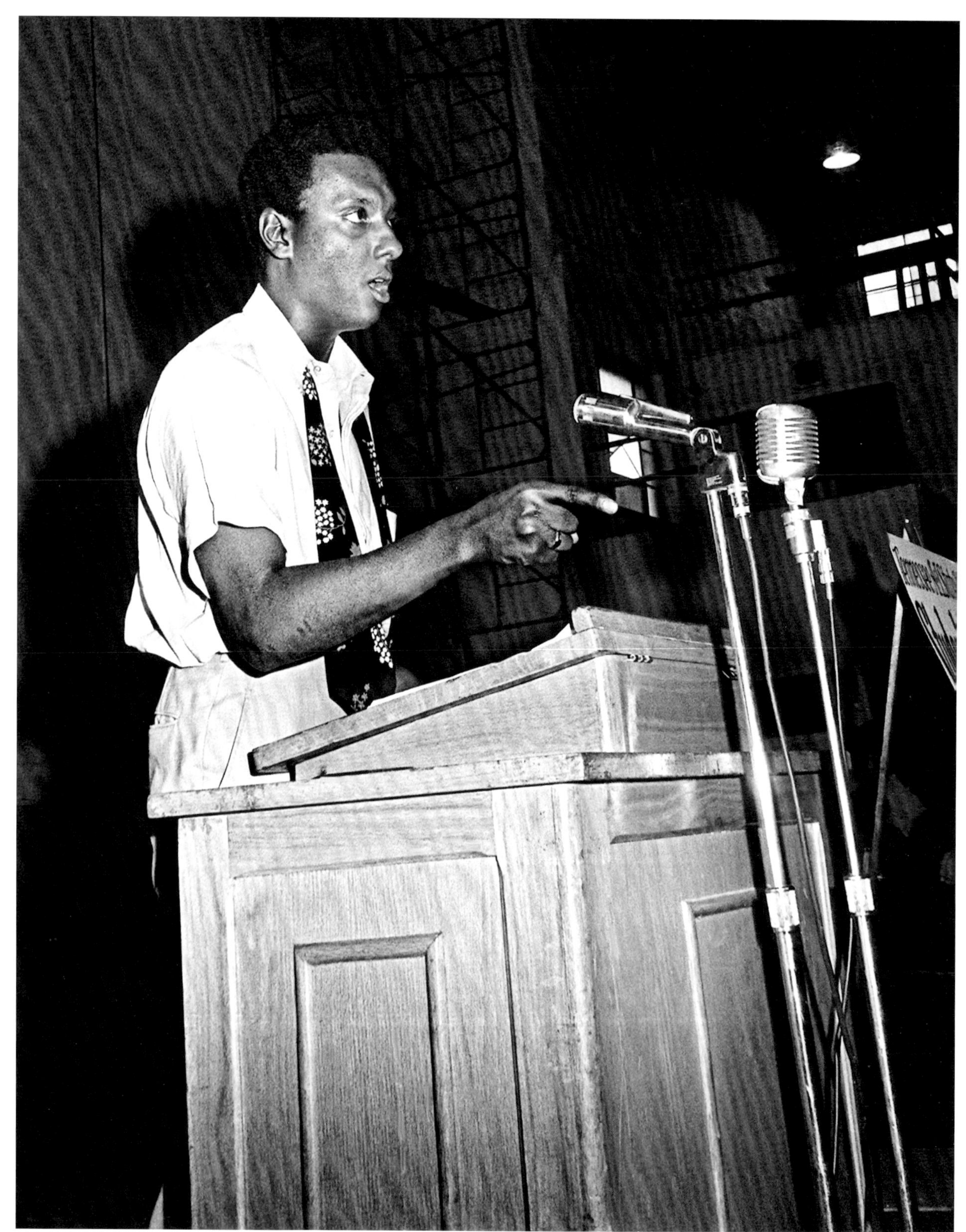

PLATE 71

Robert Johnson, *The Tennessean*

APRIL 7, 1967

Stokely Carmichael's call for Black Power was more forceful during speeches at Tennessee A&I, seen here, and Fisk University than at Vanderbilt University.

Courtesy of *The Tennessean*

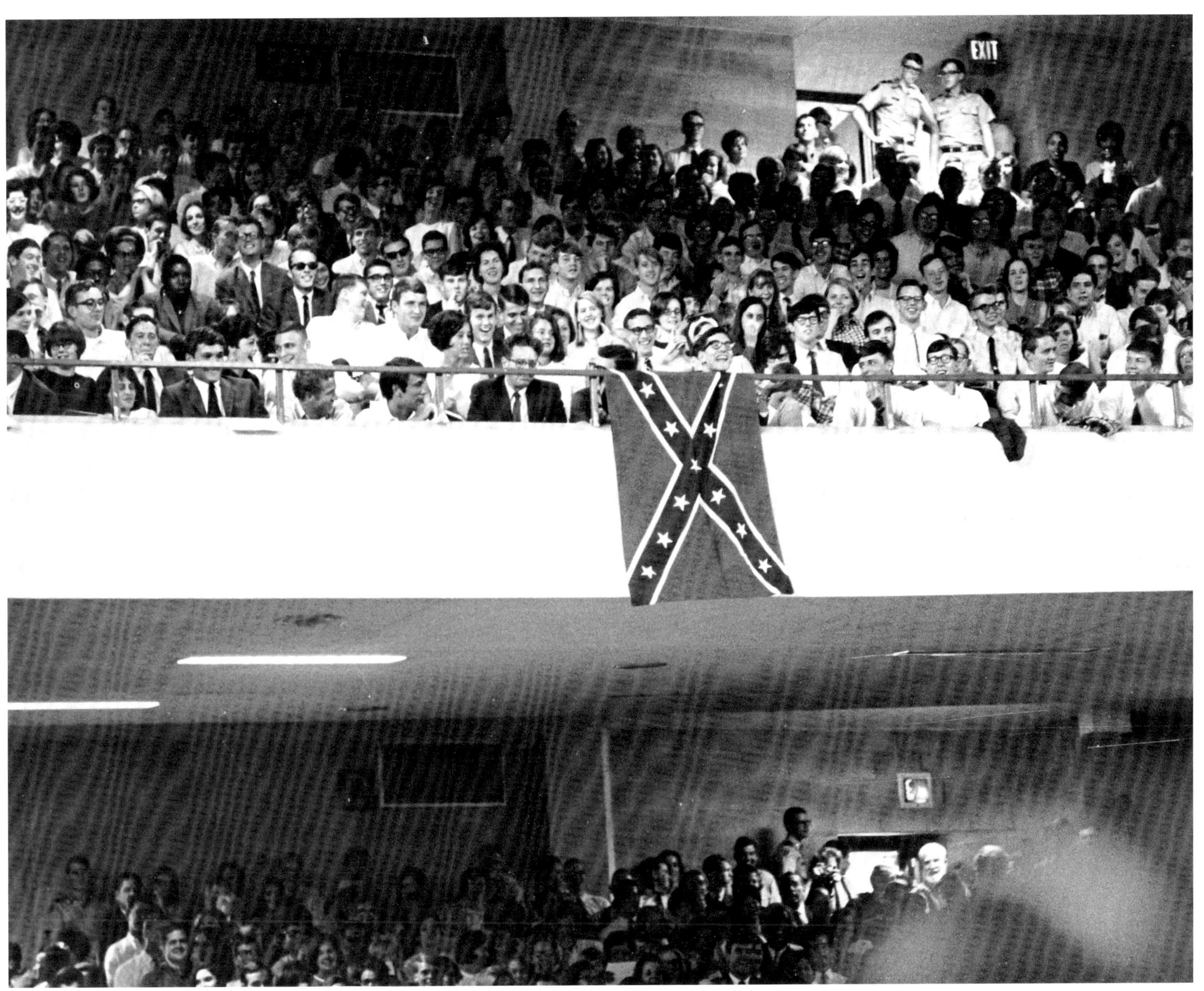

PLATE 72

Vic Cooley, *Nashville Banner*

APRIL 8, 1967

A member of the audience at the Impact Symposium unfurled a confederate flag during Stokely Carmichael's remarks. "That's ok, you can express your views," Carmichael responded, "just don't burn down my churches."

Courtesy of the Nashville Public Library, Special Collections

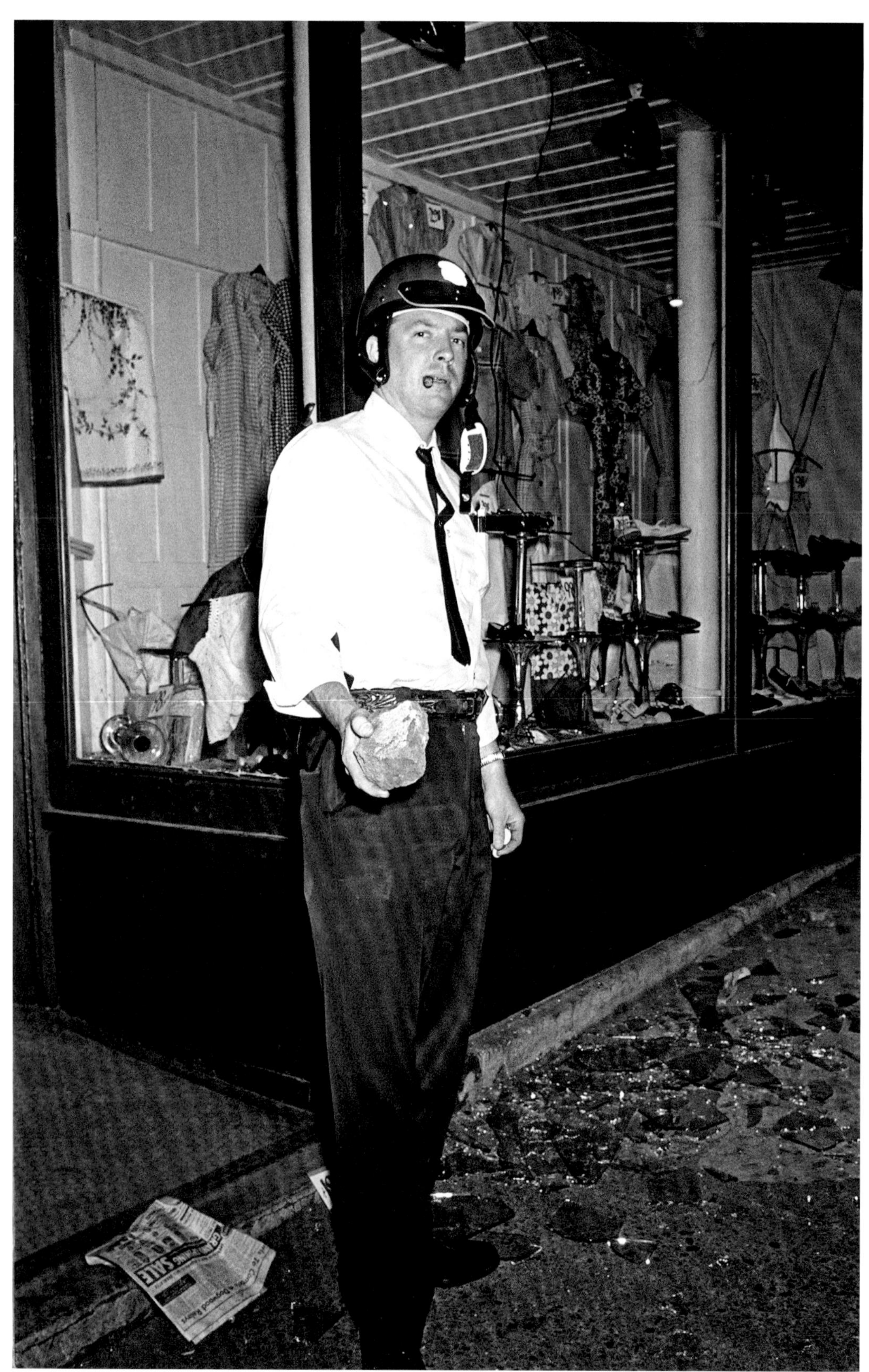

PLATE 73
Jimmy Ellis, *The Tennessean*
APRIL 9, 1967
A Metro Nashville policeman shows the rock that rioters used to damage a storefront. Rock-throwing escalated to gunfire as violence erupted, sending mobs and riot police swarming through the historically black North Nashville community.
Courtesy of *The Tennessean*

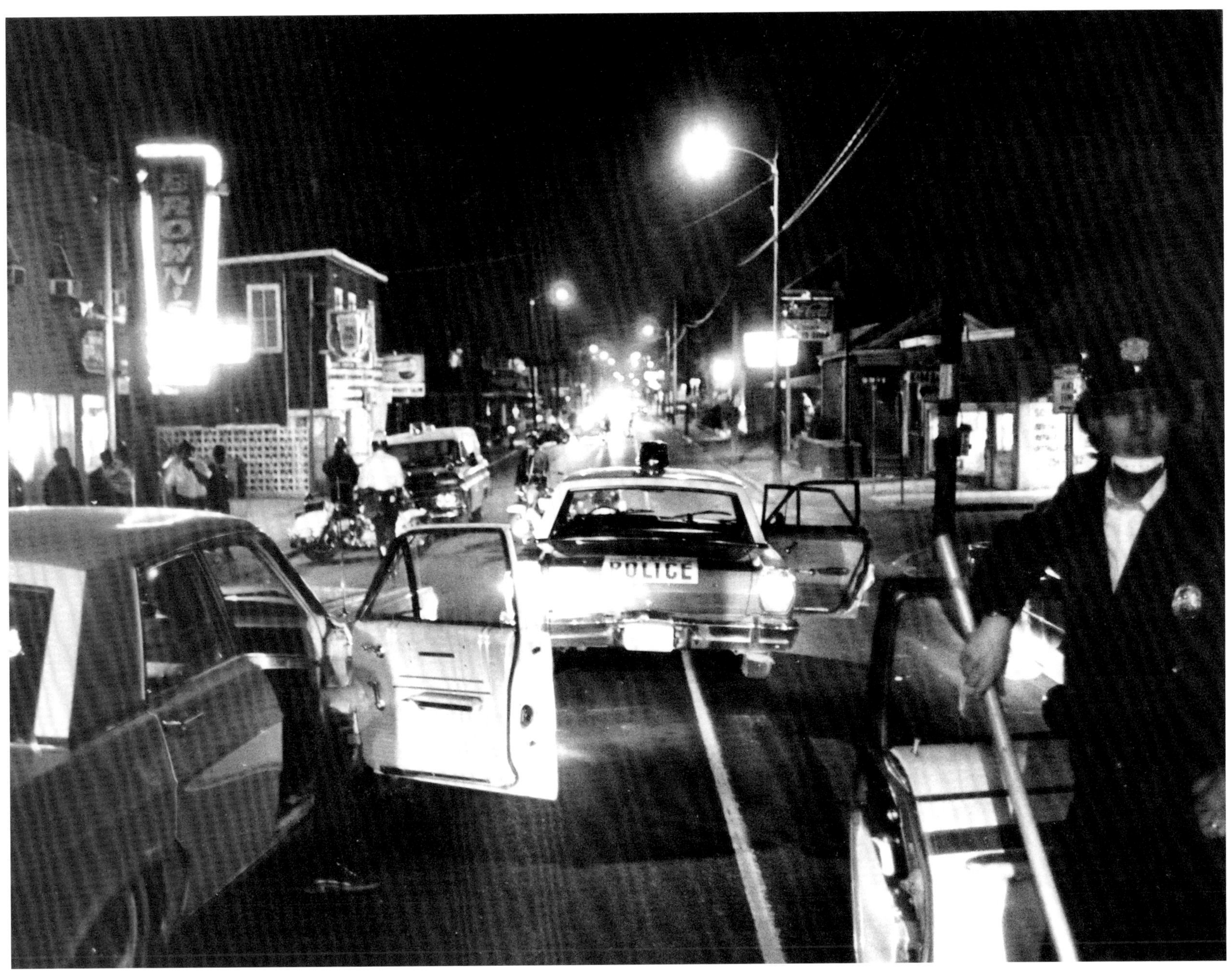

PLATE 74

Vic Cooley, *Nashville Banner*

APRIL 9, 1967

Stokely Carmichael's call for Black Power in speeches at Fisk and Tennessee A&I was blamed by some for causing three days of civil unrest in north Nashville. More than four hundred police officers took to Jefferson Street and other parts of the neighborhood.

Courtesy of the Nashville Public Library, Special Collections

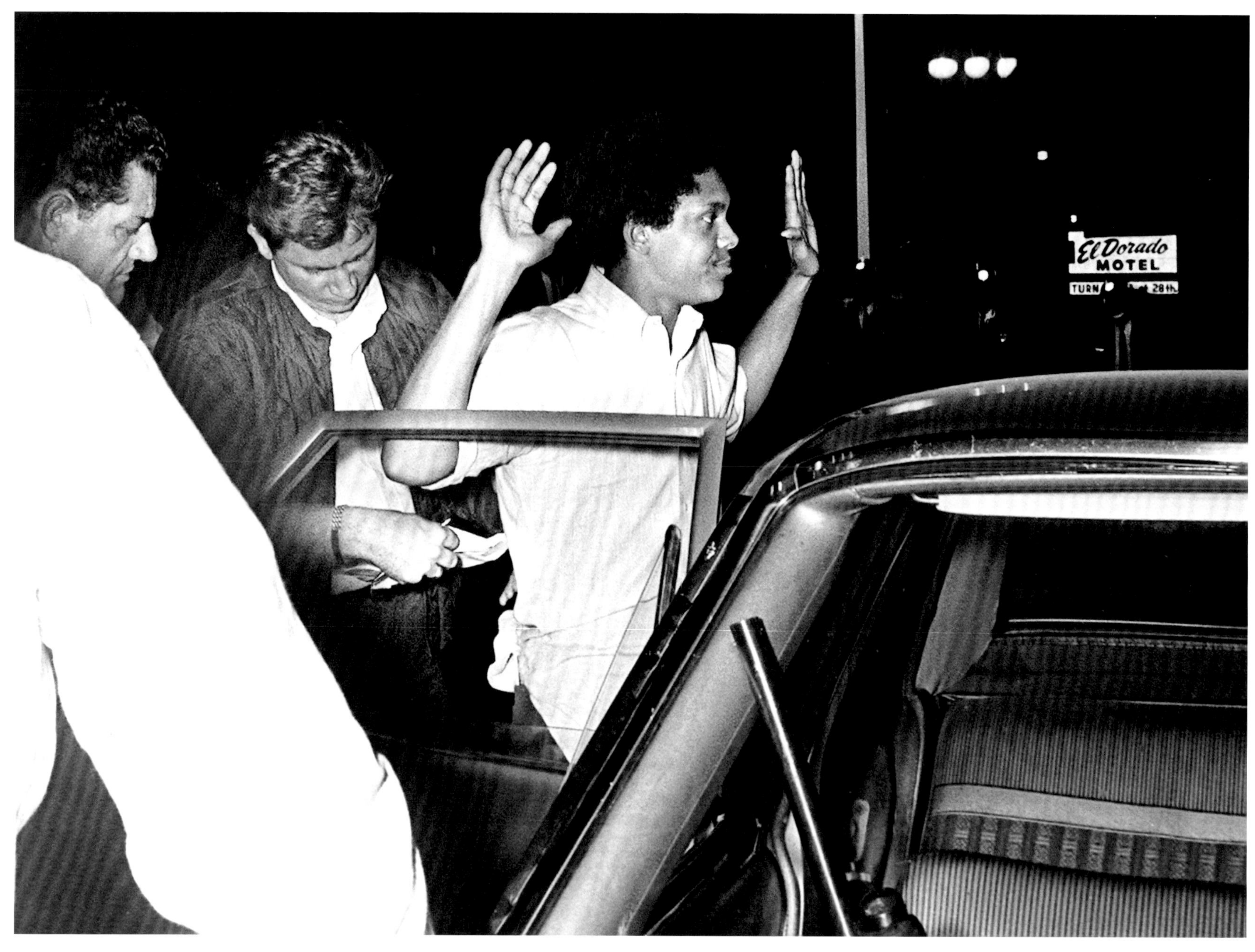

PLATE 75

Jimmy Ellis, *The Tennessean*

APRIL 9, 1967

A Metro Nashville police officer double-checks the pockets of a suspect being arrested for disorderly conduct before putting him into a patrol car on Jefferson Street.
Courtesy of *The Tennessean*

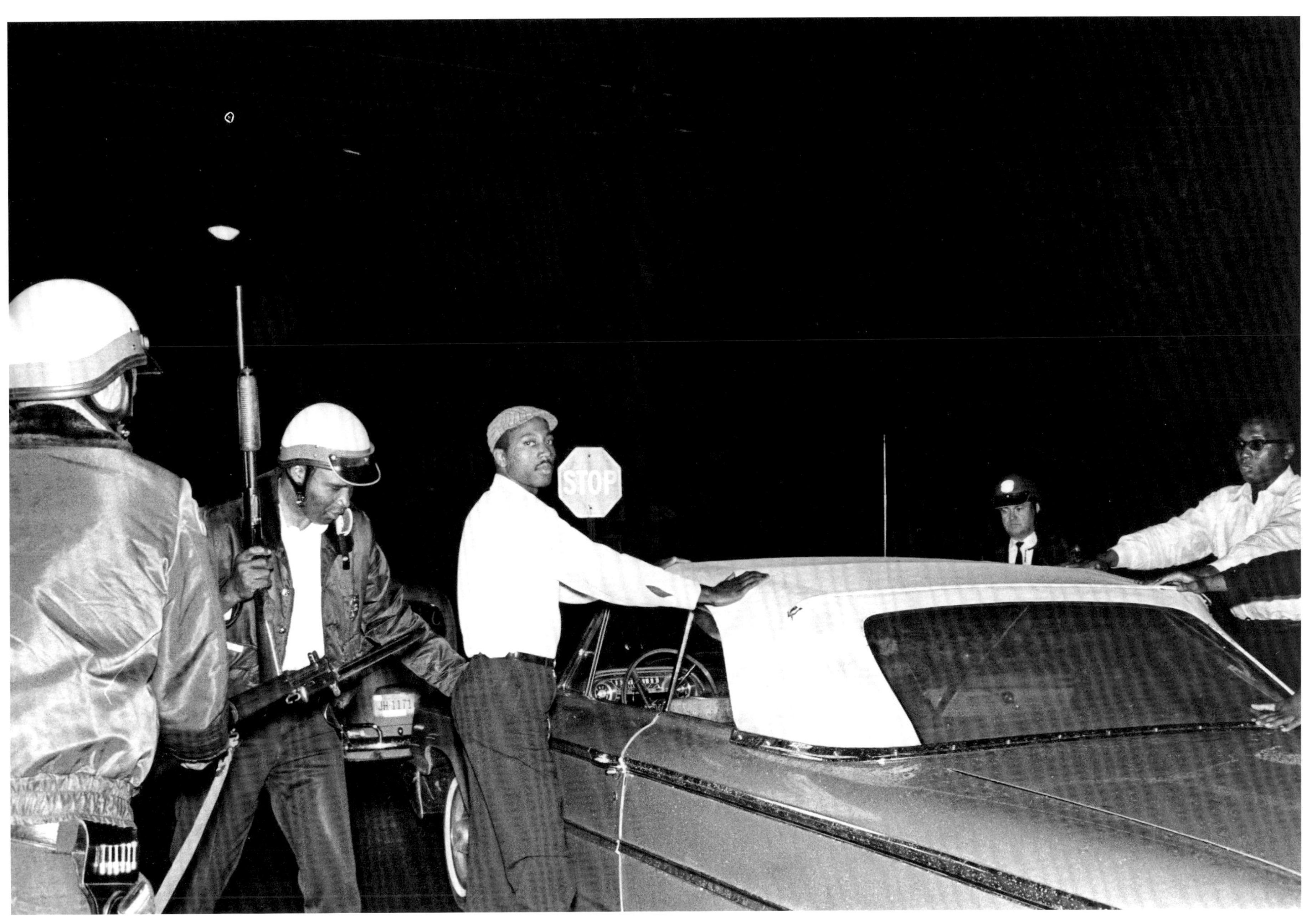

PLATE 76

Vic Cooley, *Nashville Banner*

APRIL 10, 1967

The police made multiple arrests during three days of civil unrest in North Nashville. Carmichael and his associate George Ware were later charged with inciting a riot.

Courtesy of the Nashville Public Library, Special Collections

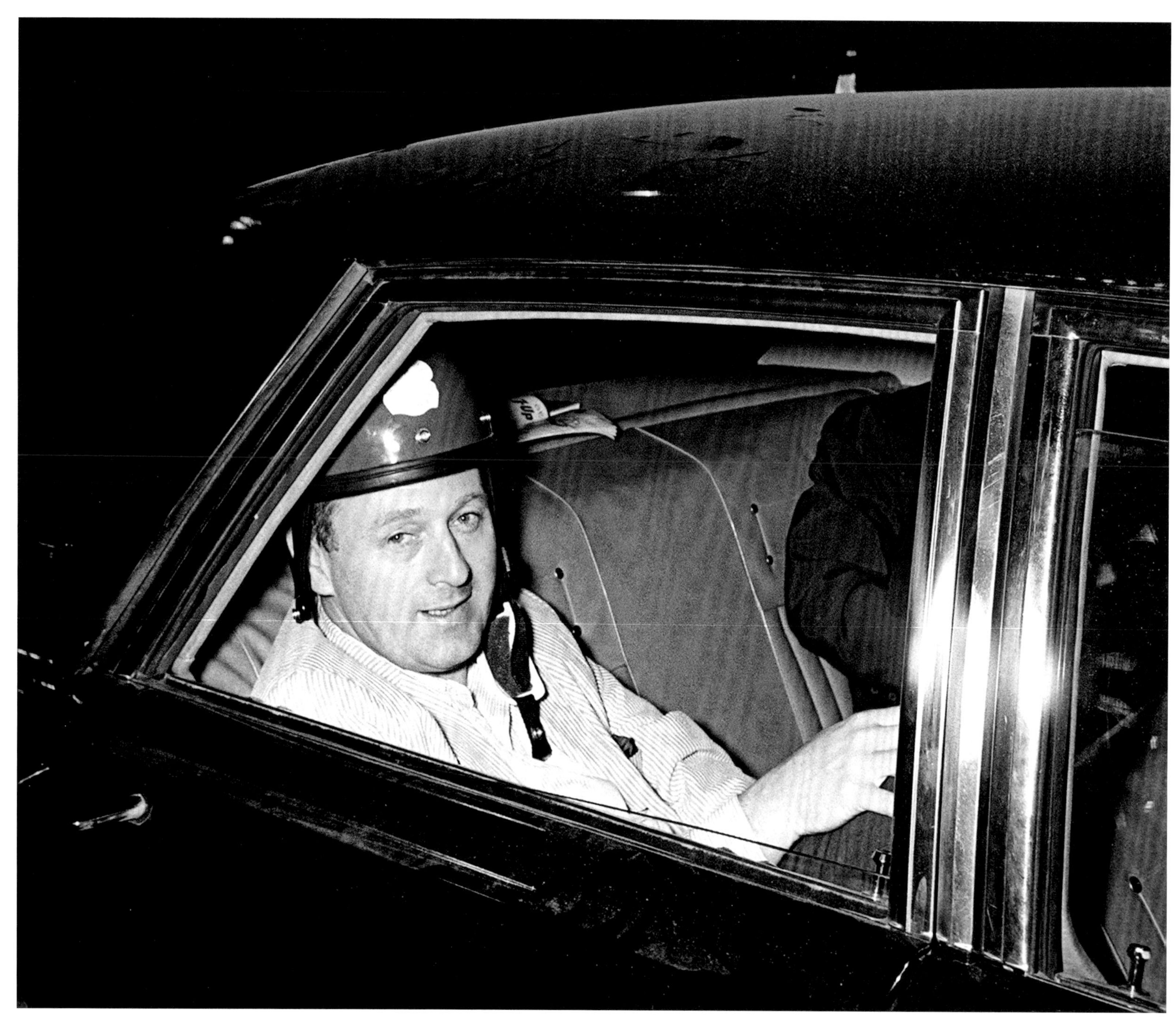

PLATE 77

Jimmy Ellis, *The Tennessean*

APRIL 9, 1967

John Seigenthaler, editor of *The Tennessean* and former aide to Attorney General Robert F. Kennedy during the Freedom Rides negotiations, came to survey the events that were unfolding in North Nashville.
Courtesy of *The Tennessean*

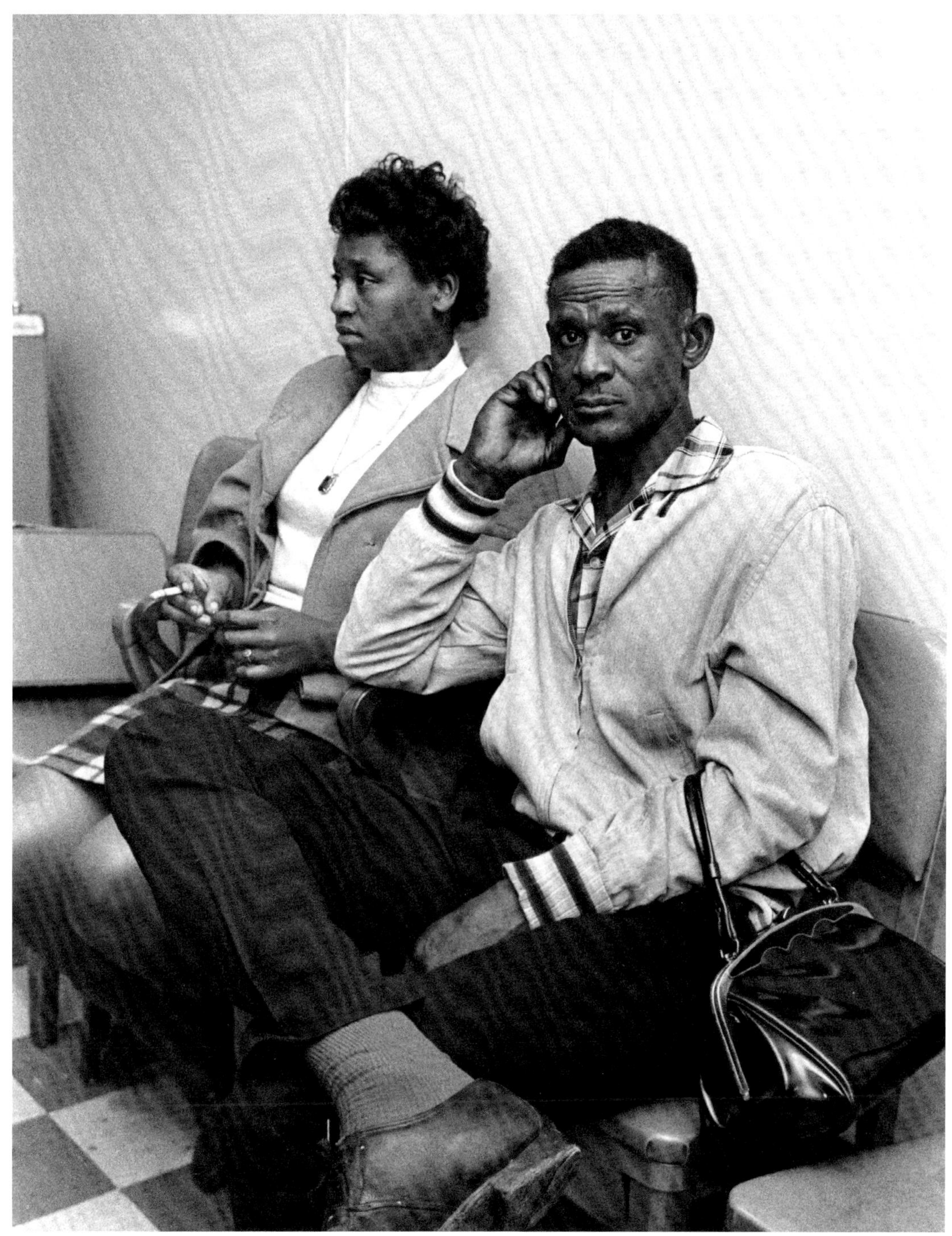

PLATE 78
Charles Warren,
Nashville Banner
APRIL 8, 1967
A couple waits in a hospital or police station, looking uneasy, the night that civil unrest began in North Nashville. Courtesy of the Nashville Public Library, Special Collections

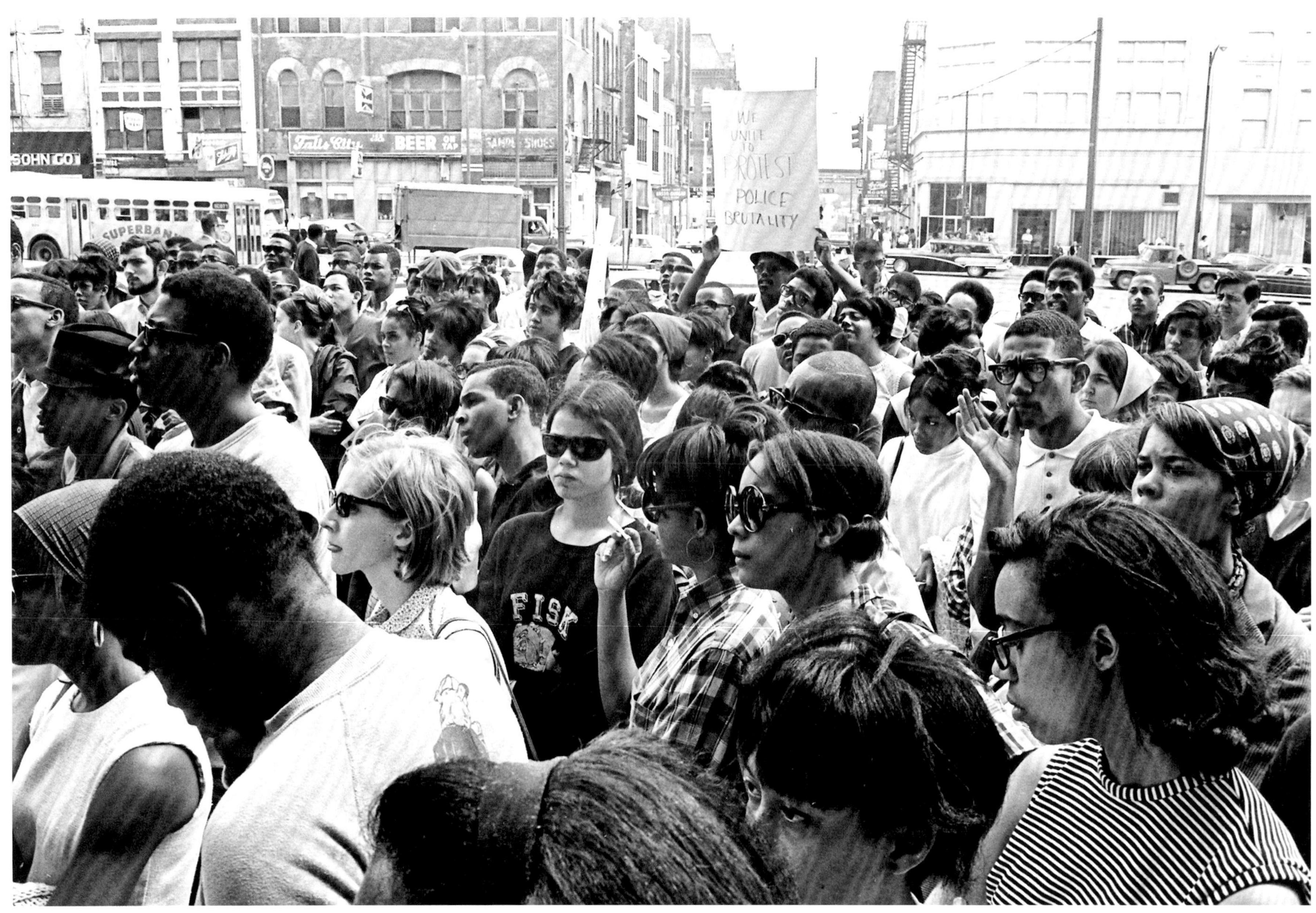

PLATE 79

Jimmy Ellis, *The Tennessean*

APRIL 14, 1967

After marching peacefully from Fisk University, more than two hundred demonstrators gather at Metro Courthouse to protest what they saw as police brutality during the so-called riot.
Courtesy of *The Tennessean*

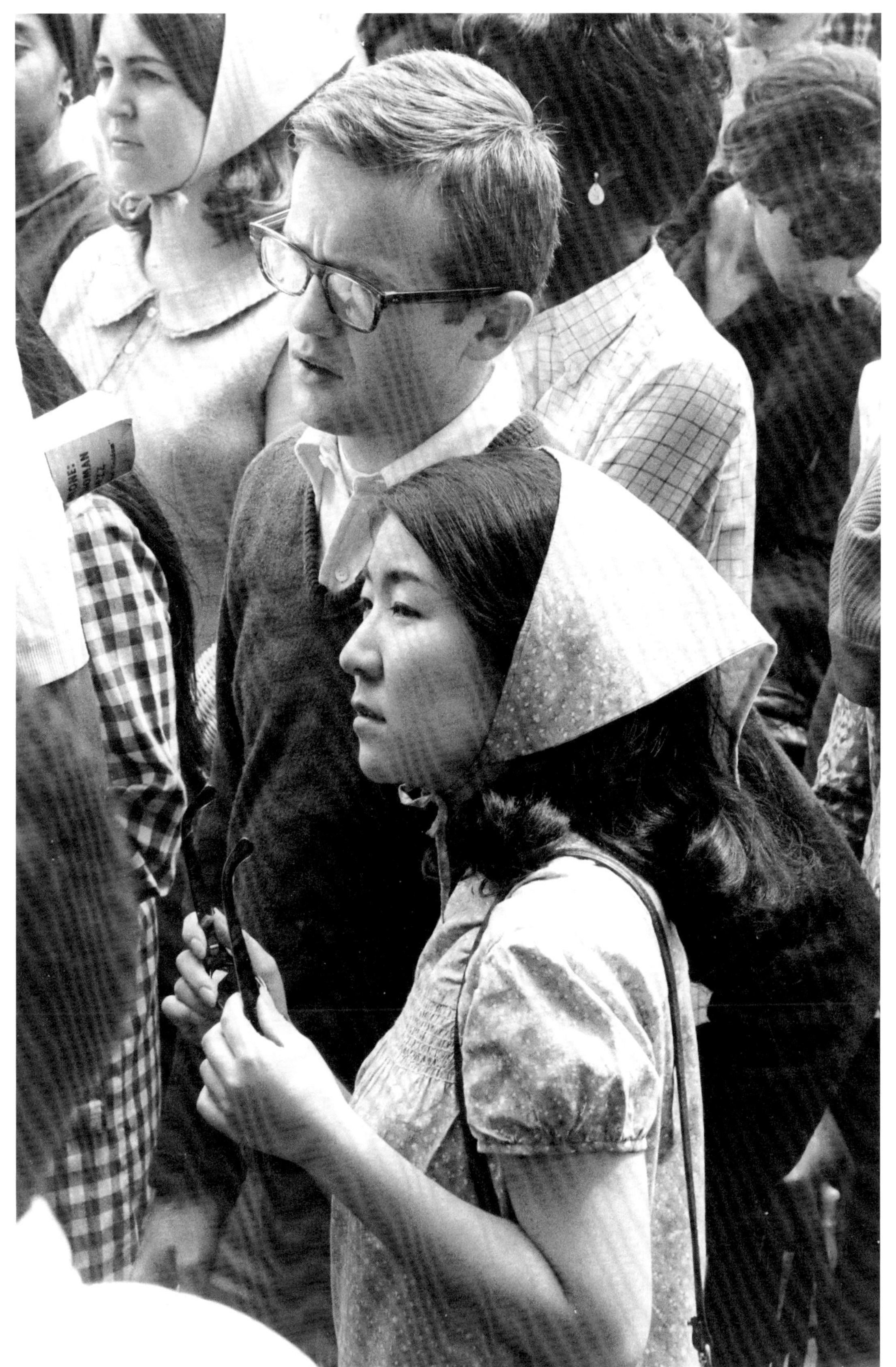

PLATE 80

Bill Goodman, *Nashville Banner*

APRIL 14, 1967

Speakers at the demonstration in the Courthouse Plaza lead the crowd in cheers for black power and condemn police actions during the unrest that occurred in North Nashville the previous week.

Courtesy of the Nashville Public Library, Special Collections

.

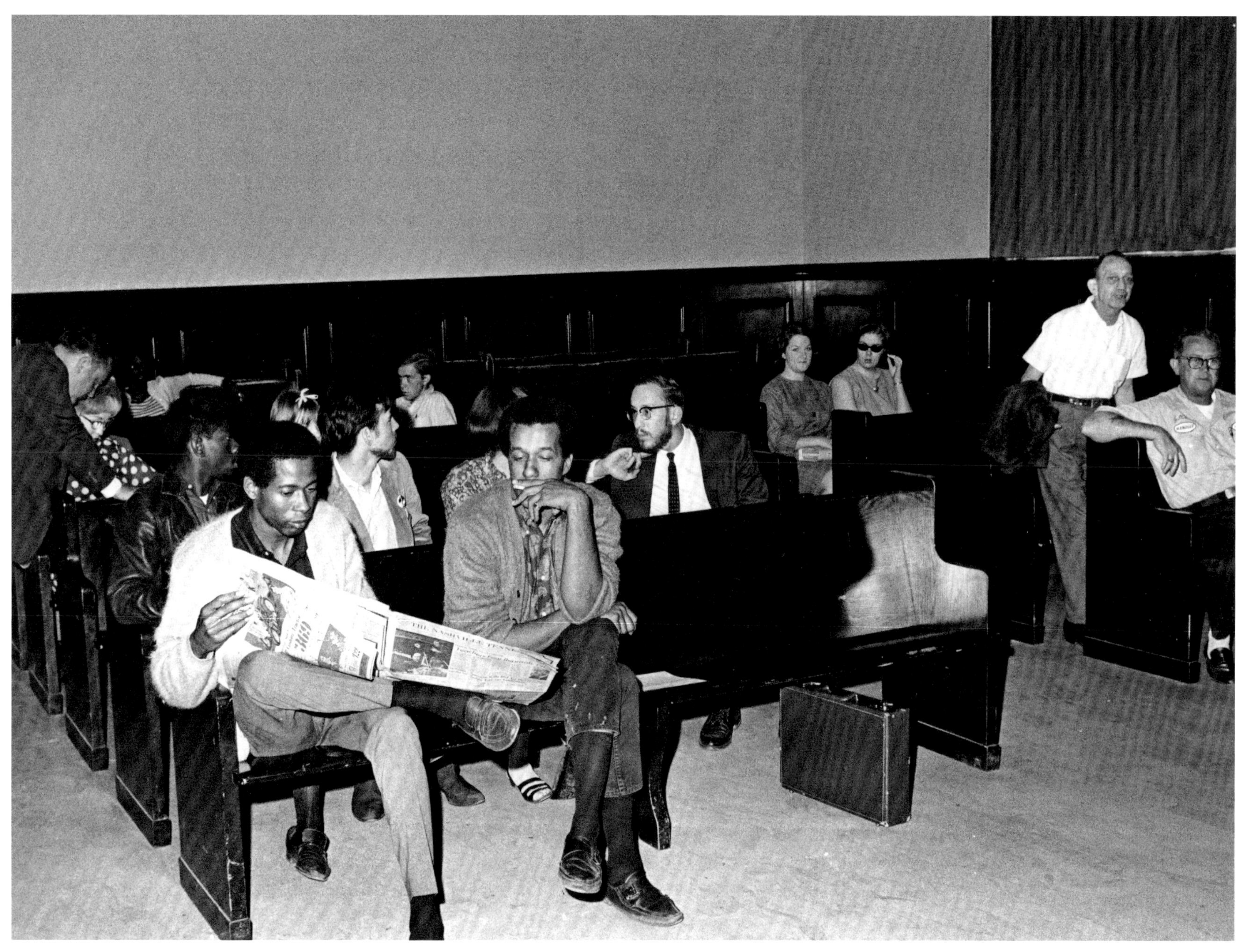

PLATE 81

Vic Cooley, *Nashville Banner*

APRIL 13, 1967

George Washington Ware (front left) and Ernest Stephens (center), two leaders of SNCC, await a court hearing in Nashville on charges of inciting to riot.
Courtesy of the Nashville Public Library, Special Collections

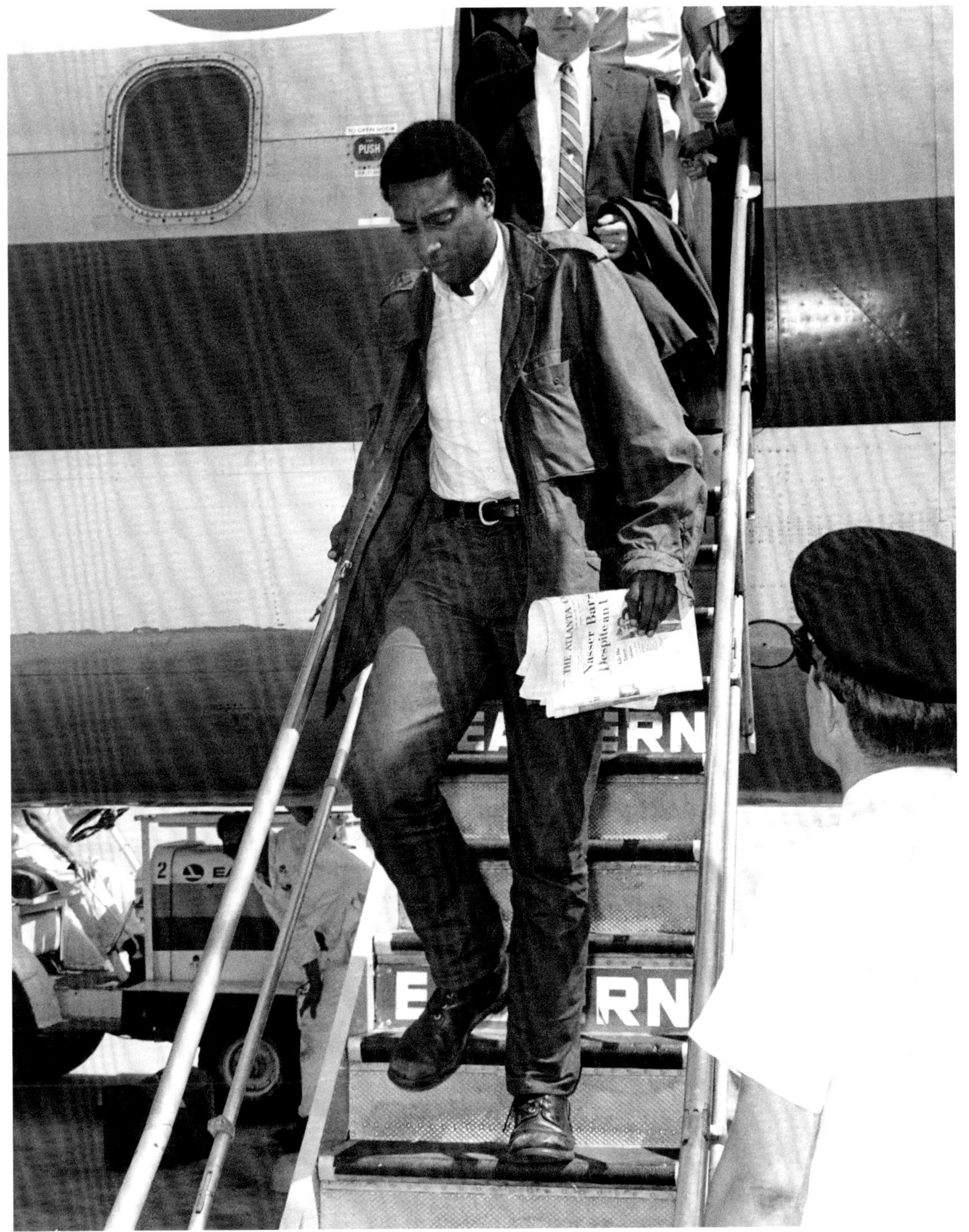

PLATE 82

Bob Ray, *Nashville Banner*

MAY 23, 1967

Stokely Carmichael returns to Nashville to face charges of inciting to riot. Many community leaders, including *Banner* editor James Stahlman, blamed the destruction of property on Carmichael's forceful call for Black Power during speeches at Fisk University and Tennessee A&I in April.

Courtesy of the Nashville Public Library, Special Collections

PLATE 83

Bill Preston, *The Tennessean*

APRIL 5, 1968

A mourner throws up her arms as she sees the body of Dr. Martin Luther King Jr., who had been slain by an assassin at the Lorraine Motel the day before. Mourners in Memphis paid their last respects before the body was flown home to Atlanta.

Courtesy of *The Tennessean*

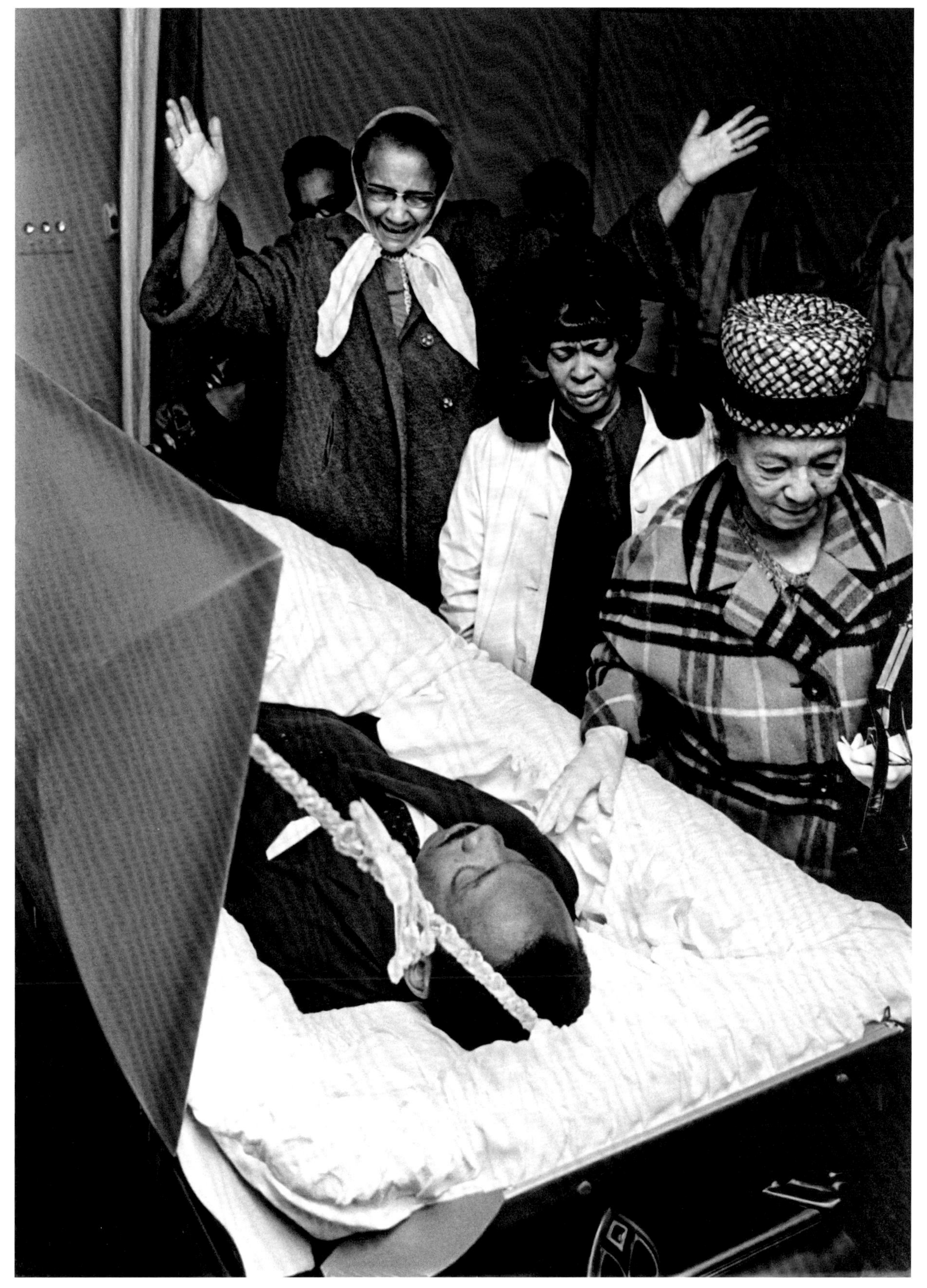

PLATE 84
Bill Preston, *The Tennessean*
April 5, 1968
Ralph Abernathy, successor to King as head of the Southern Christian Leadership Conference, stands at the top of the ramp as the body of the slain civil rights leader is moved onto an Atlanta-bound plane chartered by Senator Robert F. Kennedy.
Courtesy of *The Tennessean*
Printed in the paper on April 6, 1968

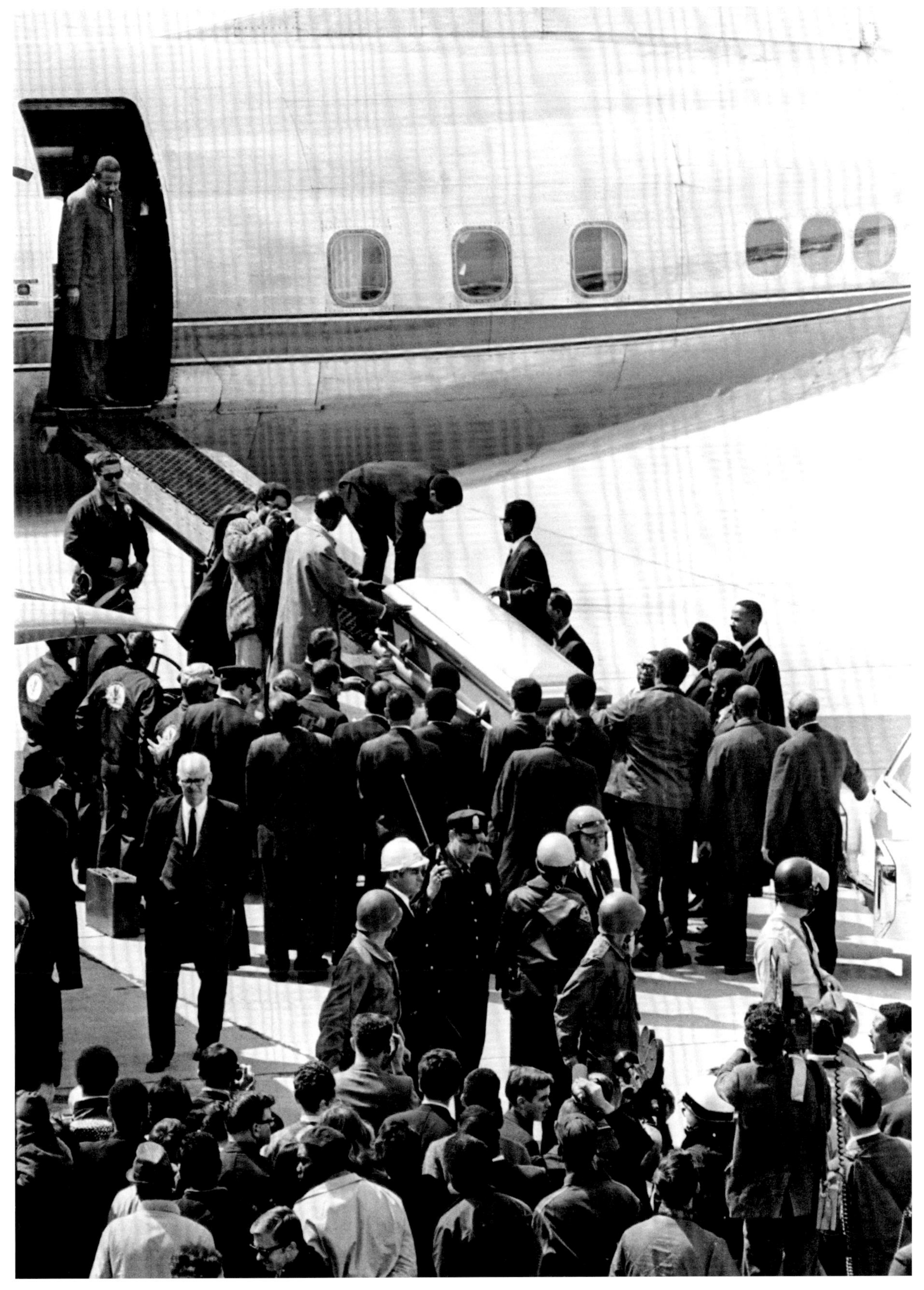

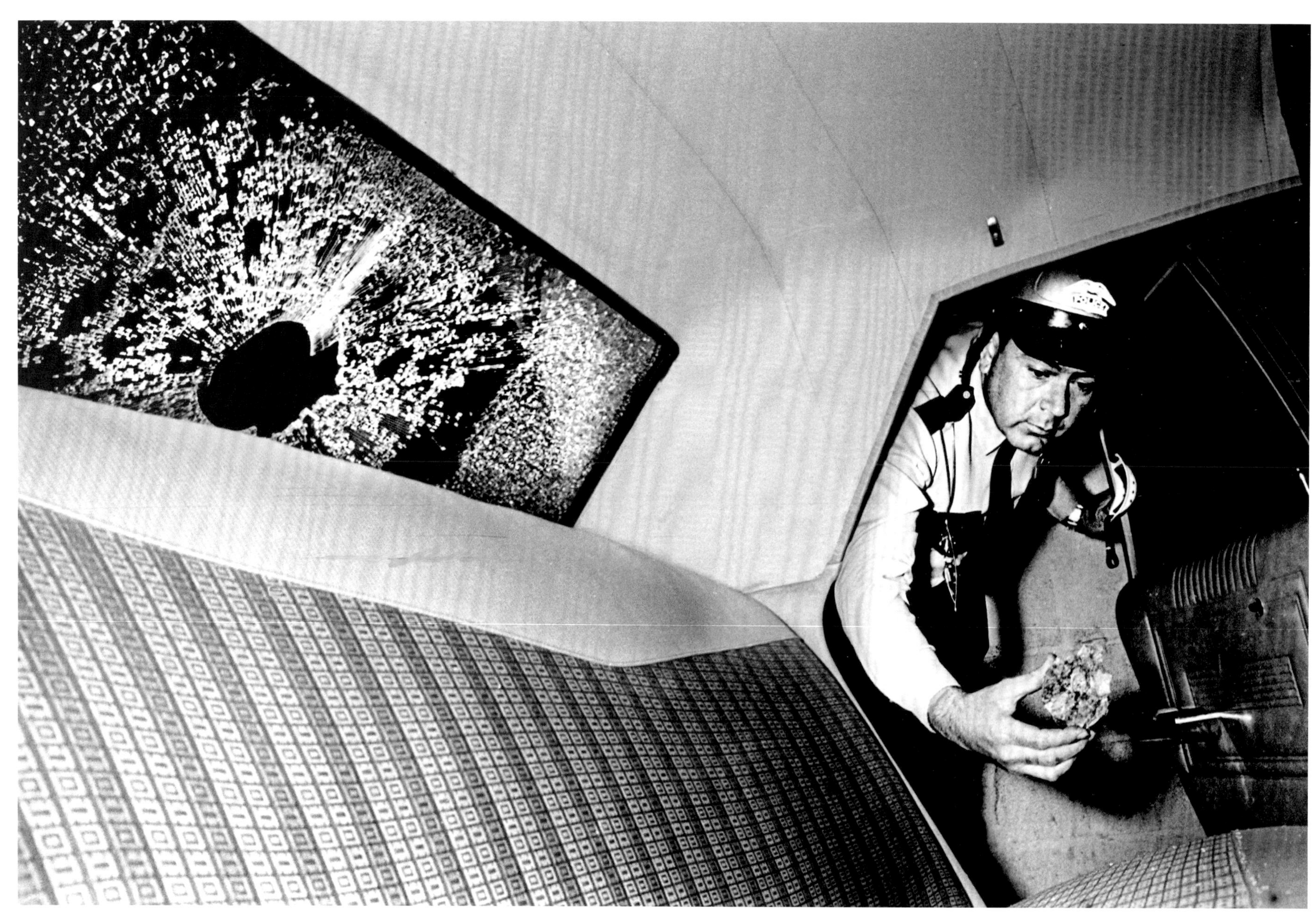

PLATE 85

Jimmy Ellis, *The Tennessean*

APRIL 4, 1968

A Metro Nashville police officer shows the rock that smashed into the back window of his patrol car in North Nashville.

Courtesy of *The Tennessean*

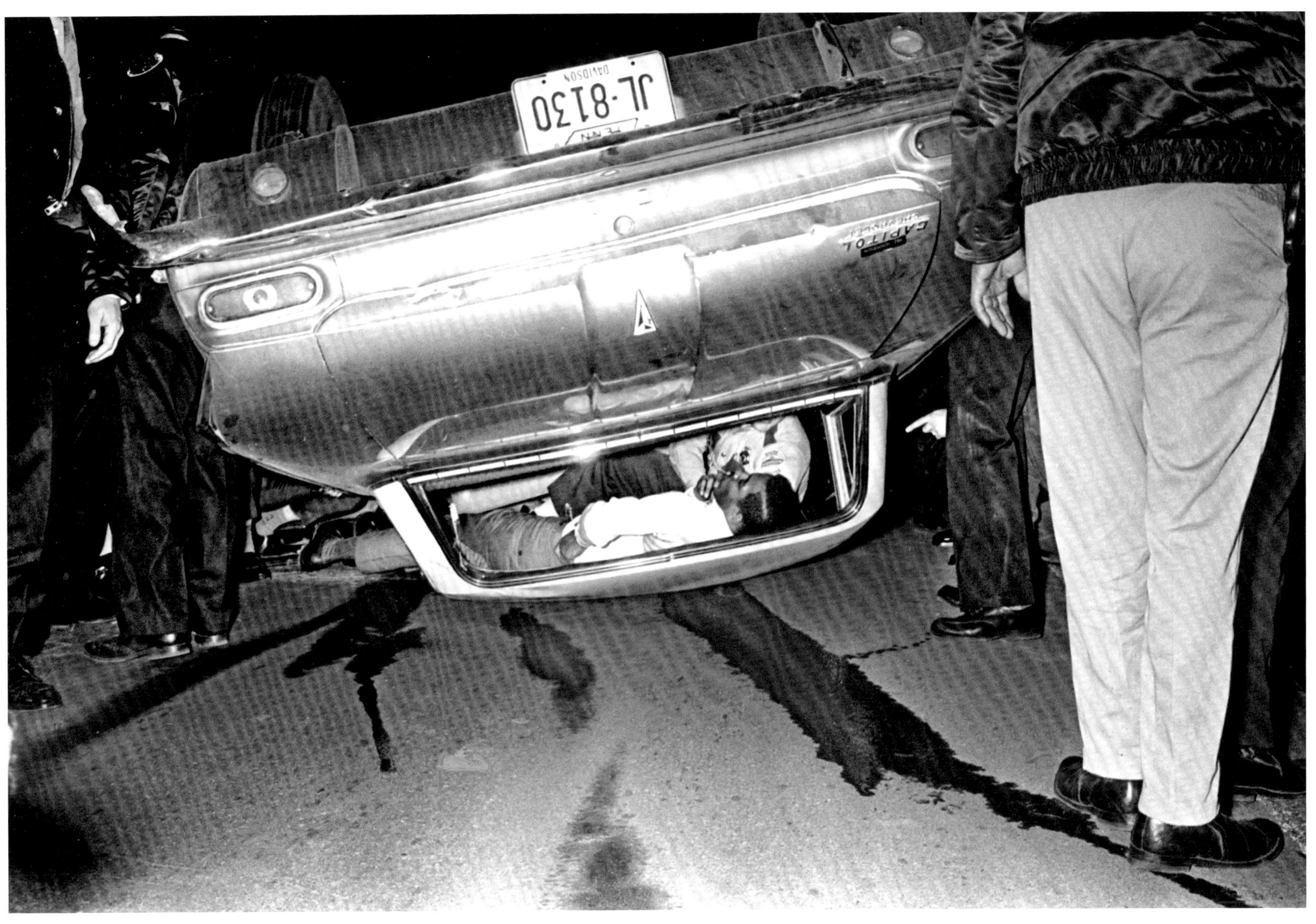

PLATE 86

Jimmy Ellis, *The Tennessean*

APRIL 4, 1968

A Tennessee state trooper aids a person inside an overturned car. Tension escalated in Nashville, as it did in cities throughout the country, just hours after the assassination of Dr. Martin Luther King Jr.

Courtesy of *The Tennessean*

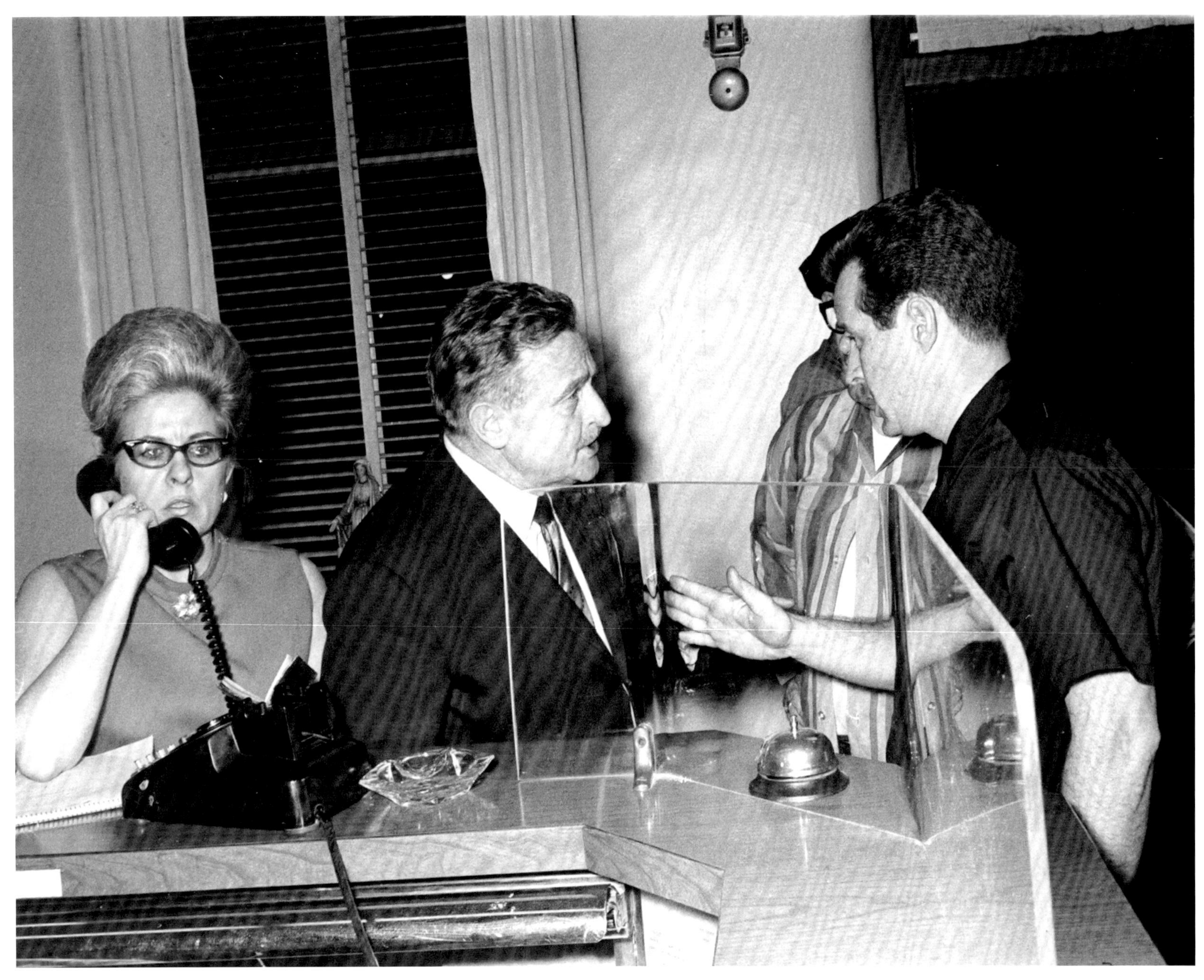

PLATE 87

Charles Warren, *Nashville Banner*

APRIL 5, 1968

On the day after the assassination of Dr. Martin Luther King Jr., Mayor Beverly Briley is briefed on conditions in North Nashville while his secretary, Lavergne Green, receives a report from police headquarters.

Courtesy of the Nashville Public Library, Special Collections

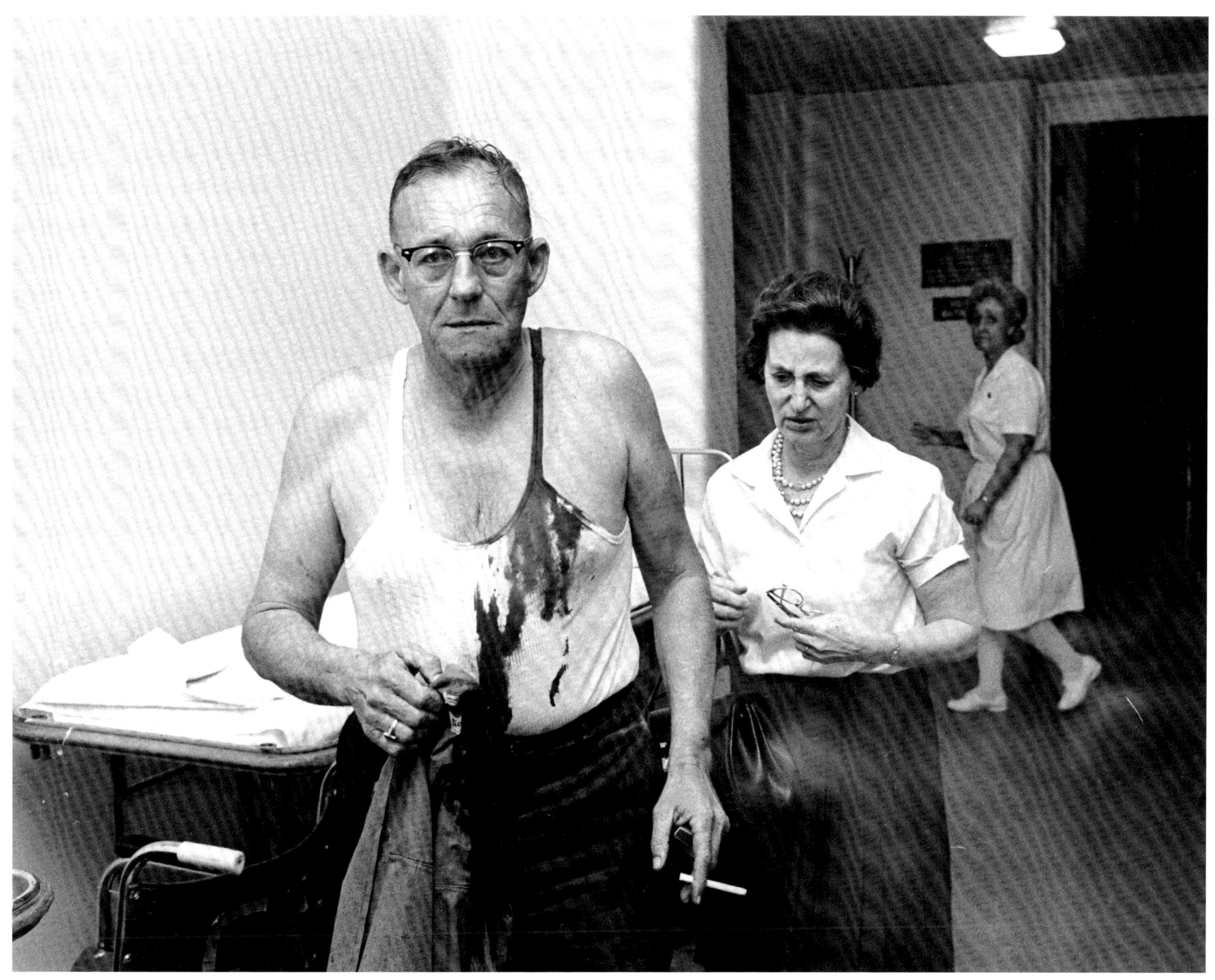

PLATE 88

Charles Warren, *Nashville Banner*

APRIL 5, 1968

T. R. Wienke and his wife had rocks thrown at them as they drove near the Fisk University campus. The rocks destroyed their car's windshield, injuring him in the process.

Courtesy of the Nashville Public Library, Special Collections

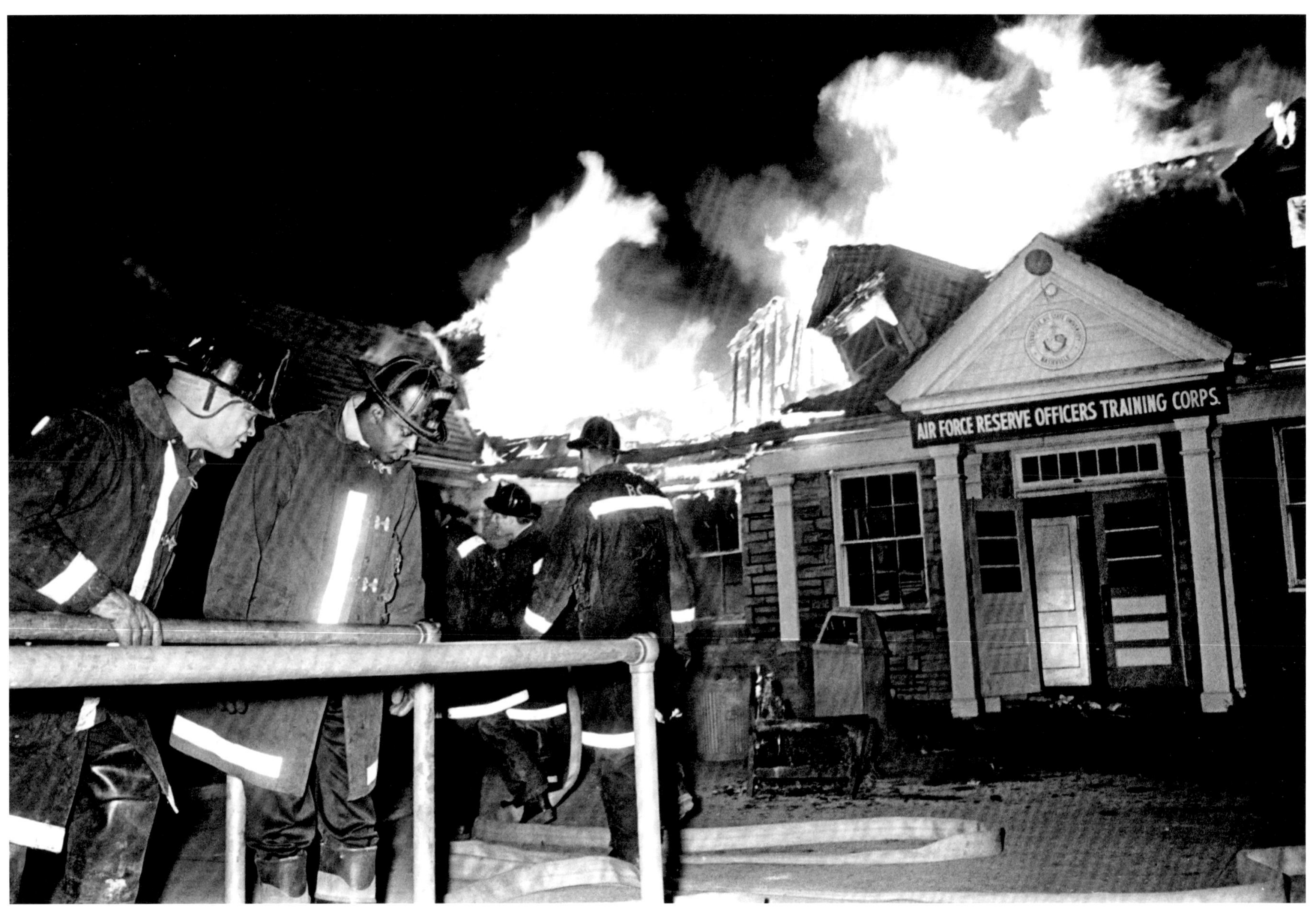

PLATE 89

Jimmy Ellis, *The Tennessean*

APRIL 7, 1968

A fire rages out of control at the Air Force ROTC building on the Tennessee A&I campus.

Courtesy of *The Tennessean*

Printed in the paper on April 9, 1968

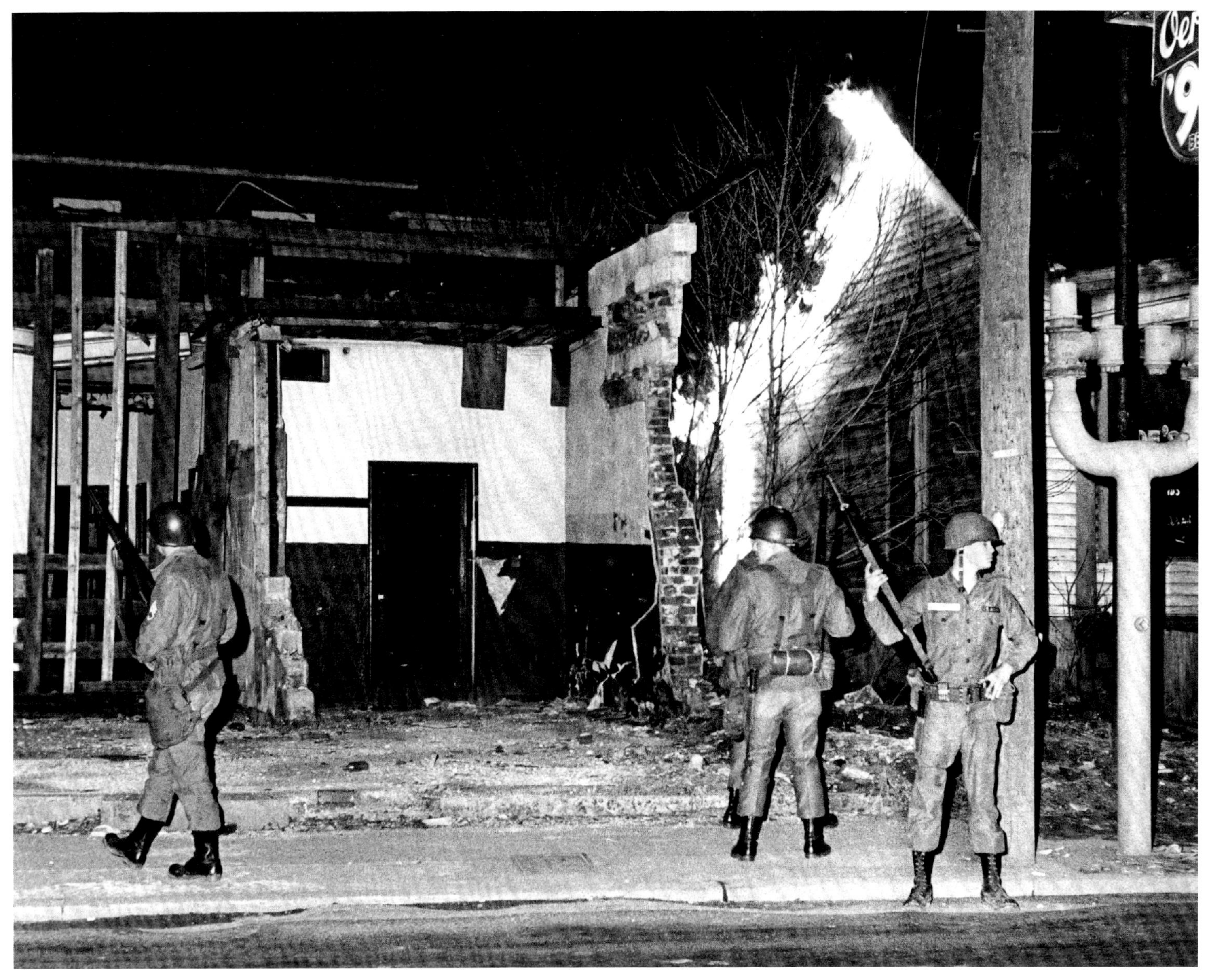

PLATE 90

Jack Gunter, *Nashville Banner*

APRIL 11, 1968

Tennessee National Guard troops take up positions to protect firemen battling a house fire. The guardsmen remained to prevent looting. Courtesy of the Nashville Public Library, Special Collections

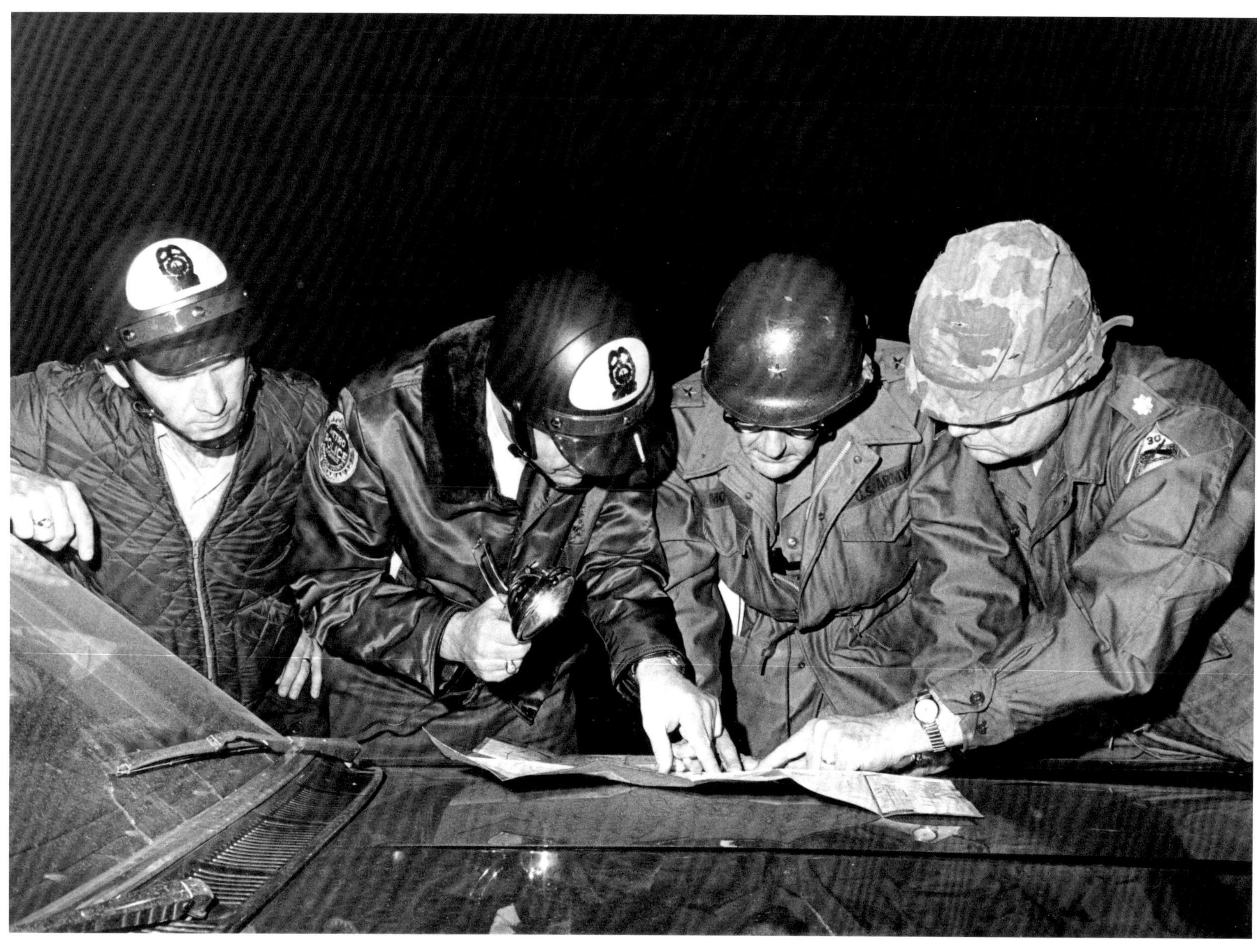

PLATE 91

Vic Cooley, *Nashville Banner*

APRIL 5, 1968

After civil unrest developed following the assassination of King, the National Guard was called to Nashville. Police Major Joe Casey, Brigadier General Hugh Mott, and Lieutenant Colonel William O. Jarris look at a map of the area into which Governor Buford Ellington sent guardsmen earlier that day.

Courtesy of the Nashville Public Library, Special Collections

Printed in the paper on April 5, 1968

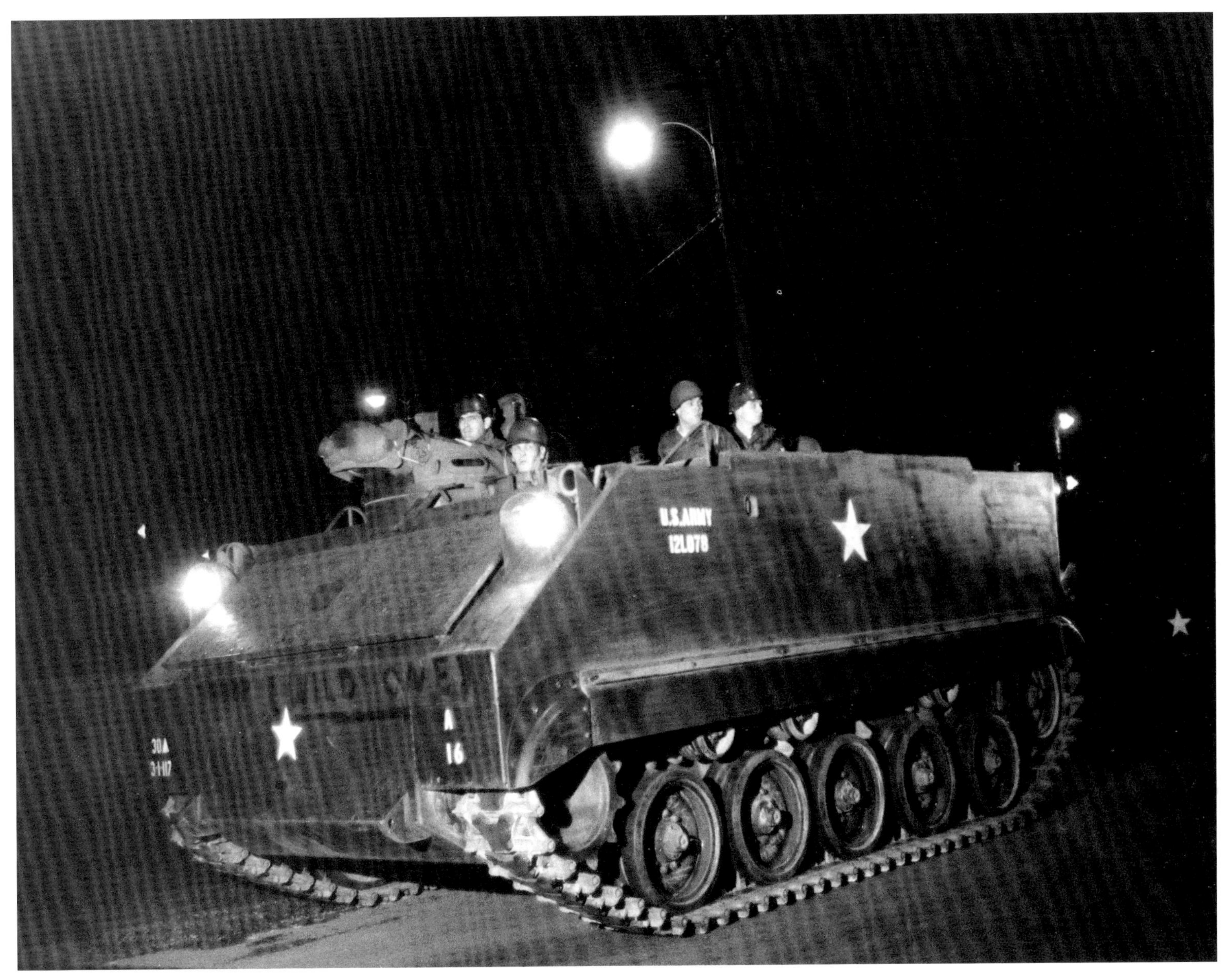

PLATE 92
Vic Cooley, *Nashville Banner*

APRIL 4, 1968

An armored personnel carrier of the Tennessee National Guard moves into the North Nashville area to restore order after a series of rock-throwing and looting incidents broke out the night of King's assassination.
Courtesy of the Nashville Public Library, Special Collections

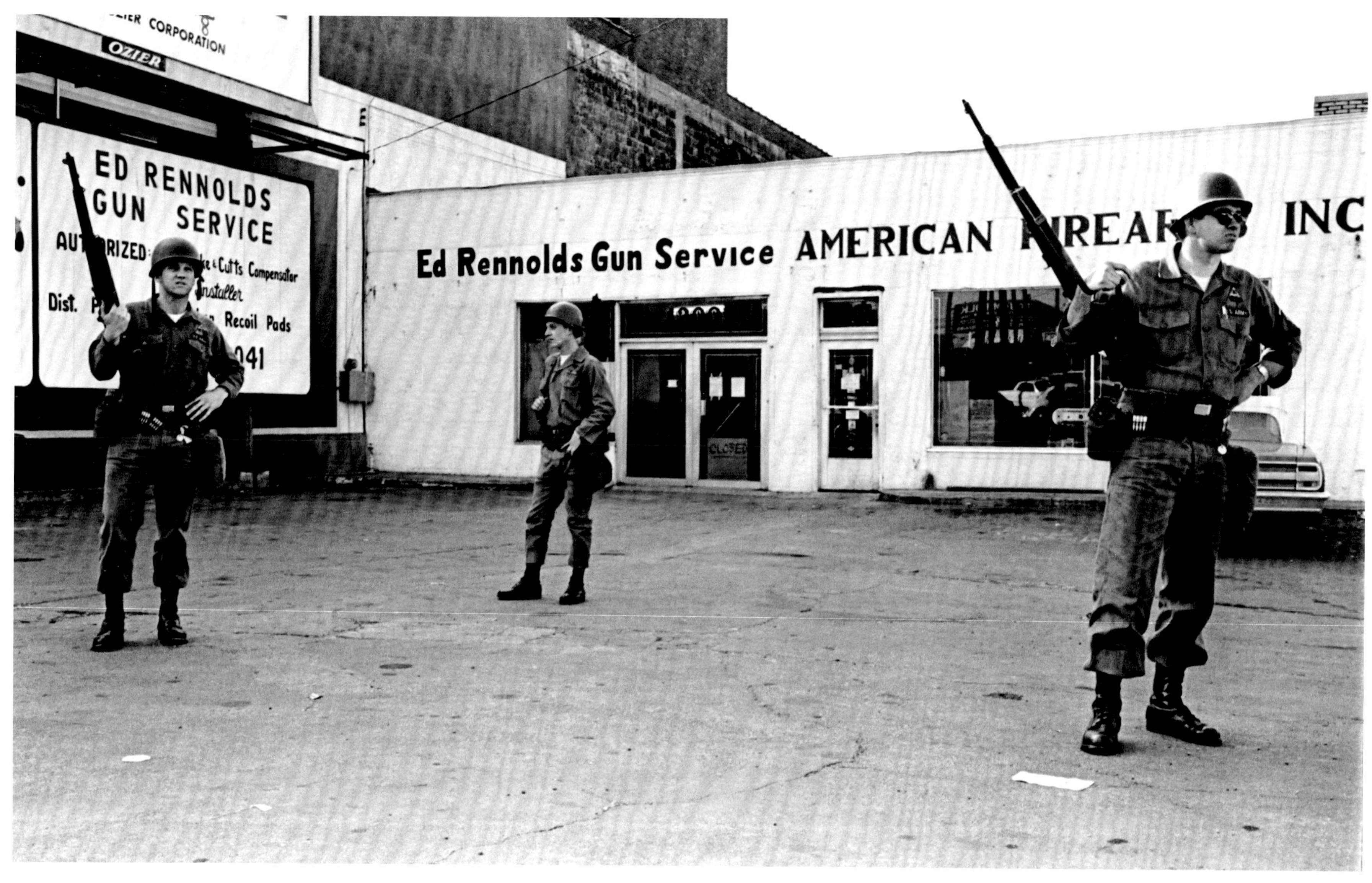

PLATE 93

Robert Johnson, *The Tennessean*

APRIL 6, 1968

Three National Guardsmen stand on duty at Ed Rennolds Gun Service and American Firearms at Broadway and Twelfth Avenue in Nashville. Courtesy of *The Tennessean*

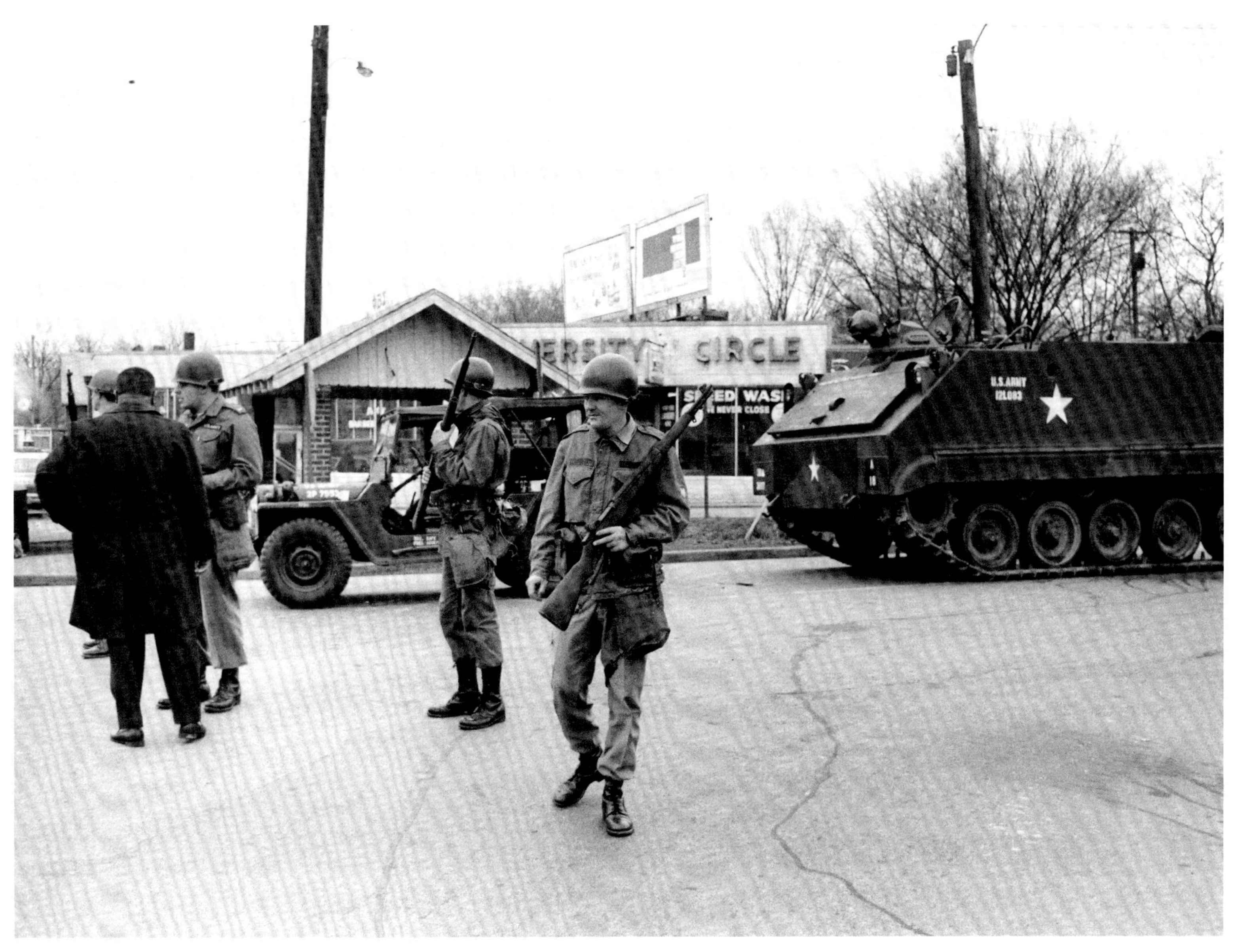

PLATE 94

Bob Ray, *Nashville Banner*

APRIL 5, 1968

National Guardsmen stand their post at Twenty-Eighth Avenue North and Jefferson Street.

Courtesy of the Nashville Public Library, Special Collections

Printed in the paper on April 5, 196

PLATE 95

Frank Empson, *The Tennessean*

APRIL 6, 1968

Two young observers watch a National Guardsman at a checkpoint on the corner of Twenty-Eighth Avenue and Clifton Avenue. Mayor Beverly Briley kept the guardsmen on duty to control the situation in the North Nashville area.

Courtesy of *The Tennessean*

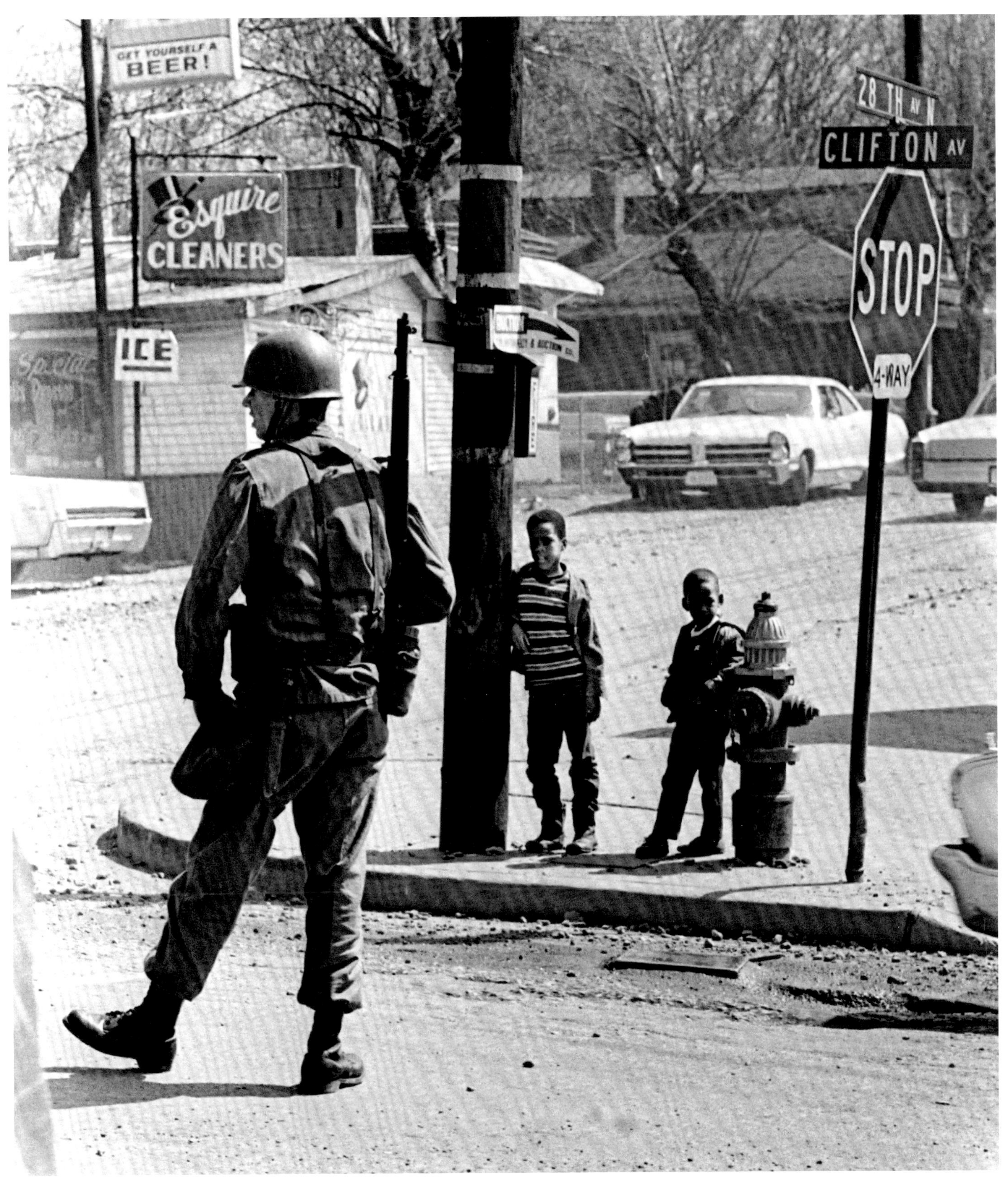
GET YOURSELF A
BEER!
28 TH AV N
CLIFTON AV
Esquire
CLEANERS
ICE
STOP
4-WAY

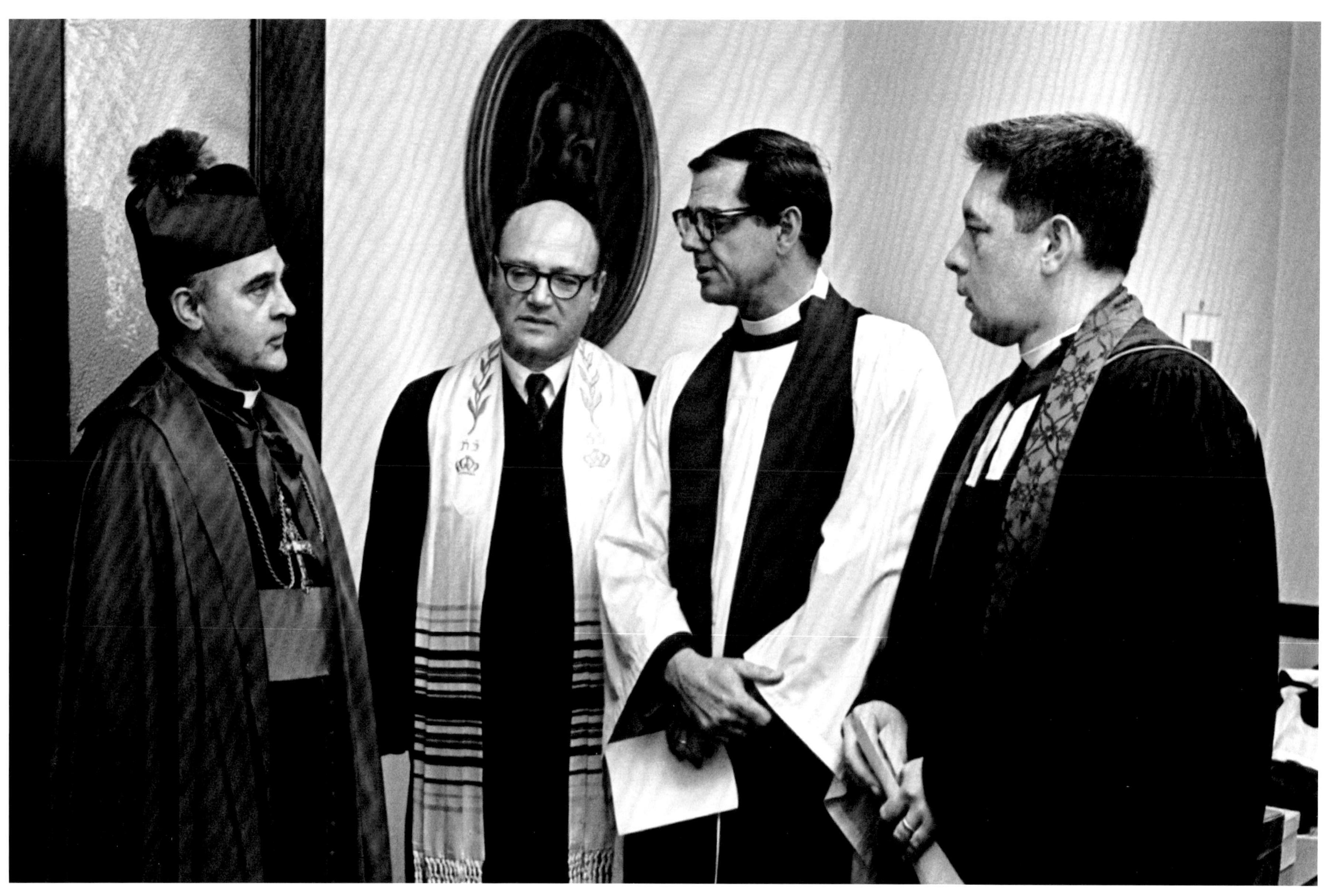

PLATE 96

Frank Empson, *The Tennessean*

APRIL 5, 1968

Clergy of four faiths await the beginning of a memorial service at St. Mary's Catholic Church for Dr. Martin Luther King Jr. From left are Bishop Joseph A. Durick of the Nashville Catholic Diocese, Rabbi Randall Falk of The Temple, the Rev. John Lane Denson of Christ Episcopal Church, and the Rev. D. P. McGeachy III of Westminster Presbyterian Church.
Courtesy of *The Tennessean*

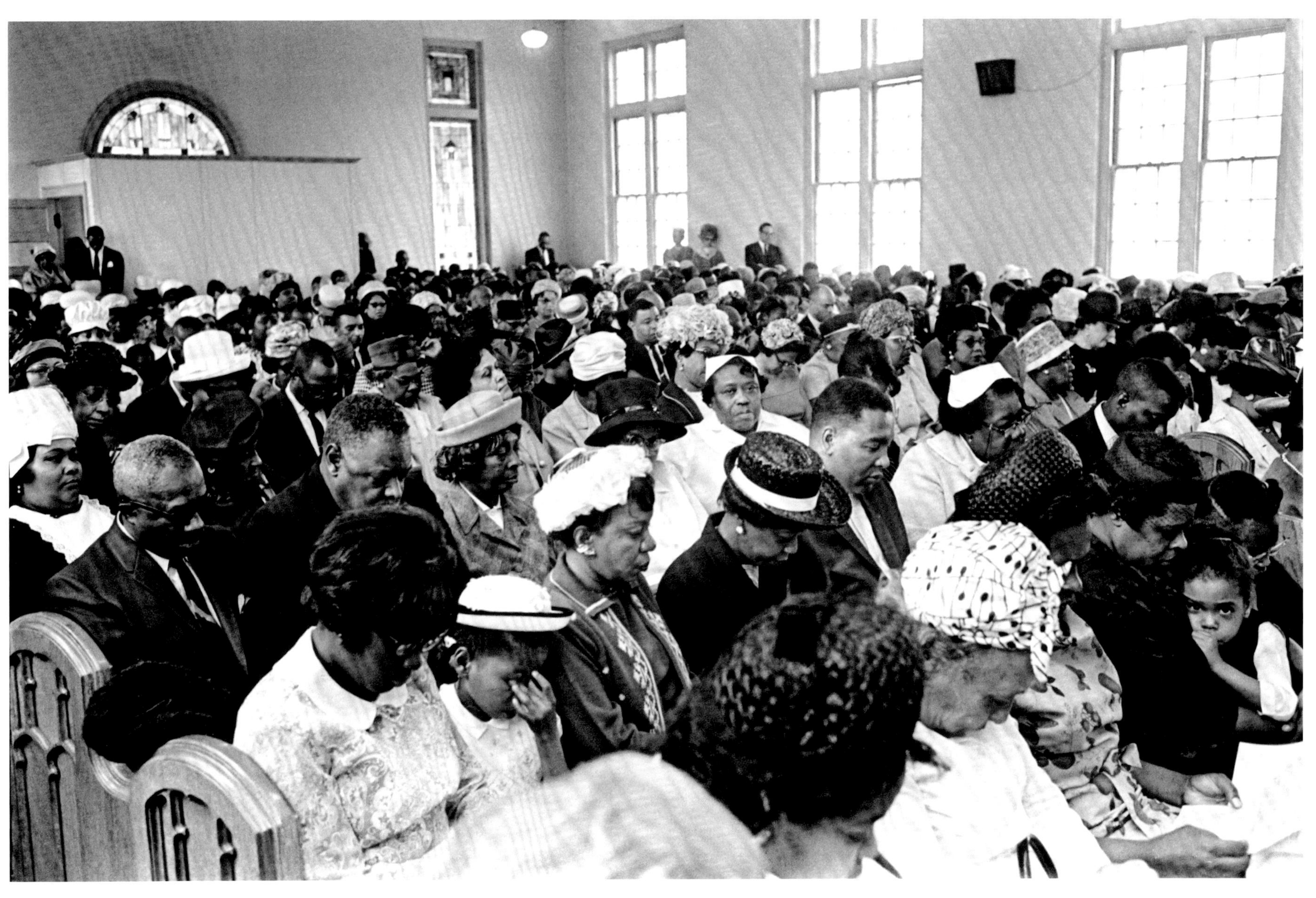

PLATE 97

Frank Empson, *The Tennessean*

APRIL 7, 1968

A packed house of 1,500 people pray during an interracial, interdenominational memorial service for King at the Gordon Memorial Church in North Nashville. Courtesy of *The Tennessean*

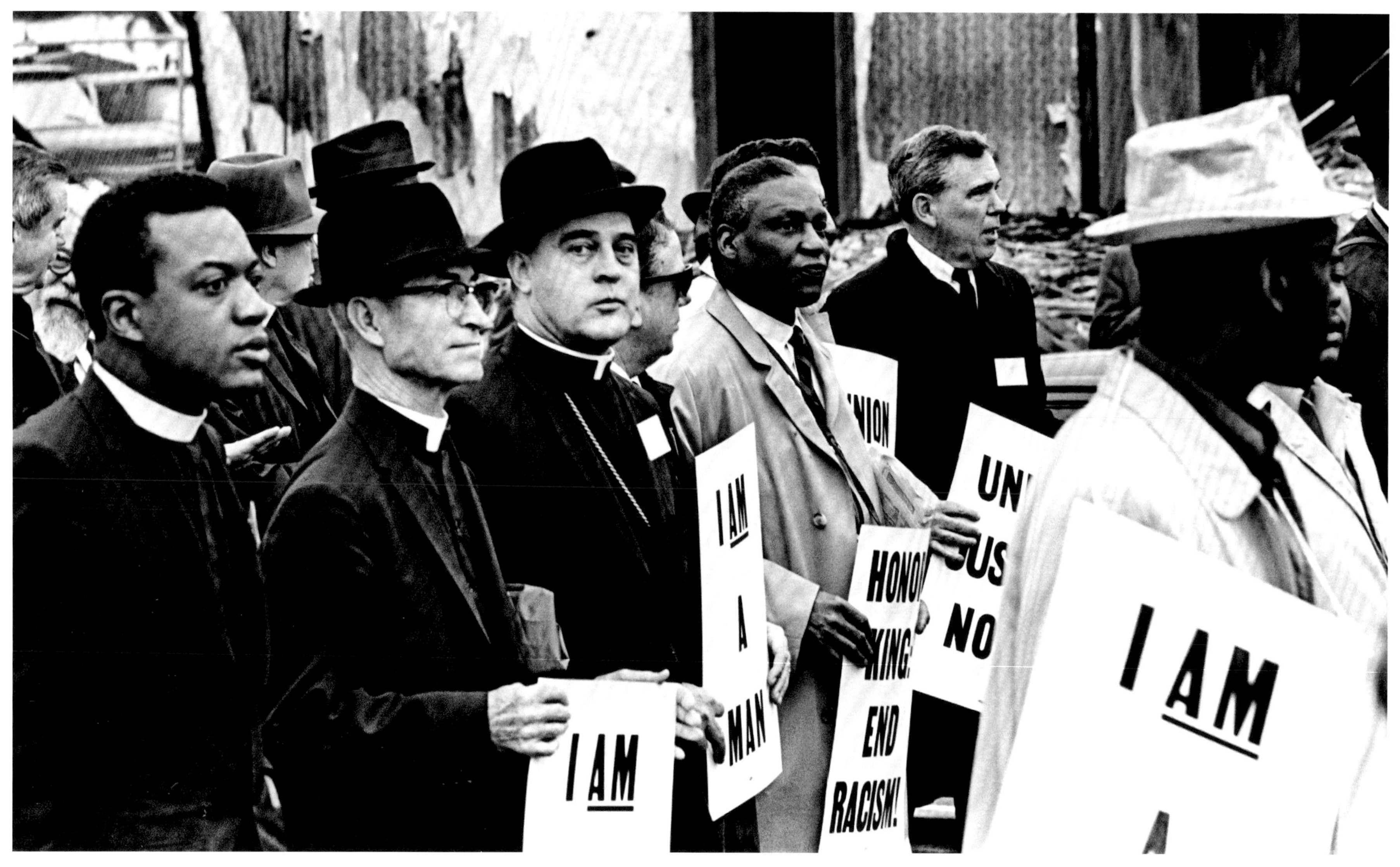

PLATE 98

Bill Preston, *The Tennessean*

APRIL 8, 1968

Bishop Joseph A. Durick (third from left) is one of forty-two thousand participants in a silent march of mourning for the civil rights leader in the streets of Memphis. Bishop Durick, apostolic administrator for the Diocese of Nashville, was one of the speakers at the three-hour rally after the march.

Courtesy of *The Tennessean*

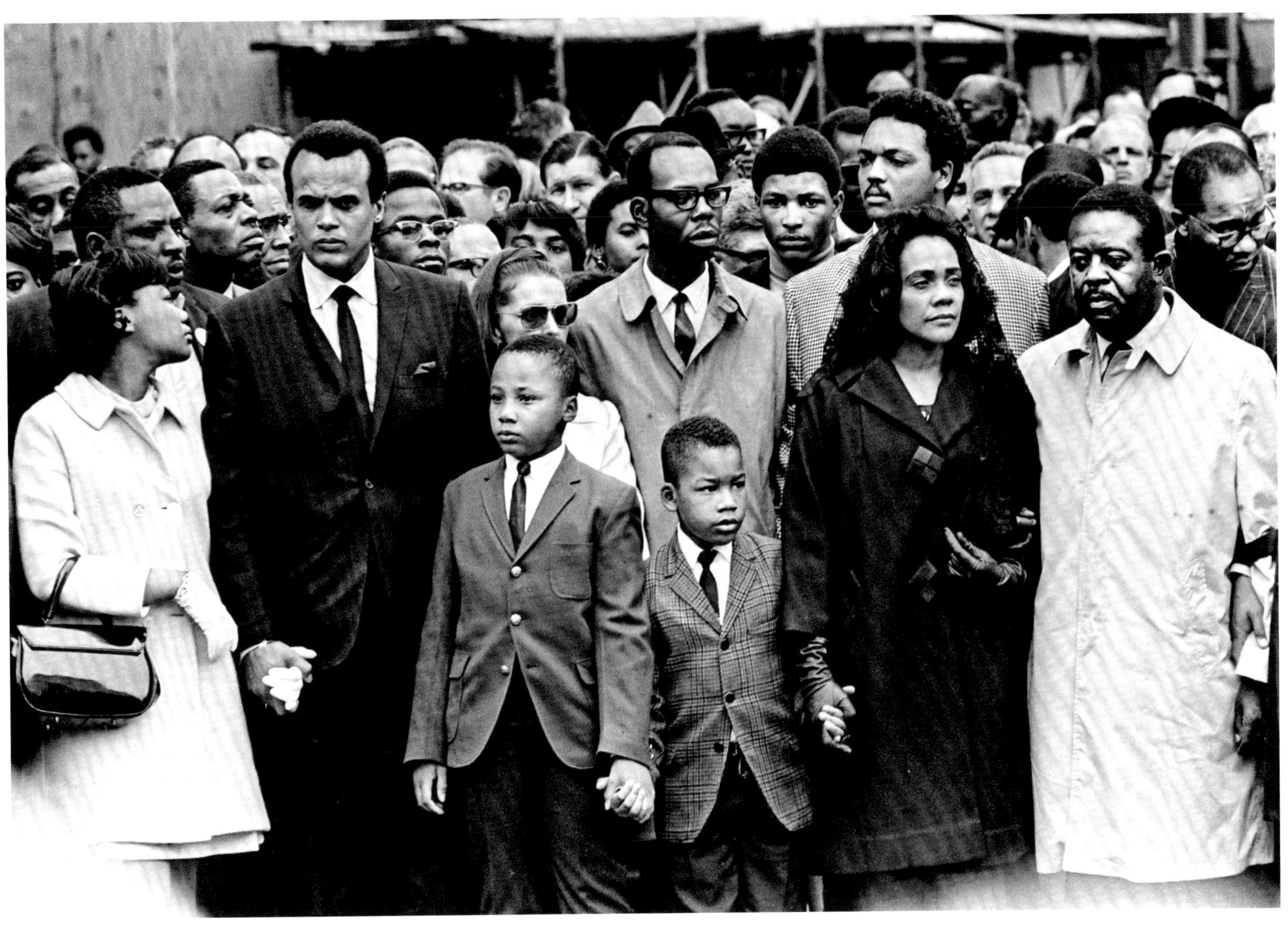

PLATE 99

Bill Preston, *The Tennessean*

APRIL 8, 1968

Mourners get ready for a silent march from Clayborn Temple, in the black section of Memphis, to city hall. From left to right: Yolanda King, Harry Belafonte, Martin Luther King III, Dexter King, Coretta Scott King, and the Reverend Ralph Abernathy, the successor to King. The Reverend Jesse Jackson stands behind the widow.
Courtesy of *The Tennessean*

PLATE 100

Bob Ray, *Nashville Banner*

APRIL 6, 1968

National Guardsmen, some with fixed bayonets on their rifles, surround the Tennessee State Capitol in case violence erupts there.

Courtesy of the Nashville Public Library, Special Collections

A very similar image was printed in both papers on April 6, 1968

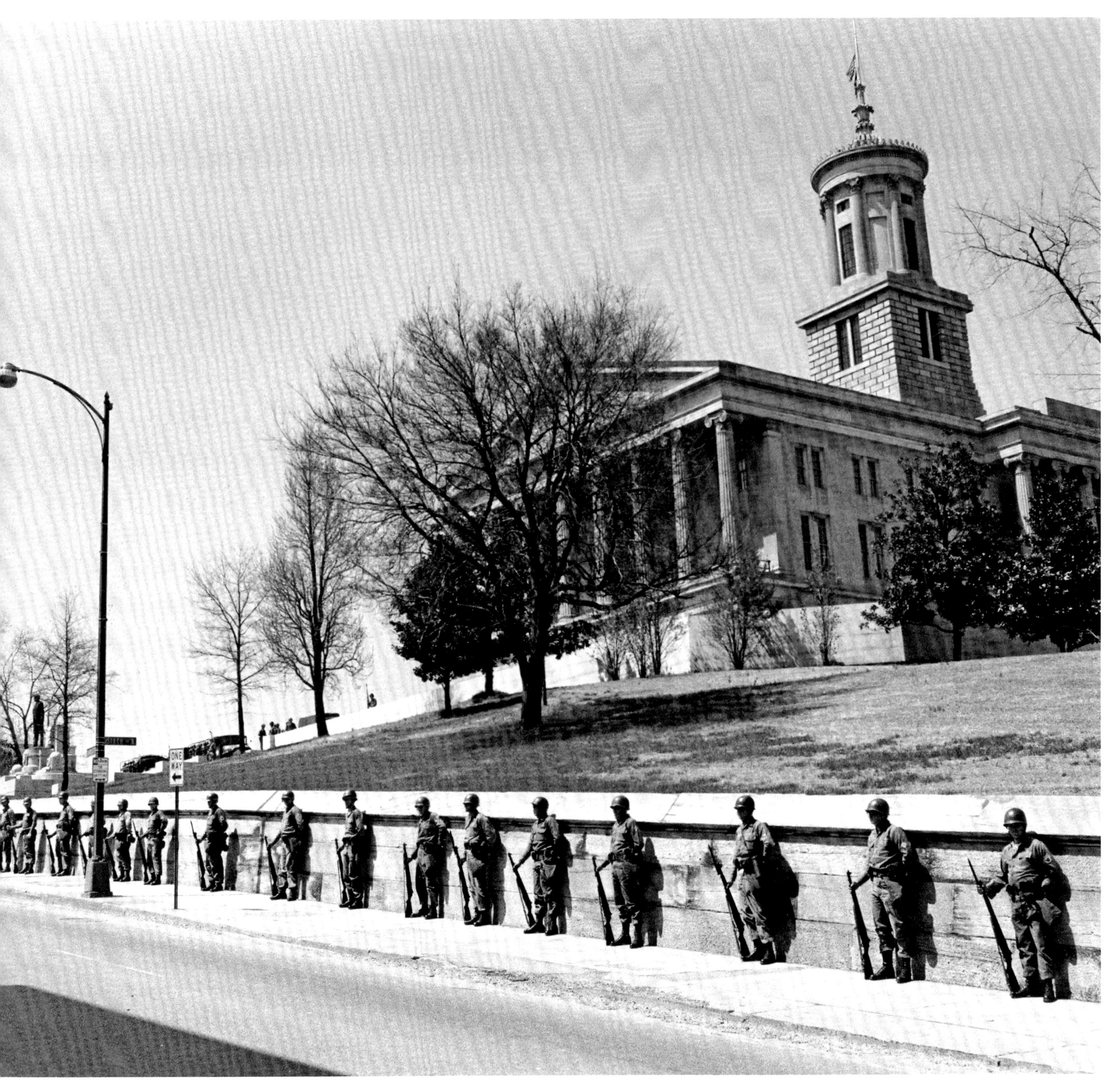
ONE
WAY

TIMELINE

Text in gray boxes indicates events that happened in Nashville.

1954

May 17 — The US Supreme Court rules unanimously in *Brown v. Board of Education of Topeka* that racial segregation in public schools is unconstitutional.

1955

July 23–August 3 — Highlander Folk School in Monteagle, Tennessee, sponsors a summer workshop on public school desegregation, which is attended by Rosa Parks of Montgomery, Alabama.

August 28 — Fourteen-year-old Emmett Till is kidnapped and murdered in Money, Mississippi, for allegedly whistling at a white woman.

September 23 — **A. Z. Kelley and twenty-one other black plaintiffs file suit on behalf of their children to end segregation in Nashville public schools.**

December 1 — Rosa Parks is arrested in Montgomery when she refuses to give up her seat on a bus to a white man. The resulting boycott of the bus system lasts for 381 days.

1956

March 12 — Only three of twenty-two senators from former Confederate states refuse to sign the Southern Manifesto, a declaration of defiance of the *Brown* decision: Estes Kefauver and Albert Gore Sr. of Tennessee and Lyndon B. Johnson of Texas.

December 21 — The US Supreme Court outlaws segregated seating, and the Montgomery bus boycott ends.

1957

January 10 — The Southern Christian Leadership Conference (SCLC) is founded, with a young Baptist minister, Dr. Martin Luther King Jr., as its first president.

January 21 — **Courts approve the Nashville Board of Education's plan to desegregate schools at the rate of one grade per year. The "Nashville Plan" is soon copied by other school systems in the South.**

September 4 — Governor Orval Faubus calls on the Arkansas National Guard to prevent nine black students from entering Central High School in Little Rock.

September 9 — **Nineteen black first-graders enter eight formerly all-white schools as Nashville becomes the first city in the South to successfully begin the desegregation process for a public education system.**

September 10 — **At approximately 12:30 a.m. a dynamite blast destroys the east wing of Hattie Cotton School in East Nashville.**

September 23–25 — President Dwight D. Eisenhower calls on federal troops to protect the "Little Rock Nine" as they enter Central High School.

1958

January **James Lawson arrives in Nashville to enroll as a graduate student at Vanderbilt University Divinity School.**

June **The Nashville Christian Leadership Conference is organized as an affiliate of the Southern Christian Leadership Conference and becomes the umbrella organization under which the city's nonviolent civil rights strategies will be shaped.**

September Governor Faubus and the Arkansas legislature close all of Little Rock's public high schools. They remain closed until the fall of 1959.

1959

November **James Lawson begins workshops on nonviolent protest at First Baptist Church, Capitol Hill.**

November and December **The first test sit-ins take place at several downtown Nashville lunch counters.**

1960

February 1 Four freshmen at North Carolina A&T State College stage a sit-in at the Woolworth lunch counter in downtown Greensboro.

February 13 **The first large-scale sit-ins take place in Nashville as more than one hundred protesters from four local historically black colleges converge on downtown lunch counters.**

February 27 **More than four hundred young people take part in a mass sit-in. Many are assaulted; eighty-one are arrested.**

March **Black community leaders announce plans for an economic boycott of downtown Nashville stores, coinciding with the pre-Easter shopping season.**

March 3 **Vanderbilt University trustees expel James Lawson for his participation in the local civil rights movement. Most divinity school faculty members resign in support of Lawson.**

March 4 **James Lawson is arrested for conspiring to violate the state's trade and commerce law.**

March 25 **CBS television prepares a special news report on the Nashville sit-in movement titled "Anatomy of a Demonstration."**

April 1 Highlander Folk School holds a workshop attended by participants in the sit-ins. Folk singer Guy Carawan and others teach them new words to an old song and rename it "We Shall Overcome."

April 17 At Shaw University in Raleigh, North Carolina, young civil rights activists organize the Student Nonviolent Coordinating Committee (SNCC).

April 19 **A predawn bomb explodes at the home of civil rights attorney and city council member Z. Alexander Looby and his wife.**

As many as four thousand demonstrators march in silent protest to the county courthouse, where Mayor Ben West agrees that Nashville's downtown lunch counters should be desegregated.

April 20 **Dr. King speaks at Fisk University: "I came to Nashville not to bring inspiration, but to gain inspiration from the great movement that has taken place in this community."**

May 6 **Negotiators for both sides in the Nashville sit-in dispute agree on a detailed plan that calls for small groups of African Americans to sit at lunch counters and be served on May 10, without public announcement or news coverage until after the fact.**

May 10 **Lunch counters are desegregated without incident. Nashville becomes the first major city in the South to permit white and black customers to eat together openly in public places.**

September 2 and 3 — Wilma Rudolph, a native of Clarksville, Tennessee, wins three gold medals at the Rome Olympics.

December 20 — **NBC television news broadcasts *White Paper #2*, "Sit-In." This fifty-six-minute news program presents the Nashville student sit-in movement to a national audience.**

1961

January 20 — John F. Kennedy is sworn in as the thirty-fifth president of the United States.

May 4 — Members of various civil rights groups under the direction of James Farmer and the Congress for Racial Equality (CORE) begin an interstate bus trip through the South to test desegregation of public transportation and accommodations.

May 14 — The Freedom Riders are attacked in bus stations in Anniston and Birmingham, Alabama. One of the buses is firebombed six miles outside of Anniston.

May 17 — **Under the leadership of Diane Nash, Nashville students travel to Birmingham to continue the Freedom Rides after the original riders are forced to abort the journey. The Nashville students are quickly arrested.**

May 19 — **Notorious commissioner of public safety Bull Connor drives the Nashville students to the Tennessee state line where he drops them off. Diane Nash orchestrates transportation for the riders back to Birmingham.**

May 20 — **After tense negotiations between Attorney General Robert Kennedy and Alabama governor John Patterson, facilitated by John Seigenthaler, the second group of riders, most of them from Nashville, leaves Birmingham for Montgomery under the promise of protection by the state. The riders and Seigenthaler are brutally attacked at the Montgomery bus stop.**

May 21 — Robert Kennedy sends federal marshals to Montgomery.

May 24 — The Freedom Riders leave Montgomery for Mississippi. There is no more violence, but they are arrested at the Jackson bus stop. They eventually spend sixty days in Parchman State Penitentiary. Throughout the summer, reinforcements arrive and the Freedom Rides continue.

June — **Tennessee governor Buford Ellington expels fourteen student Freedom Riders from Tennessee A&I State University.**

June 16, 1961 — Robert Kennedy meets with student leaders of the Civil Rights Movement and urges them to focus on voter registration projects.

1962

September 30 — James Meredith registers at the University of Mississippi, thereby integrating the previously all-white school.

1963

May 3 — Police respond to street protests involving many high school students in Birmingham with attack dogs and fire hoses. Photographs from the incident are seen around the world and spark outrage at the brutality.

June 13 — Medgar Evers, president of the Mississippi NAACP, is killed in the doorway of his Jackson home.

August 28 — About a quarter of a million people participate in the March on Washington for Jobs and Freedom, where Dr. King delivers his "I Have a Dream" speech.

September 15 — A bomb explodes on this Sunday morning at the Sixteenth Street Baptist Church in Birmingham, killing four young girls and wounding twenty-one others.

November 22 — President Kennedy is assassinated in Dallas when a sniper fires on his motorcade.

1964

Freedom Summer	Civil rights groups launch a massive voter registration drive in Mississippi, staffed by hundreds of young volunteers.
June 21	Three civil rights workers—James Chaney, Andrew Goodman, and Michael Schwerner—are reported missing in Philadelphia, Mississippi. Their bodies are found six weeks later.
July 2	The Civil Rights Act of 1964 is signed into law by President Lyndon B. Johnson.
December 10	Dr. King is awarded the Nobel Peace Prize for his leadership of the nonviolent Civil Rights Movement in the United States.

1965

February 21	American black nationalist leader Malcolm X is assassinated in New York City.
March 7	Marchers in support of voting rights, led by John Lewis and Hosea Williams, are attacked by police and troopers at the Edmund Pettus Bridge in Selma, Alabama.
March 22–25	The Selma to Montgomery March takes place.
August 6	The Voting Rights Act is signed into law by President Johnson.
August 11–16	A major riot that began with an incident between police and a young black man spreads through the Watts section of Los Angeles.

1966

March 19	**Nashville's Pearl High School wins the state boys' basketball championship in the first year of integrated high school athletic competition in Tennessee.**
May 16	SNCC leaders choose Stokely Carmichael to replace John Lewis as chair of the increasingly militant organization.
June	John Lewis resigns from SNCC.
June 6	While on a solitary "March against Fear" from Memphis to Jackson, James Meredith is shot and seriously wounded. As supporters continue the march, Stokely Carmichael coins the term "black power."
October 1	In Oakland, California, Huey P. Newton and Bobby Seale form a black nationalist group called the Black Panther Party for Self-Defense.

1967

April 7–8	**Dr. King and Stokely Carmichael are featured speakers at Vanderbilt University's annual Impact Symposium.**
April 8	**Violence breaks out in north Nashville and continues for three nights.**
April 10	**George Ware and Ernest Stephans of SNCC are arrested for inciting to riot. Stokely Carmichael, not at the scene, is later charged with the same crime.**
June 5	**John Lewis graduates from Fisk University, earning a BA in religion and philosophy.**
Summer	Race riots erupt in more than one hundred cities, including Detroit and Newark.
October 2	Thurgood Marshall becomes the first black justice of the Supreme Court.

1968

April 3	Dr. King addresses participants in a sanitation workers' strike in Memphis.
April 4	Dr. King is assassinated by a sniper at the Lorraine Motel. James Earl Ray pleads guilty and is sentenced to life in prison.
April 8	Coretta Scott King and SCLC members lead a silent march in Memphis. Forty-two thousand people participate.

Adapted from the timeline in the Civil Rights Room at the Nashville Public Library, Main Branch

FURTHER READING

Albert, Peter J., and Ronald Hoffman, eds. *We Shall Overcome*. New York: Da Capo Press, 1990.

Allen, Ivan, Jr., and Paul Hemphill. *Mayor: Notes on the Sixties*. New York: Simon and Schuster, 1971.

Arsenault, Raymond. *Freedom Riders: 1961 and the Struggle for Racial Justice*. New York: Oxford University Press, 2006.

Ashmore, Harry S. *Civil Rights and Wrongs: A Memoir of Race and Politics, 1944–1996*. Columbia: University of South Carolina Press, 1997.

Associated Press and David Halberstam. *Breaking News: How the Associated Press Has Covered War, Peace, and Everything Else*. New York: Princeton Architectural Press, 2007.

Bailey, Ronald W., and Michèle Furst, eds. *Let Us March On! Selected Civil Rights Photographs of Ernest C. Withers, 1955–1968*. Boston: Massachusetts College of Art, 1992.

Baldwin, Frederick C., photographer. *Freedom's March: Photographs of the Civil Rights Movement in Savannah by Frederick C. Baldwin*. Savannah: Telfair Books, 2008.

Baldwin, James. *The Fire Next Time*. New York: Dial Press, 1963.

Bass, Amy. *Not the Triumph, but the Struggle: The 1968 Olympics and the Making of the Black Athlete*. Minneapolis: University of Minnesota Press, 2002.

Beals, Melba Patillo. *Warriors Don't Cry: A Searing Memoir of the Battle to Integrate Little Rock's Central High*. New York: Washington Square Press, 1994.

Belfrage, Sally. *Freedom Summer*. Charlottesville: University Press of Virginia, 1990.

Bell, Janet Dewart. *Lighting the Fires of Freedom: African American Women in the Civil Rights Movement*. New York: The New Press, 2018.

Berger, Martin A. *Seeing through Race: A Reinterpretation of Civil Rights Photography*. Berkeley: University of California Press, 2011.

Blumberg, Rhoda Lois. *Civil Rights: The 1960s Freedom Struggle*. Boston: Twayne Publishers, 1984.

Booker, Simeon. *Black Man's America*. Englewood Cliffs, NJ: Prentice-Hall, 1964.

Branch, Taylor. *Parting the Waters: America in the King Years, 1954–63*. New York: Simon and Schuster, 1988.

———. *Pillar of Fire: America in the King Years, 1963–65*. New York: Simon and Schuster, 1998.

———. *At Canaan's Edge: America in the King Years, 1965–68*. New York: Simon and Schuster, 2006.

Brinkley, Douglas. *Rosa Parks*. New York: Viking, 2000.

Bullard, Sara, ed. *Free at Last: A History of the Civil Rights Movement and Those Who Died in the Struggle*. Montgomery, AL: Southern Poverty Law Center, 1989.

Carawan, Guy, and Candie Carawan. *Sing for Freedom: The Story of the Civil Rights Movement through Its Songs*. Bethlehem, PA: Sing Out Publications, 1990.

Carbone, Teresa A., and Kellie Jones. *Witness: Art and Civil Rights in the Sixties*. Brooklyn, NY: Brooklyn Museum/Manacelli Press, 2014.

Carmichael, Stokely, and Charles V. Hamilton. *Black Power: The Politics of Liberation in America*. New York: Random House, 1967.

Carson, Clayborne. *In Struggle: SNCC and the Black Awakening of the 1960s*. 1981. Reprint, with new introduction and epilogue. Cambridge, MA: Harvard University Press, 1995.

Carson, Clayborne, David J. Garrow, Vincent Harding, and Darlene Clark Hine, eds. *Eyes on the Prize: A Reader and Guide*. New York: Penguin Books, 1987.

Chapnick, Howard. *Truth Needs No Ally: Inside Photojournalism*. Columbia: University of Missouri Press, 1994.

Chappell, David L. *Inside Agitators: White Southerners in the Civil Rights Movement*. Baltimore: Johns Hopkins University Press, 1994.

Conkin, Paul. *Gone with the Ivy: A Biography of Vanderbilt University*. Knoxville: University of Tennessee Press, 1985.

Cook, James Graham. *The Segregationists*. New York: Appleton-Century-Crofts, 1962.

Counts, Will, Will Campbell, Ernest Dumas, and Robert S. McCord. *A Life Is More Than a Moment: The Desegregation of Little Rock's Central High*. Bloomington: Indiana University Press, 1999.

Cox, Julian. *Road to Freedom: Photographs of the Civil Rights Movement, 1956–1968*. Atlanta, GA: High Museum of Art, 2008.

Crawford, Vicki L., Jacqueline Anne Rouse, and Barbara Woods, eds. *Women in the Civil Rights Movement: Trailblazers and Torchbearers, 1941–1965*. Bloomington: Indiana University Press, 1993.

Davidson, Bruce. *Time of Change: Civil Rights Photographs, 1961–1965*. Los Angeles: St. Ann's Press, 2002.

Doyle, Don H. *Nashville since the 1920s*. Knoxville: University of Tennessee Press, 1985.

Duganne, Erina. *The Self in Black and White: Race and Subjectivity in Postwar American Photography*. Lebanon, NH: Dartmouth College Press, 2010.

Durr, Virginia Foster. *Outside the Magic Circle*. Tuscaloosa: University of Alabama Press, 1985.

Edwards, Harry. *The Revolt of the Black Athlete*. New York: Free Press, 1969.

Eskew, Glenn T. *But for Birmingham: The Local and National Movements in the Civil Rights Struggle*. Chapel Hill: University of North Carolina Press, 1997.

Evans, Sara. *Personal Politics: The Roots of the Women's Liberation Movement in the Civil Rights Movement and the New Left*. New York: Knopf, 1979.

Fager, Charles E. *Selma: The March That Changed the South*. Boston: Beacon Press, 1985.

Fairclough, Adam. *To Redeem the Soul of America: The Southern Christian Leadership Conference and Martin Luther King Jr.* Athens: University of Georgia Press, 1987.

Farmer, James. *Lay Bare the Heart: An Autobiography of the Civil Rights Movement*. New York: Arbor House, 1985.

Gaillard, Frye. *With Music and Justice for All: Some Southerners and Their Passions*. Nashville: Vanderbilt University Press, 2008.

Garrow, David J. *Bearing the Cross: Martin Luther King Jr. and the Southern Christian Leadership Conference*. New York: Vintage Books, 1988.

———. *The FBI and Martin Luther King Jr.* New York: Penguin Books, 1981.

———. *Protest at Selma: Martin Luther King and the Voting Rights Act of 1965*. New Haven, CT: Yale University Press, 1978.

Gitlin, Todd. *The Sixties: Years of Hope, Days of Rage*. New York: Bantam, 1989.

Graham, Hugh Davis. *Crisis in Print: Desegregation and the Press in Tennessee*. Nashville: Vanderbilt University Press, 1967.

Guthman, Edwin O., and C. Richard Allen, eds. *RFK: Collected Speeches*. New York: Viking, 1993.

Halberstam, David. *The Children*. New York: Random House, 1998.

Hampton, Henry, and Steve Fayer. *Voices of Freedom: An Oral History of the Civil Rights Movement from the 1950s through the 1980s*. New York: Bantam Books, 1990.

Hansberry, Lorraine. *The Movement: Documentary of a Struggle for Equality*. New York: Simon & Schuster, 1964.

Harding, Vincent. *Hope and History: Why We Must Share the History of the Movement*. Maryknoll, NY: Orbis Books, 1990.

Harris, Mark. *Pictures at a Revolution: Five Movies and the Birth of the New Hollywood*. New York: Penguin, 2008.

Heard, Alexander. *Speaking of the University: Two Decades at Vanderbilt*. Nashville: Vanderbilt University Press, 1995.

Holsaert, Faith, ed. *Hands on the Freedom Plow: Personal Accounts by Women in SNCC*. Urbana: University of Illinois Press, 2010.

Honey, Michael K. *To the Promised Land: Martin Luther King and the Fight for Economic Justice*. New York: W. W. Norton, 2018.

———. *Going Down Jericho Road: The Memphis Strike, Martin Luther King's Last Campaign*. New York: W. W. Norton, 2008.

Houston, Benjamin. *The Nashville Way: Racial Etiquette and the Struggle for Social Justice in a Southern City*. Athens: University of Georgia Press, 2012.

Hunter-Gault, Charlayne. *In My Place*. New York: Farrar Straus Giroux, 1992.

Jacobs, Barry. *Across the Line: Profiles in Basketball Courage; Tales of the First Black Players in the ACC and SEC*. Guilford, CT: Lyons Press, 2008.

Joseph, Peniel E. *Stokely: A Life*. New York: Basic Civitas, 2014.

Kasher, Steven. *The Civil Rights Movement: A Photographic History, 1954–68*. New York: Abbeville Press, 1996.

King, Martin Luther, Jr. *A Testament of Hope: The Essential Writings of*

Martin Luther King Jr. Edited by James Melvin Washington. New York: HarperCollins Publisher, 1991.

———. *Why We Can't Wait*. New York: New American Library, 1964.

King, Martin Luther, Jr., and Cornel West. *The Radical King*. Boston: Beacon Press, 2014.

King, Mary. *Freedom Song: A Personal History of the 1960s Civil Rights Movement.* New York: William Morrow, 1987.

Kotz, Nick. *Judgment Days: Lyndon Baines Johnson, Martin Luther King Jr., and the Laws that Changed America*. Boston: Houghton Mifflin, 2005.

Lentz, Richard. *Symbols, the News Magazines, and Martin Luther King*. Baton Rouge: Louisiana State University Press, 1990.

Levine, Ellen, ed. *Freedom's Children: Young Civil Rights Activists Tell Their Own Stories*. New York: Avon Books, 1994.

Levy, Peter B. *Documentary History of the Modern Civil Rights Movement*. New York: Greenwood Press, 1992.

Lewis, Anthony. *Portrait of a Decade: The Second American Revolution*. New York: Random House, 1964.

Lewis, John. *Across That Bridge: A Vision for Change and the Future of America*. New York: Hachette Books, 2012.

Lewis, John, Andrew Aydin, and Nate Powell. *March: Book One*. Marietta: Top Shelf Productions, 2013.

———. *March: Book Two*. Marietta: Top Shelf Productions, 2015.

———. *March: Book Three*. Marietta: Top Shelf Productions, 2016.

Lewis, John, and Michael D'Orso. *Walking with the Wind: A Memoir of the Movement*. New York: Simon & Schuster, 1998.

Long, Worth, Linn Shapiro, and Bernice Johnson Reagan. *We'll Never Turn Back*. Exhibition catalogue. Washington, DC: Smithsonian Performing Arts, 1980.

Lovett, Bobby L. *The Civil Rights Movement in Tennessee: A Narrative History*. Knoxville: University of Tennessee Press, 2005.

Lyon, Danny. *Memories of the Southern Civil Rights Movement*. Chapel Hill: University of North Carolina Press, 1992.

Marable, Manning. *Freedom: A Photographic History of the African American Struggle*. New York: Phaidon Press, 2002.

McAdam, Doug. *Freedom Summer*. New York: Oxford University Press, 1988.

McGill, Ralph. *The South and the Southerner.* Boston: Little, Brown, 1963.

McWhorter, Diane. *Carry Me Home: Birmingham, Alabama: The Climactic Battle of the Civil Rights Revolution*. New York: Simon & Schuster, 2001.

Meier, August, and Elliot Rudwick. *CORE: A Study in the Civil Rights Movement, 1942–1968*. Urbana: University of Illinois Press, 1975.

Meier, August, John Bracey Jr., and Elliot Rudwick, eds. *Black Protest in the Sixties*. New York: Markus Wiener Publishing, 1991.

Meredith, James. *Three Years in Mississippi*. Bloomington: Indiana University Press, 1966.

Mills, Kay. *This Little Light of Mine: The Life of Fannie Lou Hamer*. New York: Dutton, 1993.

Moody, Anne. *Coming of Age in Mississippi.* New York: Dell, 1968.

Moore, Charles, and Michael Durham. *Powerful Days: The Civil Rights Photography of Charles Moore*. New York: Stewart, Tabori & Chang, 1991.

Morgan, Edward P. *What Really Happened to the 1960s: How Mass Media Culture Failed American Democracy*. Lawrence: University Press of Kansas, 2010.

Murray, Paul T. *The Civil Rights Movement: References and Resources*. New York: G. K. Hall, 1993.

Myrdal, Gunnar, Richard Sterner, and Arnold Rose. *An American Dilemma*. New York: Harper & Brothers, 1944.

Ollman, Leah. *Camera as Weapon: Worker Photography between the Wars*. San Diego: Museum of Photographic Arts, 1991.

Olsen, Jack. *The Black Athlete: A Shameful Story*. New York: Time-Life Books, 1968.

Olsen, Lynne. *Freedom's Daughters: The Unsung Heroines of the Civil Rights Movement from 1830 to 1970*. New York: Scribner, 2001.

Oppenheimer, Martin. *The Sit-in Movement of 1960*. Brooklyn: Carlson Publishing, 1989.

Oshinsky, David. *"Worse Than Slavery": Parchman Farm and the Ordeal of Jim Crow Justice*. New York: Free Press, 1996.

Pearce, Gene. *Field of Dreamers: Celebrating Tennessee High School Sports*. Hermitage: Tennessee Secondary School Athletic Association, 2005.

Peck, James. *Freedom Ride*. New York: Simon & Schuster, 1962.

Powledge, Fred. *Free at Last? The Civil Rights Movement and the People Who Made It*. Boston: Little, Brown, 1991.

Raiford, Leigh. *Imprisoned in a Luminous Glare: Photography and the African American Freedom Struggle*. Chapel Hill: University of North Carolina Press, 2011.

Randall, Herbert, and Bobs M. Tusa. *Faces of Freedom Summer*. Tuscaloosa: University of Alabama Press, 2001.

Reeves, Richard. *President Kennedy: Profile of Power*. New York: Simon & Schuster, 1993.

Roberts, Gene, and Hank Klibanoff. *The Race Beat: The Press, the Civil Rights Struggle, and the Awakening of a Nation*. New York: Alfred A. Knopf, 2006.

Robinson, Jo Ann Gibson. *The Montgomery Bus Boycott and the Women Who Started It*. Knoxville: University of Tennessee Press, 1987.

Romano, Renee C., and Leigh Raiford, eds. *The Civil Rights Movement in American Memory*. Athens: University of Georgia Press, 2006.

Sayres, Sohnya, Anders Stephanson, Stanley Aronowitz, and Fredric Jameson, eds. *The 60s Without Apology*. Minneapolis: University of Minnesota Press, 1984.

Schlesinger, Arthur M., Jr. *Robert Kennedy and His Times*. Boston: Houghton Mifflin, 1978.

Schulke, Flip. *He Had a Dream: Martin Luther King Jr. and the Civil Rights Movement*. New York: W. W. Norton, 1995.

———. *Martin Luther King Jr.: A Documentary, Montgomery to Memphis*. New York: Norton, 1976.

Seeger, Pete, and Bob Reiser. *Everybody Says Freedom*. New York: W. W. Norton, 1989.

Sitkoff, Howard. *The Struggle for Black Equality, 1954–1980*. New York: Hill and Wang, 1981.

Smith, Kelly Miller. *Social Crisis Preaching: The Lyman Beecher Lectures, 1983*. Macon, GA: Mercer University Press, 1984.

Sokol, Jason. *There Goes My Everything: White Southerners in the Age of Civil Rights, 1945–1975*. New York: Alfred A. Knopf, 2006.

Squires, James. *The Secrets of the Hopewell Box: Stolen Elections, Southern Politics, and a City's Coming of Age*. New York: Times Books, 1996.

Weisbrot, Robert. *Freedom Bound: A History of America's Civil Rights Movement*. New York: Plume, 1991.

West, Cornel. *Race Matters*. Boston: Beacon Press, 1993.

Whitfield, Stephen J. *A Death in the Delta: The Story of Emmett Till*. New York: Free Press, 1988.

Wiggins, David K., ed. *Out of the Shadows: A Biographical History of African American Athletes*. Fayetteville: University of Arkansas Press, 2006.

Williams, Juan. *Eyes on the Prize: America's Civil Rights Years, 1954–65*. New York: Viking Press, 1987.

Withers, Ernest C. *I Am a Man: Photographs of the 1969 Memphis Sanitation Strike and Dr. Martin Luther King Jr.* Memphis, TN: Memphis Publishing, 1993.

———. *Let Us March On! Selected Civil Rights Photographs of Ernest C. Withers, 1955–1968*. Boston: Massachusetts College of Art and Northeastern University, 1992.

Young, Andrew. *An Easy Burden: The Civil Rights Movement and the Transformation of America*. New York: HarperCollins, 1996.

Zinn, Howard. *SNCC: The New Abolitionists*. Boston: Beacon Press, 1964.

CONTRIBUTORS

KATHRYN E. DELMEZ is a curator at the Frist Art Museum.

SUSAN H. EDWARDS is the executive director and CEO at the Frist Art Museum.

CONGRESSMAN JOHN LEWIS represents Georgia's 5th district.

LINDA T. WYNN is a professor of history and political science at Fisk University and assistant director for state programs at the Tennessee Historical Commission.